BRIT GUIDE

DISNEYLAND PARIS

AND PARIS ATTRACTIONS

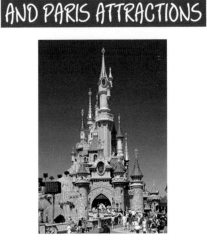

Simon & Susan Veness
with Andy De Maertelaere

D0543371

foulsham
LONDON • NEW YORK • TORONTO • SYDNEY

foulsham

Capital Point, 33 Bath Road, Slough, Berkshire, SL1 3UF, England

Foulsham books can be found in all good bookshops and direct from
www.foulsham.com

ISBN: 978-0-572-03914-1

Text copyright © 2012 Simon and Susan Veness
Series, format, logo and layout design copyright © 2012 W. Foulsham & Co. Ltd

Cover photographs © Superstock (top left); Matthew Hotson (top right);
Eurostar (bottom); Walt Disney Co. Ltd (back)

A CIP record for this book is available from the British Library

Dedicated to Anthony, Mark and Ben – our perfect research team!

Special thanks to Andy de Maertelaere for doing so much of the hard work with the
research for this edition. Great work, Andy! And also to our editors, Jane Hotson
and Wendy Hobson, for putting so much care and attention into all that we do.

Look out for the latest editions in this series:

Printed in Great Britain by Scotprint

CONTENTS

Brit Tips

Got a red-hot Brit Tip to pass on; the latest info on how to beat the
queues or the best new restaurant? We want to hear from YOU to
keep improving the guide each year. Drop us a line at: Brit Guides
(Disneyland Paris), W. Foulsham & Co. Ltd, Capital Point, 33 Bath Road,
Slough SL1 3UF. Or email us at britsguide@yahoo.com. You can also see
more of Simon and Susan's work at **www.venesstravelmedia.com**.

Sleeping Beauty Castle at the centre of the Magic

© DISNEY

FOREWORD

Simon says ... It's 20 years since we started writing about Disney parks, and the thrills and excitement of all our time in the House of Mouse are as strong as ever. Any Disney resort is a wonderful experience, and *Disneyland Paris* is a special gem in the company's crown, celebrating its 20th anniversary in 2012 and still adding to its unique rides and attractions. That means it remains a busy, dynamic and *challenging* place to visit to ensure you get the best out of your holiday here. With two parks, a village area of shops, restaurants and nightlife, six hotels, sport and more, it is also MUCH bigger than when it first opened, which means a good guide (i.e. this one!) is essential in helping you prepare, anticipate and enjoy everything in store. We hate the idea of visitors not being able to enjoy Europe's No. 1 tourist attraction to the full, so please let us help you to get it right. From the moment you start planning, to your journey there, how to enjoy it all and the many extra things to appreciate in the area, we can be your good companion for the whole adventure. It is a remarkable and astounding place – just remember to take us with you!

Simon 'n' Dale

Susan says ... Happy 20th Anniversary, *Disneyland Paris*! 'Le Parc Disneyland' is smartening up for her big 2-0, and that means even more reason to visit. And what better way to celebrate a milestone birthday than with a new parade and fireworks? It brings out the kid in all of us, and makes the perfect end to a magical day. But what's a birthday without gifts? With the 2012 debut of the amazing World of Disney store at *Disney Village*, it's hard to imagine there could be anything on your wish list that can't be found here. So head on over and join the festivities – just remember to leave plenty of extra space in your luggage – we guarantee you'll find lots to bring back! And now, it's on with the fun ...

Susan 'n' Chip

ACKNOWLEDGEMENTS

The authors wish to acknowledge the help of the following in the production of this book: The Walt Disney Company, Eurostar, Leger Holidays, P&O Ferries, Port of Dover, Cityrama, Thomas Cook Explorers Hotel, La Vallée Outlet Shopping Village, Planet Hollywood, Sea Life Paris, Seaview.

In person: David Coombs, Laura Farrow and Richard Leclerc, plus Disney Ambassador Osvaldo Del Mistero and Mathias Dugoujon (Walt Disney Company), Lucy Drake and Lucie Thevenon (Eurostar), Anita Rogers (Leger Holidays), David Simpson (Seaview), Rachel Bushell (Port of Dover), Michelle Ulyatt (P&O Ferries), Sara Whines (SeaFrance), Sarah Whelband (DFDS Seaways), Gualtiero Raimondi Cominesi (Planet Holywood), Neottie Olivier (Thomas Cook Explorers Hotel), Chantal Villeneuve (Sea Life), Cécile Naulet (La Vallée).

Reader feedback via email for this edition from: Kay and Andy Mead, Richard Hulland, Johnny Sharp, and James McCulloch.

PHOTOGRAPH ACKNOWLEDGEMENTS

The authors would like to thank everyone who provided photographs for the book, in particular, our readers Hilary White, Kirsty Dickson, Matthew Hotson and Daniëlle Todd.

Indications denote: top left and right, t tl tr; centre, c; bottom left and right, b, bl, br

Hotel Abbaye du Golf 89b; Chris Brewer 36tr, 153; Brittany Ferries 37, 40, 36tl, 81b; Clévacances 93b; Comfort Inns 93t; Thomas Cook Explorers Hotel 61, 84; Kirsty Dickson 8tl, 13, 16c, 16 above br, 20, 28t, 36bl, 57, 77b, 96 below tr, 105b, 129t, 144bl, 145, 161, 180, 200c; Walt Disney Co. Ltd 1, 8tr, 24, 45, 96tr, 101t, 120, 121 b, 132b, 141b, 144 tl, 156, 157, 160, 165; Eurostar 36 above br, below tl; Wendy Hobson 188tl, 188c, 188bl, 188br, 189, 192; Matthew Hotson 9, 12t, 16tl, 16bl, 21, 100, 105t, 120, 129, 181; Hotel Kyriad Chelles 93cl; LD Lines 48; Novotel Collegien 92b; P&O 41, 36br;

Sea Life Centre 164tr; SeaFrance 44; Daniëlle Todd 12b, 108b, 108tr, 112t, 124t, 136t, 137b, 140b, 144br, 148; Val d'Europe 164bl, 184; Vienna International Dream Castle Hotel 88b, 89t; Hilary White 16 below tl, 16 tr, 32, 53, 56, 60, 65, 68t, 69b, 69t, 76t, 80t, 96tl, 104b, 108, 117b, 117t, 141t, 144 below tl, 144tr, 164c, 164tl, 172, 173, 176, 200 below tl, 200br, 200tl, 200tr; http://reisewarnung.blogspot.com/ 124b; www.df82.blogspot.com 28b; www. dlpfoodguide.com 128b; www.gallery.nen.gov.uk 52; www.holidaycheck.com 77t, 88t; www.holidayholiday.co.uk 68b; www.myparisnet.com 8cr, 97, 108cr, 112b, 116t, 121, 133, 168t, 193; www.parisbytrain.com 49b; www.travelling-in-europe.net 197t; www.yves. marsal.free.fr 76b; www.chateauversailles.fr 196; www.provins.net 192b

FURTHER READING

Disneyland Paris – From Sketch to Reality, by Alain Littaye and Didier Ghez (Nouveau Millenaire Editions $176.44, out of print and now collectable, on amazon.com). A sumptuous book, in full colour and with a wealth of brilliant photography, it charts the building of the Disneyland Park, Disney Village and the hotels, with magnificent insight into the creativity of the Imagineers.

Walt Disney Imagineering – A Behind the Dreams Look at Making the Magic Real by The Imagineers (Hyperion, £21.99). Another lavish 200-page volume providing a riveting look at how Disney's creative force thinks and works, from original concepts to the finished attractions.

Disney – The First 100 Years (David Smith and Steven B. Clark; Disney Publications, $50). For true Disney fans, this 203-page epic charts the story of Walt and his creations, from his humble beginnings to the 100th year after his birth, looking at the landmarks of the man and his company.

TOP 10 CAMPAIGN TIPS

After years of tramping the parks and ending up at the back of more queues than we like to admit, we have a pretty well-honed method for tackling any visit to the House of Mouse. Here is our personal ten-point plan of campaign:

1. Decide what you want to do well in advance and try to plan at least a rough daily schedule (especially in summer and other busy times of the year).

2. Work out if you really want to try to Do It All (opening hours are longest in summer, and everything is available but queues are going to be longer, too) or have a quieter time (in spring or autumn with shorter hours and more unpredictable weather).

3. Are you looking to stay in the *Disneyland Paris* resort or outside? The former offers unequalled convenience and all the essential 'Magic' pretty much round the clock, but staying off-site is usually cheaper and can also be less frenetic and more relaxing.

4. Choose your mode of transport from the four main options – by the direct train of Eurostar, by self-drive (via either the ferry or Eurotunnel), by an organised coach service or by air, flying in to any of the three Paris airports. Where you stay will determine which one of these is the most convenient as each have a few limitations (see Chapter 3).

5. Are you looking for just a long weekend trip or a fully-fledged 5- to 7-day holiday? The temptation is to try to pack it all into a weekend, and the ease of the Eurostar service makes this rather appealing. But the weekends are invariably busier and going for 4–5 days instead allows you more variety and the chance to take things at a slower pace.

6. Take a break. Whether you have a day in Paris, an outing to Provins or Versailles or just a shopping expedition to Val d'Europe, you'll benefit from a Disney break at some stage on anything other than a weekend trip. Going at the parks non-stop for more than two days in a row is likely to be a recipe for exhaustion!

7. Stop and admire the scenery – often. There is SO much clever design and architecture about both parks – and the *Disneyland Park* in particular – that it rewards those who take their time and don't just rush from attraction to attraction.

8. Enjoy the fact you can have a glass of wine or a beer in the *Disneyland Park*. Alcohol is not served in *Walt Disney World*'s Magic Kingdom in Florida and it makes a great lunch or dinner addition!

9. Try a little French. The locals are usually more hospitable and forthcoming if you make a polite effort to speak their language. See our special section on French–English on Page 15 to jog your memory.

10. Get everyone in your party to read this book!

Would you like one of your pictures to appear in the *Brit Guide to Disneyland Paris* or on the website? Send us one or two of your favourites. Name a high-resolution jpeg with your name and email address, then send it to marketing@foulsham.com. Submitting photos implies permission to reproduce the images.

1 Introduction

There is one simple reason why Disney's theme parks are the world's most-visited attractions, be they in America, Japan or, in this case, France. They are simply the best family entertainment you will find anywhere.

And the fun is not restricted to families either. Sure, children do find the allure of Mickey and Co. almost irresistible, but there is something for everyone in a Disney park – young or old, singles, couples or with the whole family in tow. In fact, we reckon there is more all-round entertainment value here than anywhere else we've seen.

It is a great short-break destination, perfect for a week (or longer, given the attractions of the Paris region) and is easy to reach; it is ideal for those with young children, yet also attracts honeymooners and other couples; and its appeal is timeless, harking back to a nostalgic yesteryear but remaining contemporary in so many ways.

Pixie dust

A holiday at *Disneyland Paris* is a beguiling prospect and is also sure to bring out the child in everyone. If you can envisage grown-ups rushing to hug Mickey or Minnie, then you can imagine the effect Disney's 'Pixie dust' has on just about everyone who walks through the gates.

Indeed, Roy Disney, nephew of the great Walt himself, opened the Paris park with words his uncle first used for *Disneyland California* in 1955. He said:

Toy Story on parade

'To all who come to this happy place, welcome! This is your land. Here age relives fond memories of the past and here youth may savour the challenge and promise of the future. We hope it will be a source of joy and inspiration to the world.' It certainly shapes up that way.

BRITTIP

Disneyland Paris is just 2hrs from Ashford in Kent on the direct Eurostar service and only 2hrs 35mins from London St Pancras. For the great convenience the train provides, it's definitely worth considering.

But, if that's the broad outline, let us fill in the detail and provide you with a good understanding of how it all works – because this is a complicated business and you must keep your wits about you at all times. Holidaying the Disney way is immense fun but it can be confusing and tiring. When the crowds flock to the parks, it is a challenge to keep up with the ebb and flow of it all. When the queues for many rides top an hour, you need a strategy and the basic tool of all park-goers: a Plan!

In fact, planning is an essential component of your holiday. At quieter times you might just get away with a free-wheeling, make-it-up-as-you-go-along approach. But there are plenty of pitfalls that await the unwary and unprepared even at only moderately busy times. This is not like Alton Towers or Thorpe Park, where a day visit is enough to 'do it all'.

With two fully fledged parks in the *Disneyland Paris* experience, there is always an element of choice. Behind that lies a matter of scale that is hard to convey in advance and that includes an attention to detail both breathtaking and a little bewildering. It is easy to get side-tracked by some of the clever scenery, shops and other frippery, so that's why planning is so important.

The very name *Disneyland Paris* should convey the fact that this is a city-sized experience, and that means a multi-dimensional approach in all things: from the attractions to the hotels, the restaurants and even the shops. There is fun almost everywhere you turn and a host of options at any one time. Therefore, you *must* do your homework in advance.

Chequered history

The *Disneyland Paris* story began in the mid-1980s when Michael Eisner, then the new Chief Executive Officer of the Walt Disney Company, came to Europe in search of a new outlet for their theme park creativity. Both France and Spain were firmly in the frame, and the former was chosen for a variety of reasons, not least the strong French connection in many Disney films (*Cinderella, Sleeping Beauty, Hunchback of Notre Dame*) and the wonderful central location offered by the Paris region.

As far back as December 1985, Mr Eisner signed a letter of intent with France to build a park in Marne-la-Vallée, 32km/20mls east of Paris. That agreement was formalised with Jacques Chirac in March 1987 and what was then about 1,900ha/4,700 acres of beet fields became the planning ground for a great adventure in architecture and engineering, or Imagineering, as the Walt Disney Company likes to call it.

The first earth-moving equipment moved in on 2 August 1988, and a 4-year construction period began. Despite some challenges from Mother Nature, the *Euro Disney Park* (as it was then known – the name soon changed to *Euro Disneyland*) opened on time on 12 April 1992 to a blaze of publicity and an awkward first few years. A sceptical French press, over-optimistic attendance forecasts and cost over-runs all contributed to a painful initiation for the new park, despite 10.8m visitors in the first 12 months.

Major financial restructuring was necessary in 1994, at which time it became *Disneyland Paris*, and, from there, the story has been one of recovery. Attendance grew through the late 1990s and more development

Who owns *Disneyland Paris?*

The Walt Disney Company actually owns only 39.8% of *Disneyland Paris*, but runs 100% of the management. The other 60.2% is owned by a number of private investors, including 10% by Prince Al-Waleed of Saudi Arabia.

began to spring up around Marne-la-Vallée, both commercial and residential.

The eventual success of Disney's on-site hotels (6 of them, plus the ranch-style self-catering of *Davy Crockett Ranch* a short drive away) encouraged a mini proliferation of hotels in the vicinity, while the development extended to a new town centre at neighbouring **Val d'Europe**, a combination of businesses, shopping and housing, which adds even more to the picture locally. Here, the immaculate shopping mall is part of an excellent centre that includes the outlet shopping of **La Vallée**, the **Sea Life Centre** and some enticing restaurants.

At the same time, a Disney-run **golf complex**, with three 9-hole courses, was developed just minutes from the parks, offering yet another diversion for people wanting to enhance their theme park experience.

The second park

The original plans for the resort included a sister park along the lines of *Disney's Hollywood Studios* in *Walt Disney World Resort* in Florida. This was scheduled to open 3 years after the first park, but the financial woes of 1994 meant the concept went into storage until 1998. Construction began in earnest shortly afterwards. The eagerly awaited *Walt Disney Studios* opened on 16 March 2002 with another burst of publicity – and a new name, *Disneyland Resort Paris* (new CEO Philippe Gas then removed the 'Resort' part of the name once more in 2009).

Here, finally, was the true resort expansion as originally envisaged by Eisner and his Imagineers,

completing a well-rounded picture of accommodation, shopping, restaurants and theme parks, and providing a multi-day experience, even out of busy periods. *Festival Disney*, now known more appropriately as *Disney Village*, has grown to encompass 13 restaurants and cafés, a 15-screen cineplex (including an IMAX screen theatre), a dinner show (the family-friendly Buffalo Bill's Wild West Show), a games arcade and a choice of shops, including the brand new World of Disney store. There is also the wonderful Panoramagique tethered balloon ride and other games and activities (see Chapter 8).

With the Marne-la-Vallée railway station at the heart of the whole development linking the resort with central Paris, Charles de Gaulle Airport and, more importantly, London via Eurostar, it is a wonderfully convenient location. It is easy for arrival and well organised to allow access either straight to the theme parks, the hotels (using an efficient bus service) or directly to *Disney Village*.

Anyone familiar with the vast Orlando resort set-up – 12,173ha/30,080 acres of 4 parks, 2 water parks, 21 hotels and a mini-town area called *Downtown Disney* – will almost certainly be impressed by the comparative ease with which you can move around this one. As everything is within a 20-minute walk at most, the scale is big enough to be exciting yet manageable enough not to be daunting. Indeed, it is a triumph of the designers' art in making this hugely complex development one of very human dimensions, a riot of visual stimulation and yet easy to negotiate. Yes, there is a lot going on here, but it is easy to enjoy it all.

Disney Village

Offering a positive riot of sights and sounds, both by day and night (when the contrast is quite startling, from the peaceful Lake Disney in early morning to the near-party proportions of the late-evening hubbub), *Disney Village* acts as a conduit between the parks

The wonderful world of Alice in Wonderland

INTRODUCTION

and hotels. It is an exit for weary park-goers (and you can be pretty tired by park closing!) and offers a new source of fun for all those who enjoy their nightlife. It is a heady cocktail but also requires much forethought, especially if you have the family in tow, to ensure you get the most out of it (whether for a meal, shopping or the games and other activities) before retiring to your hotel.

Of course, *Disney Village* is not reserved purely for Disney's on-site guests; it also attracts a good number of locals (especially on Fridays and Saturdays). Its large car park makes it easily accessible for guests at nearby

Pizzeria Bella Notte

Facts and figures

- The whole of *Disneyland Paris* covers 1,943ha/4,800 acres, or one-fifth the area of Paris.
- Ground-breaking took place in August 1988.
- 51km/32mls of roads were built and 120,000,000m³/157,000,000yd³ of earth moved.
- Around 450,000 trees and shrubs were planted.
- It directly employs more than 14,000 people.
- All Disney employees are known as Cast Members to signify they are part of 'the show'.
- The *Disneyland Park* covers 57ha/140 acres.
- The *Walt Disney Studios* stands on 27ha/67 acres.
- The 7 themed hotels have a total of 5,800 rooms.
- There are 68 counter and full-service restaurants throughout the resort.
- In all, there are more than 50 different shops and boutiques.
- More than 200m people have visited since it opened.
- Around 51% of visitors are French, 12% British, 12% Belgian and Dutch, 9% Spanish, 4% Italian, 3% German, with 9% from other nations.

hotels, while the RER service (the main local commuter train) runs until after midnight.

The European touch

Disneyland Paris is a wonderfully impressive set-up and is easily the equal of any of Disney's other resorts around the world. In fact, we believe the clever 'Europeanisation' of the traditional Disney style gives it extra appeal. There is more than a hint of French flair, Italian chic, Spanish partying, German organisation and Dutch friendliness about the resort, which come together best in the Village. Yes, there are some drawbacks – the price of the Euro against the pound can make things seem expensive – and the mixture of mind and the willingness to try those few words of school French they can dredge from memory.

More importantly, it is guaranteed to put a smile on the faces of young and old alike, and reaffirm simple family values. When Walt built Disneyland in California back in 1955, his most famous statement (now etched on the bronze Walt 'n' Mickey statue in front of the Sleeping Beauty Castle) was: 'I think most of all what I want Disneyland to be is a happy place … where parents and children can have fun together.'

So, don't forget to take time out to enjoy that aspect during your visit; watch your children's faces at the parades, on the Dumbo ride or as they meet the characters (or just look at the reaction of other children); and ensure you do things together, however silly they may be! There is artistry all around you, in the rides, the architecture and the Cast Members, but the most meaningful feeling you can invoke is the bond with your loved ones – and nowhere brings that to the fore quite like a Disney park, whether it be for kids of 6 or 60.

cultures occasionally causes some awkwardness. The toilets could be kept cleaner in many instances (for some reason, this seems a bit of a blind spot in all public areas) and there is occasionally a bit of push and shove (which you don't usually find at the American parks), notably in the scrimmage for character autographs, getting in position for the parades or trying to board a hotel bus at the end of the evening.

It won't be a restful holiday, unless you go out of season in winter and are lucky enough to be blessed by mild, dry weather, and it can make a serious dent in your bank balance. But, all in all, it offers great value and richly rewards those who go with an open

However, perhaps the question most seasoned Disney-goers will want to ask is: 'If I have already been to *Walt Disney World* in Florida, do I need to go to *Disneyland Paris*?' We would say unequivocally 'Yes!' Apart from the obvious advantage of this being a

Lightning McQueen

closer and more convenient short-visit destination (no 9-hour flights and long queues at Immigration to deal with), we believe the more luxurious theming of the *Disneyland Park*, the updated versions of classic rides like Space Mountain, Haunted Mansion (or Phantom Manor as it is here) and Big Thunder Mountain, and the all-new thrills of most of the *Walt Disney Studios* make it an absolute must to visit. For some, it is also a handy 'refresher' of Disney Magic in between visits to Orlando (and, of course, it is cheaper to spend a few days in Paris than 2 weeks in America). Anyone familiar with the vast Florida resort will also appreciate the convenience of being able to walk everywhere!

See the city

Another big bonus of the location is the lure of nearby Paris. You certainly do not need to have a car to get to the city (in fact, driving into the city is not advisable). The reliability of the RER service and local buses means you can easily enjoy an evening along the Champs-Elysées or the Bastille district and get the train back to the resort.

BRITTIP

Need to find your way around Paris public transport? Options are the Métro (the underground), RER train service (regional rail, part underground), Transilien SNCF (suburban rail – not strictly relevant to *Disneyland Paris*), bus and tram. Visit **www.ratp.fr** for more info.

A highly recommended night out for couples is the *Lido de Paris* show in the Champs-Elysées, while a really handy option is the **Cityrama** bus tour of the city, picking up at *Disney's Hotel New York* every day. The latter provides an excellent whistle-stop tour of all the main features of this fabulous city, with the great convenience of staying outside the crowds and hubbub. It is only about 40 minutes on the RER train into central Paris, however, and it is then easy to negotiate either on foot or by the Métro and bus. It is a magnificent city with a wealth of history, architecture, art and amazing

INTRODUCTION

Our top 10 thrill attractions

1	Rock 'n' Roller Coaster starring Aerosmith
2	Twilight Zone Tower of Terror
3	Space Mountain: Mission 2
4	Indiana Jones and the Temple of Peril
5	Big Thunder Mountain Railroad
6	Star Tours
7	Armageddon
8	Panoramagique
9	Crush's Coaster
10	Driving in central Paris!

monuments, plus a dazzling array of fine restaurants and shops. If you are planning a 4-day Disney visit, you should definitely think about spending at least half a day and an evening in Paris itself.

Those who bring the car can benefit from exploring further afield – and there are some wonderful towns and villages in this region of France, notably the medieval walled town of Provins to the south-east. The road links are good (France also has a superb system of toll roads) and are rarely subject to the kind of congestion we experience in the UK – apart from in central Paris.

You can also stock up on some wonderful food and wine along the way, as well as in Val d'Europe, where the **Auchan hypermarket** is a highly civilised alternative to the rather tired supermarkets of Calais.

The main focus, however, should be the theme parks themselves. The original *Disneyland Park* remains the heart and soul of the Magic, especially for families with children under 10, while the *Walt Disney Studios* adds an element of excitement and thrills for the older age group. These provide a complementary experience, but the time requirements of each are slightly different. Don't be fooled into thinking you can spend 2 days here and do it all, even during off-peak times. The original park will require at least 2 days

Speaking French

The resort has been a multi-lingual operation since day one and all Disney employees (or Cast Members) should be able to speak at least 2 languages (many speak 4 or 5). This means you shouldn't have any trouble being understood. However, it is still good practice (and simple good manners) to try to remember a few words of French from time to time. All Cast Members wear a badge with their name and home country, so you can easily spot the occasional Brit working here but, for those who can't remember their basic school French, here is a quick guide to those handy vital words:

ENGLISH	FRENCH
Do you speak English?	Parlez-vous Anglais?
Good morning/Hello	Bonjour
Good evening	Bonsoir
Please	S'il vous plaît
Thank you	Merci
I would like…	Je voudrais…
Do you have…?	Avez-vous…?
How much is…?	Quel est le prix de…?
How much?	C'est combien?
A receipt	Un reçu
The bill, please	L'addition, s'il vous plaît
Coffee	Café
White coffee	Café au lait
Where are the toilets?	Où sont les toilettes?
Toll booths	Les péages
Motorway service areas	Aires
Autoroutes (toll roads)	Autoroutes des péages
Hypermarket	Hypermarché

to ensure you've seen and done most of what is on offer, while the *Studios* needs a full day now that its new attractions are up and running.

Seasonal fun

Disneyland Paris also provides terrific added value with a unique range of seasonal celebrations. While all their other resorts lay on a brilliantly themed backdrop for Christmas and Halloween, only here will you find a real in-depth and broadly arranged series of attractions throughout the year. There are special winter festivities, St Patrick's and St David's Day events each March, extra summer entertainment, a Bastille Day extravaganza in July, the amazing transformation of Main Street USA for Halloween in October, a bonfire spectacular in November and the Disney-style magic of Christmas.

BRIT TIP

In keeping with their seasonal approach, the New Year period from January to Easter has become the great 'family value' time to visit, with plenty of Kids Go Free (with each adult) deals.

Rain and shine

This is still Western Europe and the climate can be depressingly like our own at times – wet, grey and cold. However, much of both parks has been built with rain and wind in mind, which means there is nearly always somewhere you can escape to if the weather turns nasty – indeed, almost 80% of the *Walt Disney Studios* is under cover. Providing you pack a light raincoat you will be well prepared to carry on enjoying the fun. In fact, spring and autumn can offer some of the best times for visiting *Disneyland Paris* as they rarely come up with any seriously anti-social weather, the crowds are more manageable and the queues shorter. And, while the delight of Paris in the springtime is a wonderful cliché, that doesn't also mean it isn't true. In fact, the months of April (after Easter) and May are just about the best time to visit, with a heavenly combination of pleasant weather, convivial atmosphere and generally lower-than-average attendances.

Yes, this is the biggest tourist attraction in Europe – with a record 15m visitors in 2010, 1.8m from the UK alone – but it can easily be a breeze of a place to visit if you get your tactics right.

And so, with that in mind, it's time to move on to the subject of Planning …

Planning

or How to Do It All and Stay Sane!

Before 2002, you could pop across the Channel to Marne-la-Vallée, have a fun day out and be back home for tea the next day, safe in the knowledge you had 'done' Disney. Not any more.

The addition of the *Walt Disney Studios*, the expansion of the surrounding area and continuing development mean this is now a more demanding holiday choice. It is not quite in the same league as *Walt Disney World* in Florida, where any visit has to be planned like a military campaign, but you must have a good idea of what you're getting into and prepare accordingly.

First of all, the two parks are a complete contrast from each other, with different sizes, time requirements and appeal. They provide a complementary experience and you will certainly want to visit both. You'll probably find you need 2 full days to explore the *Disneyland Park* plus a day for the *Studios*.

Disneyland Park

The *Disneyland Park* follows the main formula of the *Magic Kingdom Park* in Orlando, and *Disneyland California* in Anaheim, Los Angeles. It is subdivided into 5 'lands' around a central hub and features almost 50 attractions

Beauty and the Beast feature in the daily parade

in the form of rides, shows, parades and other live entertainment. There is an impressive choice of shops and restaurants, all themed to the various lands and offering useful browsing opportunities. At 57ha/140 acres, it requires some serious legwork to see it all. You'll be amazed at how time-consuming it can be to get from one land to another, especially with the number of diversions on the way.

This is the park families with younger children tend to focus on (although there are terrific thrill rides, like Space Mountain: Mission 2 and Indiana Jones and the Temple of Peril). There is a huge choice of dining and wonderful character meals (that kids adore), but you need to pace yourself as it's easy to get worn to a frazzle – and end up with fractious children – with too much to-ing and fro-ing.

Walt Disney Studios

This park is subdivided into 4 areas and, at slightly less than half the size of its sister park, it is easier to negotiate. As the name suggests, it is themed around the magic of the film world, but it is different to *Disney's Hollywood Studios* in Orlando (although 3 of the rides are similar and another is a transplant from Orlando's *Magic Kingdom*). It is more show-based, hence its attractions take place at specific times of the day (like the amazing Stunt Show), and more of it is indoors, which is handy when the weather is bad. The dining options are pretty ordinary, but you still have the all-important Disney characters and some wonderful live entertainment.

Beyond the theme parks

Once you have visited the parks, the delights of *Disney Village* await. You can dine, drink, shop, go to the cinema or catch a dinner show in this lively, bustling hub, which is great at night, with its periodic live entertainment, notably in the busier seasons.

Dining and shopping: The choice of dining is terrific, with the superb theming of international duo Planet Hollywood and Rainforest Café, the unique Steakhouse, great value of Earl of Sandwich, and the fun Bavarian-style of King Ludwig's Castle the pick of the bunch. Then there is the 1950s Americana of Annette's Diner, the country and western style of Billy Bob's Saloon – with live bands an outstanding feature – an all-day character-fest at Café Mickey, a Sports Bar and the New York Deli, not forgetting a large McDonald's and a Starbuck's coffee house. Eight boutiques stay open usually until midnight.

Video arcade: An inevitable feature with a variety of high-tech games.

Buffalo Bill's Wild West Show: This live entertainment is a local institution, a corny but fun dinner show that is usually a huge hit with kids (even grown-up ones!). It offers the chance to shout, cheer and wave your (free) cowboy hat in support of the various acts, who perform in the indoor auditorium during a typical cowboy dinner, accompanied by Mickey and Co. In the summer there is a daily Wild West parade outside before the first of the two shows (around 6pm).

Panoramagique: Something different again, this is a breathtaking tethered balloon ride over the Village that soars to some 180m/600ft and provides an

PLANNING

awesome view of the surrounding area.

Other hands-on activities: Add pedal boats, bungee trampolines, cycling and, in winter, ice-skating and you have an interactive playground that will keep everyone amused for at least half a day. For the full details on *Disney Village*, see Chapter 8.

Val d'Europe: As if all that were not enough, there is the additional lure of the excellent shopping, dining and other attractions here. It is just 5 minutes away by RER train (free buses run between the Disney resorts and La Vallée outlet shopping village at various times) and can provide a refreshing break from the world of the Mouse after a few days. It boasts a huge indoor mall, some excellent restaurants in an upmarket food court and the child-friendly **Sea Life Aquarium**, run by the chain that owns many similar attractions throughout Europe. It is a great diversion for kids aged 2–12 especially and provides a good 2-hour lure if mum or dad want to go shopping!

When to go

The vast majority visit in full family mode, so they are usually here in the school holidays. This is unfortunate because both the cost and crowds increase at these times, while the summer can also be uncomfortably hot – in excess of 30ºC/86ºF (and 2 of the resort hotels, *Disney's Hotel Cheyenne* and *Hotel Santa Fe*, plus non-suite rooms at the Explorers Hotel, do not have air-conditioning). So you need to consider your options.

If you are confined to the holidays, try to opt for late Easter or late summer. The spring and autumn half-term holidays are also prime opportunities, although, once again, the cost increases. The big pay-off with a summer visit is the bonus of **extended opening hours** (usually to 11pm) and a full show and parade schedule. If you can avoid 'Le Weekend' crowds, you still benefit from the magic of long nights in the *Disneyland Park* with the evening finale fireworks. As ever, it is

swings and roundabouts, and you need to consider what works best for you.

Busy times

It is usually better to visit in non-peak periods, in which we include weekdays rather than weekends. While the locals didn't embrace Disney at the beginning, the theme parks and *Disney Village* have become a major source of local recreation, so French attendance on a Saturday or Sunday can top 60%. This is where much of suburban Paris comes to play at the weekend, and Saturdays can be especially hectic.

Both parks cope pretty well with the thousands who pour in during the first few hours of the day, but the queues build up quickly at the main rides (and just about everywhere in Fantasyland in the *Disneyland Park*). The wait for rides like Peter Pan's Flight and Dumbo can top an hour, which means an uncomfortable period in a queue, especially when it's hot. Disney does have a nifty virtual queuing system called **FASTPASS** (see page 105), which takes some of the sting out of the waits for many attractions, but even that has its limits, hence during Easter, summer and Christmas (and any sunny weekend), you'll spend a LOT of time on your feet.

19 PLANNING

BRITTIP

Disney's FASTPASS system is an invaluable aid to your visit, but many people overlook it because they don't understand it. It is FREE to use and simply gives you a time to return to the ride and bypass the main queue with only a short wait. It is fully explained in Chapter 5.

If you prefer to avoid school holidays, most of the summer and the weekends, when should you go? Well, the spring usually sees Paris at its best, and this tends to rub off on *Disneyland Paris*, too. Of all Disney's resorts around the world, this is designed and landscaped with European tastes in mind. There is a greater emphasis on plants and greenery, providing a naturalistic element to the *Disneyland Park* in particular, which is beautiful in the

The 4-night test

Leger Holidays are the UK's largest tour operator to *Disneyland Paris*, with the biggest variety of packages and travel options. Their stock-in-trade is a 4-night holiday using coach transport, with Disney accommodation. Here is an example of how to get best use out of one of their typical packages, using a family of 4 (with children aged 4 and 6) and leaving from the south-east:

DAY ONE: Arrive at *Disney's Hotel Santa Fe* at 9.30pm after 8½-hour journey, including P&O Ferry crossing.

DAY TWO: Up at 8am for hotel breakfast and off to the *Disneyland Park* soon after. Full day in the theme park, with lunch (pre-booked) at The Lucky Nugget Saloon. Take a break after the 3pm parade back at the hotel (nap time for youngest child). Dinner at Planet Hollywood at 6.30pm, followed by a slow wander back to the hotel through *Disney Village* (with much to sidetrack the children).

DAY THREE: A later start, with hotel breakfast at 10am, then off to the *Walt Disney Studios* just in time to catch the 11.15 Stunt Show. Take in 2 more shows before lunch at Blockbuster Café (self-service), then complete the full range of attractions by 6pm. Switch to *Disneyland Park* for dinner at Silver Spur Steakhouse at 6.30pm (pre-booked), then one last ride before catching bus back to hotel.

DAY FOUR: Today there is the option of Leger's organised day-tour of Paris, leaving the hotel at 9.30am for a short sight-seeing tour of the city and an optional cruise on the Seine. There is free time to soak up the atmosphere of the French capital, with another optional visit to the Montparnasse Tower, where the fastest lift in Europe goes up to the 56th floor in just 38secs for a view not to be missed. The coach returns to *Disneyland Paris* at 7pm. Another option is to purchase an additional 1-day ticket for a third day in the parks, or to spend time in *Disney Village* or take the RER train to Val d'Europe and indulge in some great shopping as well as a visit to the child-friendly SeaLife centre. So many choices!

DAY FIVE: An 8am breakfast, then time to pack and load luggage back on the coach. Visit the petrol station (next to *Disney's Hotel Santa Fe*) to grab a few snacks for the journey back to Calais. Coach departs at 10am, non-stop to Calais hypermarket. Home again – tired but with very happy children – at 4.30pm UK time.

PLANNING

RC Racer

spring and early summer. Both parks have year-round charm, of course, and you can have as much fun on the rides in winter as you can in spring. But, there is something special about a bright spring day that sets off the Magic provided by Disney's Imagineers, notably in the design and creativity of Adventureland.

Visiting off-peak

Spring weather in Paris tends to be more consistent than the UK – compare the temperature and rainfall charts for Paris and Birmingham on page 22. However, the winters can be just as cold and wet, so there are several factors to bear in mind if you visit Nov–Feb. The most obvious is the downturn in business, with not only the crowds dropping off, but some restaurants and attractions closing, too. All rides, shows and attractions are regularly refurbished, often in winter,

France on holiday

France has 11 public holidays when government departments, banks and shops are usually closed: 1 Jan, Easter Monday, 1 May, 8 May, Ascension Day, Whit Monday, 14 Jul, 15 Aug, 1 Nov, 11 Nov and Christmas Day. French schoolchildren also have 5 holidays a year: a week at the end of Oct, 2 weeks at Christmas, 2 in Feb, 2 in spring and the whole of Jul and Aug. Consequently, *Disneyland Paris* is noticeably busier then. More details on French school holidays at **www.education.gouv.fr/pid184/le-calendrier-scolaire.html**. You may also want to note some of the other main European school holidays on **www.eurydice.org**.

so you may find several things shut down. For example, if you enjoyed the Lion King-style dining at Hakuna Matata (in the *Disneyland Park*) during a summer visit, be aware it is frequently closed at off-peak times.

Some entertainment takes place only during peak periods, when the theme parks are open longer. A nightly Dreams fireworks show and a special evening parade, Fantillusion, are highlights in the *Disneyland Park* in summer and at Christmas, while the Winnie The Pooh & Friends show is high season only. Bad weather (notably heavy rain) can scupper some of the outdoor entertainment at any time, but this is more likely in winter. However, the Disney team is adept at creating extra Magic in the form of shows and theming at various times of the year, which make **Halloween** and **Christmas** especially appealing and provides an extra reason to visit at these times (see pages 23 and 25).

◀▷ BRITTIP

The excellent website **www.dlrpmagic.com** includes a section on Closures & Refurbishments, which lists rides due for a revamp up to 4 months in advance (go to Calendar, click on the Closures & Refurbishments tab).

The obvious advantage of visiting out of season is there are shorter queues, and nothing beats wandering around Fantasyland and Discoveryland with the choice of any ride without queuing (and without running into hordes of

Fantillusion parade

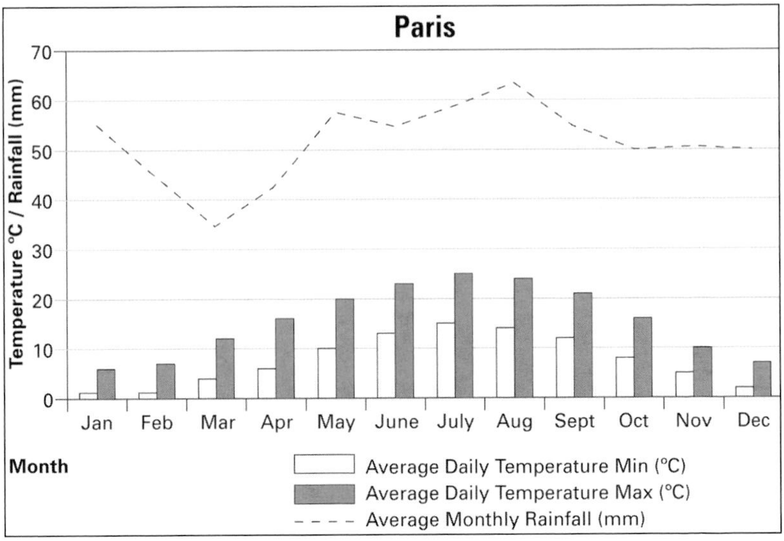
Paris
Temperature °C / Rainfall (mm)
70
60
50
40
30
20
10
0
Jan
Feb
Mar
Apr
May
June
July
Aug
Sept
Oct
Nov
Dec
Month
Average Daily Temperature Min (°C)
Average Daily Temperature Max (°C)
Average Monthly Rainfall (mm)

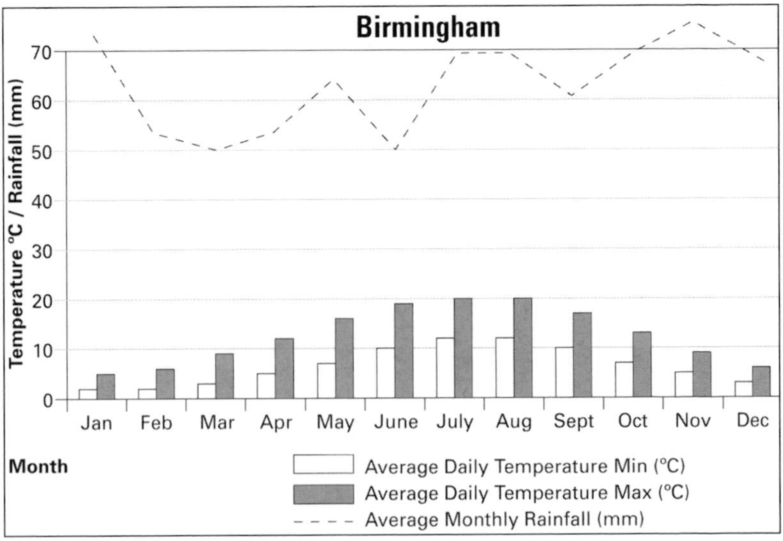
Birmingham
Temperature °C / Rainfall (mm)
70
60
50
40
30
20
10
0
Jan
Feb
Mar
Apr
May
June
July
Aug
Sept
Oct
Nov
Dec
Month
Average Daily Temperature Min (°C)
Average Daily Temperature Max (°C)
Average Monthly Rainfall (mm)

pushchairs). Cast Members have more time for you and the atmosphere is less frenetic.

Kids Go Free: The other big bonus is the regular Kids Go Free season, usually early Jan–end Mar, whereby, with any Disney hotel package, every child under 12 stays *free* with a full fare-paying adult, including continental breakfast and park entry. Park hours are shorter at these times of year (usually 10am–8pm at the *Disneyland Park* and 10am–7pm at the *Walt Disney Studios*), but it is easier to get around, so you shouldn't feel short-changed. In 2011, the offer was extended for much of the year for **children under 7**, which is well worth looking out for.

A weather eye

'Ah, but what about the weather?' you might well ask. *Disneyland Paris* can organise many things, but they have yet to discover how to keep the rain at bay. But the park designers took the weather firmly into consideration when they were busy Imagineering and you will find more attractions protected from the elements than at any other theme park. It is even possible to walk deep into the *Disneyland Park* mainly under cover (follow the route in Chapter 6).

The provision of arcades down both sides of Main Street USA (the entrance to the main park), some capacious indoor restaurants and few real 'outdoor' rides (not to mention the welcome shelter of all the shops) means much of your enjoyment should be unspoilt by the weather. In addition, if you bring a waterproof (or buy one of the cheap plastic ponchos on sale throughout the resort) you'll continue to enjoy the rides with fewer people around.

Christmas events

Foremost among the seasonal events you may want to consider when planning your visit is the Christmas programme, which features special shows, parades, fireworks, characters, decorations and other events in the theme parks, hotels and *Disney Village* early Nov–early Jan.

Disneyland Park: Main Street USA becomes the focus of the festive fun as it is transformed into a winter wonderland. There is a Yule overtone to the daily **Disney's Dreams Parade** with the addition of the 'Dreams of Christmas' float (with toy soldiers, Father Christmas and his reindeer, plus the regular Disney characters in festive costume), along with a guaranteed **snowfall** up to 5 times a day on Main Street, which is also illuminated with a series of glittering street lamps representing the Disney Princesses. New in 2011 was **Princess Aurora's Christmas Wish**, a 'magical moment' starring the Princess and Prince Philip, with the fairy godmothers adding their influence to turn the castle's roofs into a festive kaleidoscope of lights. Other highlights are **Belle's Christmas Village** – a charming medieval village

themed on *Beauty and the Beast*, with a chance to meet favourite characters from Disney's animated classic (and sample some Yuletide fare!) and **Mickey's Winter Wonderland** – a 20-minute song-and-dance ice-skating frolic with Mickey and the gang at the Chaparral Theatre in Frontierland (the one Christmas element that usually continues until early Mar). Children will also be drawn to **Santa's Christmas Village**, in the heart of Frontierland, where Father Christmas and his Elves wait to meet visitors young and old alike – and kids can post their 'wish list' at a special letter-box (and get an answer from Santa himself in due course!). Or they can meet **Santa Goofy** in full costume in Town Square. The signature **'it's a small world'** ride also gets a festive makeover dedicated to children the world over. For many, though, the twin highlights are the evening **Christmas Tree Lighting Ceremony** in Town Square, with one lucky child chosen to switch on the lights, and the nightly performance of the grand **Disney's Fantillusion** parade, which rounds out the festive events.

BRITTIP

Some of the Disney characters have different names in France and will occasionally give their autograph in French fashion. Chip 'n' Dale translate into Tic and Tac, Goofy can become Dingo and Winnie The Pooh is Winnie l'Ourson.

Walt Disney Studios: While there are not as many overtly festive elements at this park as at the *Disneyland Park*, the theme of a glamorous Hollywood Christmas is still centred on the entrance courtyard and inside Disney Studio 1, with suitably tinsel-clad style and seasonal accents. Look out also for a special Seasonal Greeting from none other than Mickey Mouse himself in the Courtyard each morning and afternoon. Finally, at the Umbrellas of Cherbourg in the Backlot area, the normal sprinkling of rain turns to snow.

Disney Village: The highly decorated theme is recurrent through all areas of the resort, including the resort's

© DISNEY

Indiana Jones

restaurant and shopping hub, with a chance to sample a host of traditional culinary specialities such as mulled wine, and festive touches to Buffalo Bill's Wild West Show.

If you have seen how brilliantly Disney prepares its Orlando theme parks for the season, we can assure you they take it to new heights in *Disneyland Paris* and it is definitely worth braving the wintry elements for the experience.

24

PLANNING

BRITTIP
If you can visit in late Nov or the first 2 weeks of Dec, you will benefit from the full Christmas festivities but without the heavy crowds they attract later in the month.

Hotels and dining: You can enjoy another great winter touch at *Disney's Hotel New York*, with a clever **ice-skating rink** outside, while all the Disney resorts feature a spectacular **Christmas Tree** in the lobby area with more decorations than you can shake a Mickey wand at, and the *Disneyland Hotel* also boasts a spectacular **Gingerbread House**, which is a visual marvel and a great photo opportunity. From 21–31 Dec, *Disney's Newport Bay Club* hotel also features a special musical gala dinner, **Mickey's Holiday Dinner Show** aboard HMS *Newport*, with Mickey, Minnie and Co. setting off on a journey of song and dance around the globe. To enjoy it, book from the UK on 00 33 1 60 30 40 50, but be aware

Party time

Disney knows how to throw a good party, and you should keep an eye out for several notable one-off events. **St David's Day** will be celebrated 8–11 Mar 2012, with Welsh-themed festivities in both the *Disneyland Park* and *Disney Village* (including a traditional Welsh choir, face-painting, live bands, a Welsh food and craft market, fireworks and a true 'red, white and green' spirit) while 17 Mar sees the high jinks of the annual **St Patrick's Day** celebration in *Disney Village*. Then 14 Jul is the big **Bastille Day** event, mixing spectacular fireworks and music in the *Disneyland Park*. Both parks celebrate their 'birthdays' in enchanting fashion too – the *Disneyland Park* on 12 Apr and the *Walt Disney Studios* on 16 Mar.

prices range from £81.60–£98.10 for adults and £17.30–£28 for children (3–11). There are even **Christmas Eve Character Dinners**, served buffet-style at *Hotel New York* and *Newport Bay Club* (for a whopping £156 adults and £48 children); Christmas Eve Dinners (without characters) in several hotels, *Disney Village*, and the *Disneyland Park* (£67–185 and £22–48); and a **Merry Christmas Lunch** with characters and Goofy as Santa Claus at the *Disneyland Hotel* on Christmas Day (£116 and £45). For **New Year's Eve**, there are character buffets at *Hotel New York* and *Newport Bay Club* (£166 and £48) and regular dinners at the hotels, Billy Bob's Saloon in *Disney Village* and the *Disneyland Park* (£84–265 and £20–48).

BRITTIP
The *Disneyland Park* stays open until 10pm 22 Dec–New Year and until 1am on New Year's Eve, when there are party festivities throughout the park and *Disney Village*.

Summer season

From mid-Jul–end Aug, the full range of park entertainment is up and running. The *Disneyland Park* is open until 11pm and crowds are at their highest. At this time of year the **Fantillusion** parade is one of

Disneyland Paris calendar

Jan–Mar: Under-12 Kids Go Free season

8–11 Mar: St David's Day festivities

16 Mar: Birthday of *Walt Disney Studios*

17 Mar: St Patrick's Day

12 Apr: Birthday of *Disneyland Paris*

14 Jul: French National Day fireworks

Mid-Jul–end Aug: Summer season

Oct: Disney's Halloween Festival

2–7 Nov: Bonfire Night Specials

Late Nov–end Dec: Christmas season

31 Dec: New Year's Eve festivities in *Disneyland Park* and *Disney Village*

the main highlights, followed by the fabulous new **Dreams fireworks** show, which bring down the curtain each evening during the launch of the 20th anniversary celebrations for *Disneyland Paris* in 2012 (and beyond!). **Goofy's Summer Camp** is another live show that goes on throughout the season at the Chaparral Theatre in Frontierland.

Halloween

The next great festive period is Halloween, and Disney makes a big feature of this. While the idea is certainly more American than European, the style with which *Disneyland Paris* has adopted this tradition is breathtaking. Not only is there a daily **Halloween Parade** (the Disney's **Dreams** parade, given a heavy 'bewitching' makeover), **Mickey's Halloween Treat in the Street** (an elaborate, themed meet 'n' greet) several times a day along Main Street USA, and **Disney's Maleficious Halloween Party** – a wonderfully villainous show in front of the Castle featuring Maleficent and other classic baddies – but the whole of Main Street is beautifully themed and decorated for the whole of October (amusing rather than scary for young children). Kids automatically gravitate towards the Halloween **face-painting** stalls and other special events, while there are also a series of **Mickey's Not-So-Scary Halloween Parties** 8–11pm (at around £23 per person, with park entry possible from 5pm) to give young 'uns their own fun evening out.

Halloween at Disneyland Paris

Special events include the Not-So-Scary show, the Merlin and The Witch Academy, Disney characters in special costume and a special parade, plus all the rides of Fantasyland are open, along with a few in Frontierland and Adventureland. There is then the one-off **Halloween Party** (31 Oct, £31 per person) 8.30pm–1am for more ghostly goings-on (see page 126), including more live entertainment and a Fantillusion parade plus a late-night party in *Disney Village*.

Finally, the **Bonfire Night specials** run for 3–4 nights each year around 5 Nov in best Guy Fawkes tradition. This magnificent fireworks and special effects spectacular takes place on and above Lake Disney, adjacent to *Disney Village*.

How long do you need?

First-time visitors should opt for the maximum time they can afford, especially at busy periods. The standard packages now offer 2-, 3- and 4-night stays and, as indicated on page 20, the 4-night duration is only just enough, especially if you have young children. If you can afford a week in summer, you will have the ideal amount of time to explore *Disneyland Paris* fully, see some of Paris and the surrounding area – and not return home too frazzled! However, because we know the majority of people book one of the standard packages, we have drawn up an example of how to plan for 3- and 5-day trips in Your Holiday Planner in Chapter 10.

If you're already familiar with the *Disneyland Park* and have yet to see the *Walt Disney Studios*, you will probably be comfortable with a 2-night stay, concentrating on the newer park during your full day on site. Couples without children or with older kids who can safely survive the demands of a bit of hectic park-hopping can probably negotiate both parks and, perhaps, Val d'Europe, on a 3-night package. But let us stress – you simply will not be able to 'do it all' in one of the peak periods!

The perfect 4-night visit would run Mon–Thurs, returning on Fri before the weekend crowds show up. However, if you can't go for this long or if you have to include a weekend, you can still have a great time. We'll tell you the dodges, tips and short cuts that will give you a head start over the rest of the crowds.

Clothing and comfort

The most important part of your holiday wardrobe is footwear – you will spend a LOT of time on your feet, even at off-peak periods. The parks may not be gigantic but that is irrelevant to the amount of time you'll spend walking and standing in queues. This is not the time to break in new sandals or trainers; comfortable shoes or trainers are essential. Otherwise, you need dress only as the climate dictates. T-shirts and shorts are quite acceptable in both parks when it's warm enough and most restaurants accept informal dress, although shoes and shirts must be worn at all times. In summer, bring a mac for those sudden showers. Warm, waterproof footwear is best in winter, along with extra-thick (or thermal) socks.

BRITTIP

Little girls love to dress up in their princess outfits to visit the parks so if your princess already has a dress, make sure you pack it. They are much more expensive in the park stores than at home.

If you feel you will need a change of clothes after a long day or some extra layers for the evening, you can leave them in a bag at the Luggage Check next to Guest Relations in both parks (€3 per bag) when you arrive. Both parks are well equipped with pushchairs for a small charge and baby-changing areas can be found in most toilets.

Disney with children

We are often asked what we think is the right age to take children to Disney for the first time, but there is no hard and fast answer. Some toddlers take to it instantly, while some 6- or even 7-year-olds are left rather bemused. Quite often, the best attractions for young children are the hotel swimming pool or the kiddie rides in *Disney Village*! Some love the Disney characters at first sight, while others find their size frightening. There is simply no predicting how they will react, but Simon's eldest boy (then 4½) loved just about every second of his first experience (apart from the fireworks). A 3-year-old may not remember much, but you can be sure they WILL have fun and provide YOU with great memories and photos. Here are a few tips, put together from personal experience and other parents.

The journey: Try to look calm (even if you don't feel it) and relaxed. Small children soon pick up on any anxieties, which makes them worse! Pack a bag with plenty of little bits for them (comics, sweets, colouring books, small surprise toys, etc) and keep vital 'extras' like Calpol® (in sachets, if possible), change of clothes, small first-aid kit (plasters, antiseptic cream, baby wipes), sunglasses, hat and suncream in your hand luggage – but remember to check on the latest security advice with regard to liquids. If they are fussy with their food, you may want to take a bottle of their favourite squash, etc. Ribena® is unheard of in European supermarkets, for example.

BRITTIP
Pushchairs are essential, even if your children have been out of them for a year or so. The distances involved can wear kids out quickly and a pushchair can save a lot of discomfort (for dads especially!). You can take your own, hire them at the theme parks or even buy one relatively cheaply at the Auchan supermarket in Val d'Europe.

Once there: Take things slowly and let children dictate the pace to a large extent. Remember to carry your small first-aid kit with you. Things like baby wipes always come in handy and it is a good idea to take spare clothes, which you can leave at the Luggage Check

at both parks. Going back to the hotel for an afternoon break is a good idea – the late afternoon and early evening are usually the best times to be at the parks in terms of cooler temperatures (in summer), fewer crowds and pure enjoyment. Both parks have a Lost Children meeting place (see page 107).

In the summer: Carry suncream and sunblock at all times and use it frequently – in queues, on buses, etc. A children's after-sun cream is also a good idea and don't forget to get them to drink lots of water or non-fizzy drinks. Tiredness and irritability are often caused by mild dehydration.

BRITTIP
The summer heat can make children irritable in no time, so take breaks for drinks and visit indoor attractions that have air-conditioning.

Dining out: Look for the all-you-can-eat buffets as these are a great way to fill the family up (you may get away with two meals a day) and cater for picky eaters. The Lucky Nugget Saloon, Plaza Gardens Restaurant (in the *Disneyland Park*), Rendezvous Des Stars (*Walt Disney Studios*) and Billy Bob's (*Disney Village*) all offer some serious buffets. But try to let your children get used to the size of the characters before you eat at a restaurant where they visit.

BRITTIP
Baby Care Centres (for changing, preparing food and feeding, with nappies and baby food for sale) are behind the Studio Services, just inside the entrance to the *Walt Disney Studios* and next door to the Plaza Gardens Restaurant in the *Disneyland Park*.

Having fun: Try to involve your children in some of the decision-making and be prepared to go with the flow if they find something unexpected they like (the Pocahontas Indian Village playground in the *Disneyland Park* is a good example). With young children, you are unlikely to see and do everything, so just take your time and

Attention to detail is a Disney hallmark

make the most of what you can all do together.

Travellers with disabilities

Disney pays close attention to the needs of guests with disabilities, and there are few rides and attractions that cannot cater for them, while wheelchair availability and access is almost always good. As the *Walt Disney Studios* is so recent, much thought and care has gone into the arrangements for people with various disabilities (from the wheelchair-bound to those

Top 10 must-do things in *Disneyland Paris*

1 Have a character meal.

2 See the daily parades (especially if Fantillusion is running).

3 Take a stroll around Lake Disney.

4 Have dinner at Planet Hollywood and then check out the live music at Billy Bob's Saloon in *Disney Village*.

5 See Buffalo Bill's Wild West Show with Mickey and Friends.

6 Have a drink in the Redwood Bar and Lounge at *Disney's Sequoia Lodge*.

7 Go shopping at La Vallée.

8 Try the Panoramagique balloon ride at *Disney Village*.

9 See the unique Cinémagique show in the *Walt Disney Studios*.

10 Dine at the California Grill restaurant.

with autism and epileptic concerns). It is worth taking time to familiarise yourself with all the ways in which you can take advantage of the facilities. The Cast Members should be fully prepared to help and assist, ensuring you get

Sequoia Lodge

Disney for seniors

If Simon's parents are anything to go by, the over-60s can also get a huge amount of enjoyment from the Disney experience. The greater ease of getting here (as opposed to the American parks) is high on their list of plus factors, while the convenience of just about everything being within walking distance or a short bus or train ride away scores highly, too. They preferred the *Disney Village* and hotel areas during the day when crowds were light. Within 2 days they were fully *au fait* with the whole resort and extremely comfortable with the set-up. Here is their own top 10 of attractions suitable for the over 60s.

1   Cinémagique (*Walt Disney Studios*).

2   Star Tours (*Disneyland Park*).

3   Pirates of the Caribbean (*Disneyland Park*).

4   Moteurs … Action! Stunt Show (*Walt Disney Studios*).

5   Studio Tram Tour (*Walt Disney Studios*).

6   Phantom Manor (*Disneyland Park*).

7   Animagique (*Walt Disney Studios*).

8   The daily spectacle of Disney Magic On Parade (*Disneyland Park*).

9   'it's a small world' (*Disneyland Park*).

10 Flying Carpets Over Agrabah (*Walt Disney Studios*).

They would even go as far as listing the walk around Lake Disney as an attraction in its own right, while they also felt the more show-based style of the *Studios* suited them better than the rather more hectic ride-orientated nature of the original park. However, they still acknowledge the essential magic of the latter is totally unmissable.

full value from all the thoughtful extra touches. The main car park also has areas closer to the park entrances set aside for guests with reduced mobility and you should ask for one of these on arrival. There are even specially adapted minibuses for transfers from the Disney hotels to the parks (on request at your hotel reception desk and at Guest Relations in the parks).

All Disney hotels (except *Disney's Davy Crockett Ranch*) have rooms accessible for guests with disabilities, and they publish a free *Guide for Guests with Special Needs*, available at hotel receptions and park Guest Services. The guide can be requested in advance from: *Disneyland Paris*, Guest Communication, PO Box 100, 77777 Marne-la-Vallée, Cedex, France.

Guidebooks in Braille are also provided and guide dogs are allowed in (although they are not permitted on certain attractions). You can ask for an **Assisted Access Card** that allows access to special waiting areas for many attractions for a person with disabilities and up to 3 companions (although this does not provide special access to the rides, as most queues have been made wheelchair-accessible). There are special areas at the many shows and parades for the disabled but not all rides at the *Disneyland Park* are fully accessible; some require transfer and therefore the help of a companion is needed.

Visitors with hearing disabilities are not terribly well catered for, apart from a handful of attractions that have subtitles on video screens rather than bilingual commentaries or headphone translators (Animagique and Cinémagique in the *Walt Disney Studios* both have induction loops, for example). The multi-lingual nature of the resort makes it difficult to use a close-captioning system effectively, as in Disney's American parks, and they still seem to be some way from solving this problem.

Animagique

Disney for grown-ups

You don't need to have children in tow to enjoy *Disneyland Paris*. In fact, we've often felt the place is actually too good for kids! There is so much clever detail and creativity that the majority of youngsters miss in their eagerness for the next ride, it is usually the grown-ups who get the most out of the experience. In fact, there are just as many couples without children and young adults on their own visiting the theme parks, making it a legitimate holiday for all ages. Certainly, when you look at some of the sophisticated dining on offer and the evening entertainment at places like Billy Bob's in *Disney Village*, it is easy to see the attraction for those aged over 18.

Paris obviously makes a wonderful honeymoon destination but newly-weds are just as likely to visit one of Disney's parks as the Eiffel Tower. Restaurants like the Blue Lagoon and Auberge de Cendrillon in the *Disneyland Park*, The Steakhouse in *Disney Village*, Hunter's Grill Restaurant at *Disney's Sequoia Lodge* and the superb California Grill at the *Disneyland Hotel* all offer a genuine romantic touch to dining à la Disney.

Being practical

When it comes to the practicalities of your holiday, your obvious needs include **passports** for all the family (double-check that the name on your passport matches that on your travel tickets) and remember all children must have their own passport. All British subjects MUST have a full, valid 10-year passport that will not expire for 3 months after you enter France. Non-British subjects should check their visa requirements in advance. For UK passport enquiries, call 08705 210410 or look up **www.passports-office.co.uk**.

Travel insurance

You can get free or reduced cost treatment in all EU countries. However, you must possess a European Health Insurance Card (EHIC), which replaced the old E111 in 2006. You can apply for the free EHIC online at **www.dh.gov.uk/**

PLANNING

travellers, by phone on 0845 606 2030 or 0845 605 0707, or by post – you can obtain a form at the Post Office (but you must know your NHS/National Insurance number). The EHIC does not cover all medical expenses, though, or the cost of bringing a person back to the UK in the event of illness or death, so it is essential to have adequate travel insurance cover as well.

You should never travel without good insurance, but you should also not pay over the odds for it. Tour operators may imply you need to buy their insurance policy, which you don't, and their policies can be expensive. Check that you don't already have cover through your home insurance or bank account as it is sometimes given as an extra.

Make sure your policy covers you for: **medical treatment** up to £1m; **personal liability** up to £1m; **cancellation or curtailment** up to £3,000; **personal property** up to £1,500 (but check on expensive items, as most policies limit single articles to £250); cash and documents, including your passport and tickets; and finally that the policy gives you a 24-hour emergency helpline.

Shop around at reputable dealers like **American Express** (0800 028 7573, **www.americanexpress.com/uk**); **AA** (0800 975 5819, **www.theaa.com**); **Aviva** (0844 891 1104, **www.aviva.co.uk); Direct Travel** (0845 605 2700, **www.direct-travel.co.uk**); **Club Direct** (0800 083 2466, **http://clubdirect.com**); **Columbus** (0870 033 9988, **www.columbusdirect.com**); **Egg** (0800 519 9931, **http://new.egg.com**); **Worldwide Travel Insurance** (01892 833338, **www.worldwideinsure.com**).

BRITTIP

If you're likely to make more than one trip abroad in a year, consider an **Annual Travel Policy** from the likes of Essential Travel (0845 803 5434, **www.essentialtravel.co.uk**) or Virgin Money (0844 888 3900 or **http://uk.virginmoney.com/virgin/travel-insurance/**).

MoneySupermarket also compares different travel insurers (**www.moneysupermarket.com/insurance**).

Key contacts

Here are the principal contact numbers for all the main agencies at *Disneyland Paris* (from the UK, omit the first 0 and add 00 33 to the number, e.g. to call Seine-et-Marne Tourist Office, dial 00 33 1 60 39 60 39):

Annual Passport Hotline: 01 60 30 60 69

Baby Care Centre: 01 64 74 26 00

Billy Bob's Buffet: 01 60 30 40 50

Buffalo Bill's Wild West Show: 01 60 45 71 00

Café Mickey: 01 60 30 40 50

Davy Crockett Ranch: 01 60 45 69 00

Davy Crockett's Adventure: 0825 150 280

Disneyland Hotel: 01 60 45 65 00

***Disneyland Paris* First Aid Centre:** 01 64 74 23 03

***Disneyland Paris* Lost Children:** 01 64 74 24 00

Disney Village: 01 60 30 20 20

Disney Village Tourist Office: 01 60 43 33 33

Euro Disney SCA, Shareholders Info & Club: 01 64 74 56 30, dlp.actionnaires@disney.com

France Tourist Office, London: 0906 824 4123 (60p/min), info.uk@franceguide.com

Golf Disneyland: 01 60 45 68 90

Hotel Cheyenne: 01 60 45 62 00

Hotel New York: 01 60 45 73 00

Hotel Santa Fe: 01 60 45 78 00

King Ludwig's Castle: 01 60 42 71 80

Lost and Found: 01 64 74 25 00

Mail Order Service: 01 64 74 48 48, dlp.mail.order@disney.com

Newport Bay Club Hotel: 01 60 45 55 00

Panoramagique: 01 60 45 70 52

Planet Hollywood: 01 60 43 78 27

Rainforest Café: 01 60 43 65 65

Resort Guest Relations: 01 60 30 60 53, dlp.guest.communication.@disney.com

Resort Restaurant Reservations (up to 2 months in advance): 01 60 30 40 50

Sea Life Aquarium: 01 60 42 33 66

Seine-et-Marne Tourist Office: 01 60 39 60 39, cdt@tourisme77.fr

Sequoia Lodge Hotel: 01 60 45 51 00

The Steakhouse: 01 60 45 70 45

UK bookings (to book a Disneyland Resort Paris stay from the UK): 08448 008 111.

VEA Airport Shuttle Bus: 01 53 48 39 53

VIP Guided Tours: 01 64 74 21 26

Write to *Disneyland Paris* Guest Relations: *Disneyland Paris*, Communication Visiteurs, BP 100, 77777 Marne-la-Vallée, Cedex 4, France

Top 10 'hidden secrets' of Disneyland Paris

Look out for the many special 'extras' that may not be so obvious to the busy visitor.

1 La Tanière Du Dragon – the 'Dragon's Lair' under the Castle at the *Disneyland Park*, which many people miss.

2 Lighting effects – you can change the lights inside Studio 1 at the *Walt Disney Studios*, in front of Club Swankadero and in the Liki Tiki Lounge.

3 Take a phone call – pick up the phone next to Walt's bureau inside the Photo Shop on the corner of the *Disneyland* Park's Town Square and listen for a message!

4 Get breezy – approach the giant fan at the exit to the Armageddon attraction in the *Walt Disney Studios*; it works via a motion sensor.

5 Heavy rock – sit on the large stone underneath the suspended bridge in Adventure Isle (*Disneyland Park*) – it rocks from side to side!

6 Puppet parade – be outside 'it's a small world' on the hour for a fun parade of ride characters on the 'clock tower'.

7 Take a ride – sit on the motorcycle outside the Café des Cascadeurs in the *Walt Disney Studios* and be startled by the sound effects!

8 Get a haircut – in Dapper Dan's, the period barber's shop on Main Street USA in the *Disneyland Park*.

9 Make it rain – stand under the Umbrellas de Cherbourg next to the Backlot Express restaurant in the *Walt Disney Studios*.

10 Make some music – try out the working keyboard in the back of the technician's van outside Rock 'n' Roller Coaster starring Aerosmith, again at the *Walt Disney Studios*.

Plus, it's not exactly 'hidden,' but Cinema Mickey inside the Videopolis restaurant/theatre in Discoveryland (in the *Disneyland Park*) is a chance to sit and watch some of the classic cartoons that made Walt's most iconic creation famous. It is fully air-conditioned and makes a great break during hotter (or wetter) periods.

PLANNING

Adventure Isle

Medical matters

There are two fully English-speaking hospitals in Paris: the **American Hospital in Neuilly**: 63 Boulevard Victor Hugo, 92200 Neuilly-sur-Seine (Métro Porte Maillot); tel. (in Paris) 01 46 41 25 25, **www.american-hospital.org**; and the **Hertford British Hospital**, 3 Rue Barbès, 92300 Levallois-Perret (Métro Anatole France); 01 46 39 22 05, **www.british-hospital.org**.

For an after-hours chemist, the **Drugstore Champs-Elysées** at 133 Avenue des Champs-Elysées (Métro Charles de Gaulle-Etoile); tel. 01 47 20 39 25, is open until 2am daily, while the **Pharmacie Dhery** at 84 Avenue des Champs-Elysées (by Métro Georges V); 01 45 62 02 41, is open around the clock. There is also a pharmacy at the entrance to the big Val d'Europe shopping mall, closest to the RER station entrance, open 10am–9pm Mon–Sat.

Disney's Newport Bay Club

Emergencies

Here are your emergency contact numbers.

- **Police:** 17 or 112.
- **Fire brigade:** 18 or 112.
- **24-hour doctor:** 01 47 07 77 77.
- **24-hour medical emergencies:** 15 or 112.
- **Less serious medical incidents:** 18 or 112.
- **Public ambulance service:** 01 45 13 67 89.

Safety first

Crime has never been a major issue at *Disneyland Paris*, but you should still use your common sense as you would in any city (especially around the RER station, where pickpockets sometimes operate). Keep your hotel door locked at all times (even if you are just popping down the corridor) and don't leave things like cameras or camcorders on view in the car when you leave it parked.

Both parks have a Lost and Found office and Guest Services can advise you of any additional security requirements (only the *Disneyland Hotel, Disney's Hotel New York* and

Disney's Newport Bay Club have rooms equipped with safety deposit boxes).

The Paris **lost property office** is located at the Préfecture de Police, 36 Rue des Morillons, 75015 Paris (Métro Convention); 08 21 00 25 25. It is open Mon, Wed and Fri 8.30am–5pm, Tues and Thurs 8.30am–8pm. If for any reason you need to contact the **British Embassy** in Paris, it can be found at 35 rue du Faubourg St Honore, 75363, Cedex 08, Paris; 01 44 51 31 00.

Money

As ever on a foreign holiday, it is advisable not to carry too much cash. Credit cards are almost universally accepted (although not by many small hotels and cafés in some areas of France) and you can also use Maestro, Visa and Mastercard at the several cash dispensers around the resort.

 BRITTIP

Want the best exchange rate for your holiday cash? Check out **www. travelmoneymax.com** from the folks at Money Saving Expert.

The currency, of course, is the euro. At the time of writing, £1 = €1.16, or €1 = 86 pence, so, roughly speaking, £10 would be a touch less than €12. There are eight coins – €1 and €2 and 1, 2, 5, 10, 20 and 50 cents – and seven notes in €5, €10, €20, €50, €100, €200 and €500 denominations.

Perhaps the best option, though, is the convenient, simple **FairFX card** (**www.fairfx.com**), a debit card that you charge in advance and use as a credit card to your pre-paid limit. The exchange rate is fixed at loading and you can save 5–10% on High Street currency rates.

Tipping: In France, a 15% service charge is sometimes added to restaurant and hotel bills but the usual practice of tipping is simply to leave a few euros at the end of a meal. A taxi driver would expect a 10–15% tip, while a porter would expect €1 a bag.

Phone calls

If you need to **phone home**, avoid using the hotel phones as they are fiendishly expensive (and Disney hotels are no exception). Your mobile phone will probably also have expensive connection charges for calling from abroad (or even for receiving calls). It is better to use a public payphone and pay with a BT Chargecard or other phone card. To call the UK from France, dial 00 44 and then the UK number (omit the first 0 from the area code).

BRITTIP
Look for a character meet 'n' greet *without* the crowds – in the first-floor lobby of the *Disneyland Hotel* twice a day, usually at 11am and at teatime. Ask at the hotel's Guest Relations desk for exact times.

Tourist info

If you are out and about in France, look for the local **Offices du Tourism and Syndicats d'Initiative** for maps, advice and info on the local sights and attractions. Most tourist attractions are open 10am–5pm, with one late opening day per week but, surprisingly, many close on public holidays (although not in *Disneyland Paris*).

Where are the characters?

The biggest question on most visitors' lips (especially those with children!) is usually 'Where can we find the characters?' Invariably, some leave frustrated because they simply miss out on this essential photo and autograph opportunity. So here's a head start on where you can usually meet Mickey and Co.

Disneyland Park:

- Various characters at the top of Main Street USA for the Main Street Park Opening at 9–9.30am (or 10–10.30am on later opening hours) every day.

- The big cheese himself in the new (for 2012) *Meet Mickey Mouse* location in Fantasyland.

- Minnie under the Gazebo on Main Street USA periodically throughout the day.

- Mary Poppins and friends also often appear in this Town Square location.

- Winnie the Pooh and Friends periodically by the Castle Theatre Stage in Fantasyland OR at Casey's Corner on Main Street USA.

- Disney Princesses can always be seen in the new Princess Pavilion in Fantasyland.

- Mickey and/or Minnie, plus *Toy Story* friends Woody, Jessie and Bullseye at Woody's Roundup Village in Frontierland (usually afternoons).

- Jungle Book/Lion King characters outside Colonel Hathi's Pizza Outpost; Peter Pan and friends after the Following The Leader show, and Aladdin outside Les Tresors de Scheherezade, all in Adventureland.

- Captain Jack Sparrow outside the Blue Lagoon restaurant.

- A wide variety of characters (including various Disney villains) can often be found outside 'it's a small world' and Alice's Curious Labyrinth in Fantasyland; at lunch or dinner at Cowboy Cookout Barbecue in Frontierland or Auberge de Cendrillon (with various Disney Princes and Princesses, plus Suzy and Perla, the mice from *Cinderella*) in Fantasyland.

Walt Disney Studios:

- Mickey, Minnie and many classic characters in the entrance courtyard in front of Studio 1, usually from 10am to noon and 2.15–4pm each day.

- Mickey and Friends in Place des Stars in Production Courtyard.

- Chip 'n Dale and others occasionally by Les Parapluies de Cherbourg in the Backlot.

- The latest Pixar Films stars at the character scenes next to the Cars Road Rally ride in Toon Studio.

- Buzz Lightyear and other Pixar classics in the central plaza of Toon Studio.

- Monsters Inc characters at the set-piece display in Toon Studio next to Studio 1.

- The Green Army Men from the *Toy Story* films at Toy Story Playland – and watch out for how they greet children in Buzz Lightyear costume.

Disney Village:

- At one of the character meals served throughout the day at Café Mickey (7.30 and 9.30am for breakfast, noon–2.30pm for lunch and 3–11pm for dinner); and also for Sunday brunch at The Steakhouse (midday–3pm).

For all character meals you need to make a reservation either when you book your Disney package, through reception at your Disney hotel or in advance by phoning (from the UK) 00 33 1 60 30 40 50 (just 01 60 30 40 50 in France) up to 2 months in advance.

Disneyland Hotel:

- At dinner at the Inventions Restaurant, and in the foyer in the morning and late afternoon.

All Disney Hotels (including Disney's Davy Crockett Ranch):

- In the lobby area at regular intervals throughout the morning.

◀◀▶ **BRITTIP**

To check exactly when and where to meet the characters in the parks, always pick up a time/location schedule as you enter the park, alongside the park maps, or available at City Hall at the *Disneyland Park* or Guest Relations at the *Walt Disney Studios*.

Know before you go

As hard as we work to keep this guide up to date, there are always things that change after our deadlines or areas we can't cover fully in this relatively small volume so here are some websites to help you stay up to date.

www.disneylandparis.co.uk: First and foremost is the official Disney website with the opportunity to book online and save money (although it can be hard to navigate).

www.dlp.info: This fan site has a wealth of useful info, news and photos, including a restaurant guide.

www.dlrpmagic.com: Another sharp fan site with great photos, videos and maps, in-depth dining and ride detail. It has a separate section for news and updates at **www.dlrptoday.com**.

www.dlpfoodguide.com: Tops for the Disney dining experience.

www.clickmagique.com: Some of the best photos and other news.

www.thedibb.co.uk: The top UK site dedicated to all things Disney, with its own *Disneyland Paris* forum.

www.disboards.com: This site also has a special forum on the Paris resort.

Other general tourist info websites are: **http://uk.franceguide.com**, **www.new-paris-ile-de-france.co.uk**, **http://en.parisinfo.com**, **www.disneylandparisguide.net** and **www.tourism77.co.uk**.

Now let's move on to another vital subject in your preparations, that of actually Getting There…

3 Getting There

or Trains, Planes and Automobiles – plus Coaches and Ferries!

In many ways, your choice of when to go to *Disneyland Paris* pales into insignificance compared with the issue of HOW to get there. The options for travel for this relatively short journey are almost as wide-ranging as the resort itself.

Obviously, your location in the UK plays a large part in your decision. The Eurostar service may be a wonderful method of transport but it is not ideal if you live in the North or Wales. Equally, going by coach and letting someone else do all the driving has a lot of appeal but it can seem the long way of doing things if you live in the South East (where Eurostar and Eurotunnel are quicker options). Flying is increasingly popular and affordable with the low-cost airlines, and the advantages are especially noticeable from regional airports like Newcastle, Aberdeen, Bristol and even Southampton. So here is an outline of the pros and cons of each of the main possibilities.

By car

With the opening of the Channel Tunnel in 1994, the dream of quick, reliable transport to the Continent became a reality. A permanent link was established along with a whole new realm of Channel-hopping

Brittany Ferries' Normandie Express

possibilities. Some 85m people used the longest undersea tunnel in the world (50km/31mls in length, 39km/24mls of them under the sea itself) in the first 10 years. In 2010 alone, the figures were: 2,125,259 cars, 56,507 coaches and 9,528,558 Eurostar passengers.

BRITTIP — If you exceed the speed limit by more than 40kph/25mph, the French police have the power to take your driving licence immediately, so you won't be able to drive. For serious offences they can even confiscate your car.

While the Channel Tunnel obviously opened in direct competition with cross-Channel ferry businesses, it actually served to increase the total traffic between the UK and Europe. Not only did the day-tripping habit pick up (as did the number of British-orientated supermarkets in the Calais vicinity), but driving holidays to France, Belgium, Holland, Spain, Germany and even Italy also received a major boost. So, just 2 years after the opening of *Disneyland Paris*, it stands to reason the tunnel would become a prime route to get there (in fact, it was one of the many reasons why Disney eventually settled on the Paris site).

The combination of the tunnel and the well-established ferry links from Dover, Newhaven and Portsmouth now provide a wealth of opportunity for routes into France by car and coach, and more people travel by car than any other mode of transport. France is also blessed with well-organised and relatively smooth-flowing motorways (certainly compared to our M25), many of which are toll-road autoroutes (autoroutes des péages). In summer 2011, the tolls still amounted to just €19.30 one way to use this quickest and most convenient routes (A26 from Calais, then A1, A104 and A4 – see maps on pages 40 and 41). Basically, it is 104km/65mls on the A26, 156km/97mls on the A1, 25km/16mls on the A104 and then another 11.5km/7mls on the A4 before

Autoroutes des péages

Tickets are issued at the beginning of each of the paid motorway networks. Payments are then calculated on the distance you travel and must be paid on leaving the motorway. You pay at the *péages* (toll-gates) with either cash or credit card. For short local journeys it is a good idea to keep some small change handy to avoid the hassle of using your credit card. Payments vary according to the type of vehicle, with different price bands for cars, vans, cars with trailers, lorries and motorbikes.

the turn-off (Exit 14) for 'Les Parcs Disneyland'.

BRITTIP — Watch out for the A26 junction with the A1, as the signposting is not very clear and it is easy to miss. The motorway turn-off signs are in white (and set off to the right-hand side) and you need to follow the big blue overhead destination signs for Paris.

Toll roads and routes: The toll-road system in France is split into 8 privately owned networks, although the one from Calais to Marne-la-Vallée is all under the control of SANEF (**www.sanef.com/en/**).

Check out:

- **www.autoroutes.fr** for more details on your journey, a handy route planner and real-time traffic info;

- **www.eurotunnel.com** for helpful route advice;

- **www.multimap.com** and **www.mapquest.co.uk** for maps and directions;

- **www.theaa.com** for a good route planner.

BRITTIP — The autoroute speed limit is 130kph/80mph, but 110kph/68mph when it is wet. It is 110kph/68mph on non-toll motorways and 90kph/56mph on other roads, 80kph/50mph when wet and 50kph/30mph in towns.

GETTING THERE

French driving rules

- Children under 10 are forbidden to travel in the front seat.
- On-the-spot fines or deposits (in cash – and you should get an official receipt) can be demanded for not wearing seat-belts (which are compulsory front AND back).
- Drink-driving, driving on a provisional licence and speeding offences will also incur heavy fines (and French police are pretty hot on the latter).
- The use of mobile phones while driving is strictly prohibited.

Driving from Calais: Most people drive from Calais. From Calais ferry port, you are directed straight on to the A26 (via the E15 – follow the clear signs for Paris, Reims), while from the Channel Tunnel, you have a short 6km/3½ml stretch south-west on the A16 (signs for Calais) before picking up the A26.

BRITTIP
It is best to navigate by the directional signs rather than the route numbers.

From Calais on the A26, initially follow the signs for Saint-Omer, Arras, Reims, Paris; at the junctions with the A1, follow signs for Paris, Arras Est; immediately after Charles de Gaulle Airport, follow signs for Bordeaux, Nantes, Lyon, Marne-la-Vallée, Paris Est, Bobigny; once on the A104, look for Lyon, Meaux, Marne-la-Vallée and 'Les Parcs Disneyland'; at the junction with the A4, follow signs for Meaux, Reims.

BRITTIP
Although *Disneyland Paris* is officially located in Marne-la-Vallée, the whole area along the A4 here is designated Marne-la-Vallée, hence it is easy to get sidetracked. From the A104, follow the signs for 'Les Parcs Disneyland'.

The only other area to watch out for is switching from the A1 to the A104 at Charles de Gaulle Airport, although there is a sign for 'Les Parcs

Disneyland' just before and after the airport, directing you on to the A104. Immediately after the airport, the autoroute splits and you need to be in the right-hand lanes for Marne-la-Vallée; it then splits again and the 2 right lanes bring you on to the A104 heading south (see map on page 41).

It should take you a shade under 3hrs to drive from Calais. You can save the toll money by taking the Routes Nationales (or N-roads), but that would add nearly an hour to your journey.

The first tollbooths you come to on the A26 are after about 61km/38mls, between Exits 4 and 5, and here you simply collect a ticket from the machine, which records the point at which you join the A-route system, and then you pay at the tollbooths just north of Charles de Gaulle Airport (after Exit 7). These are the only tolls you pay on the direct Calais–Marne-la-Vallée route.

BRITTIP
Speed camera detectors are illegal in France, and if found by police will be confiscated and incur a BIG fine.

Driving from Boulogne: From the ferry port at Boulogne, follow the 'Toutes Directions' signs and these quickly bring you on to the A16 via a stretch of dual carriageway. Once on the A16, head south for 200km/125mls until it becomes the N1, then follow N1 around until it hits the junction with D104 (after about 7.5km/4½mls. Take D104 (La Francilienne) for 16km/10mls to the A1 just north of the airport. Go south on the A1 and follow the same directions as above (A104–A4). Tolls will be about €33 and the journey will take 2½–3hrs.

Driving from Caen: If you take the Portsmouth–Caen ferry route, your journey will be around 265km/164mls via the A13, the Paris *périphérique* and the A4, and the tolls will be about €22.

Local roads: Once in the Marne-la-Vallée area, your main route to and from the theme parks is likely to be the

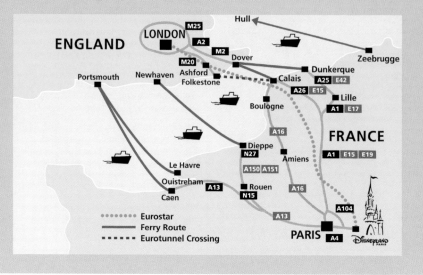

Map legend:
- Eurostar
- Ferry Route
- Eurotunnel Crossing

ENGLAND — LONDON, M25, M2, A2, M20, Dover, Ashford, Folkestone, Newhaven, Portsmouth, Hull

FRANCE — Calais, Dunkerque, Zeebrugge, Boulogne, Lille, Dieppe, Amiens, Le Havre, Ouistreham, Caen, Rouen, PARIS

Road numbers: A25, E42, A26, E15, A1, E17, A16, N27, A150, A151, A1, E15, E19, A13, N15, A16, A104, A13, A4

Disneyland Paris

GETTING THERE

A4, a busy stretch of motorway at peak periods (especially into Paris itself) but otherwise an easy-to-use arterial. There are no tollbooths on this section, hence you can use the A4 as frequently as you like at no extra cost. Once you turn off at Exit 14 for the theme parks, everything is well signposted to the hotels and main car parks. A huge ring road encompassing the whole resort (plus Val d'Europe), called the Boulevard de l'Europe, makes an interesting drive as you can get some unusual glimpses of the theme parks from it.

On board the **Normandie Express**

BRITTIP

If a French driver flashes their lights at you, it means they intend to go first, NOT that they are giving you right of way.

Parking and breakdowns: Parking and rest zones are situated every 10–20km/6–12mls on motorways, with 24-hour petrol stations about every 40km/25mls. In addition, you must not park on yellow kerbs.

If you break down, pull up on the right, put on your hazard lights and place a red warning triangle 30m/33yds behind your vehicle (compulsory for vans and cars with trailers). Orange emergency telephones are usually every 2km/1¼mls apart on motorways. If you break down and can't leave your vehicle, there are regular road patrols on all autoroutes.

Both AA and RAC members can take advantage of their organisation's European Breakdown Assistance service, valuable when travelling on the Continent. Look up **www.theaa.com** (0800 085 2721) or **www.rac.co.uk** (0800 015 6000).

Service areas: French motorway service areas (or *aires*) are generally open 24 hours and offer a combination of facilities way beyond anything in the UK in terms of quality. There are two types: one has full fuel, catering and shopping facilities, while the other is a picnic area with toilets. The latter are often pretty places to stop, but bring your own toilet paper (for some reason it is not a standard French provision!).

On board a P&O ferry

BRITTIP

Buying petrol in motorway service stations in France is as exorbitant as it is in the UK. You can save 12–15% (more on diesel) by filling up at the nearest hypermarket (*hypermarché*) in Calais or Le Havre.

Maps: The AA's *Touring Map France* series (around £4.50 each) are among the best available. Look for *Paris & The North* for the full route from Calais to Marne-la-Vallée, while you would need *Normandy* and *Paris & The North* to cover the journey from Caen. Online, the website **www.viamichelin.co.uk** also offers some valuable maps and info. All autoroutes have an information radio station. In northern France, English-language bulletins are on 107.7FM on the hour and half-hour.

By ferry

Of course, if you are taking the car, you need to decide which method of cross-Channel travel you prefer – the various ferry services from one of 3 south coast ports or the Eurotunnel service from Folkestone. If you opt for the more traditional ferry route, you can go from Dover, Portsmouth and Newhaven, or even Hull to Zeebrugge in Belgium. Here's how they break down.

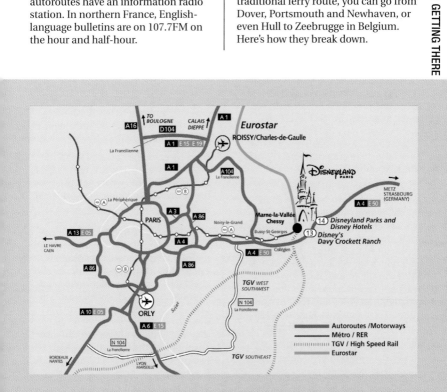

Driving in France

There are no major differences in the traffic rules in France (other than driving on the right!), but driving with dipped headlights is compulsory in poor visibility – so don't leave home without a pair of headlight beam adjusters. It is also advisable to take a set of spare bulbs, while a red hazard warning triangle is compulsory (for vans and cars with trailers) in case of a breakdown. You should take your vehicle registration document and insurance certificate, as well as your driving licence (it is a legal requirement to have it with you whenever you are driving). Check with your insurance company to ensure you have full cover while driving in France. Green cards are no longer required, but some insurance companies issue them anyway as they are a sure way of convincing local police you are properly insured. Road signs are pretty much universal, but additional signs or warnings to watch for are:

Allumez vos phares/feux	Switch on your lights	*Interdit aux piétons*	Forbidden to pedestrians
Attention au feu	Fire hazard	*Ne pas depasser*	Do not overtake
Attention travaux	Beware roadworks	*Pas de sortie*	No exit
Cedée le passage	Give way	*Rappel*	Reminder (often on speed limit signs)
Chaussée déformée	Uneven road surface		
Circulation	Traffic	*Route barrée*	Road closed
Essence sans plomb	Unleaded petrol	*Sens unique*	One way
Fin d'interdiction de stationner	End of prohibited parking	*Sens interdit*	No entry
		Supercarburant	Lead replacement petrol
Gazole	Diesel	*Verglas*	Black ice

Dover

To start with, Dover is an easy port to get to by road – either straight down the M2/A2 in north Kent or (our preferred route) via the M20/A20, both of which come off the M25. It is about 1¾hrs from central London (given a relatively traffic-free run) and you need to head to the Eastern Docks for the main ferry operators. Dover is a modern, well-organised port and should get you aboard your ferry with the minimum of fuss.

The Travel Centre includes ferry operator ticket offices, an AA shop, a café, phones, toilets and baby-changing facilities. Also, once you have driven into the terminal area itself, there are 2 mini food villages offering another café, a Burger King, a WH Smith, bureau de change and cashpoint, plus more toilets, baby-changing facilities and phones. You should arrive at least 30mins to 1 hr before your sailing time and have passports ready as you drive in.

If you have booked in advance (which is highly advisable), you proceed straight through to your ferry operator's check-in. If you don't have a ticket, you can park up in the short-stay parking area (maximum stay 15 mins) at the main entrance to the passenger terminal and buy one from the Travel Centre (6am–8pm). Alternatively, you can pass straight to check-in and purchase a ticket there. There are NO services by any operator on Christmas Day.

Once through the Eastern Docks' main reception area, follow the 'Ferry' signs to Border Control, where you will need to show your passports. Remember, all British subjects MUST have a full, valid 10-year passport that will not expire for at least 3 months after you return. Non-British subjects should check their visa requirements in advance. Then follow the ferry operator signs to check-in, where you will be allocated a numbered embarkation lane to proceed to, from where you will be directed to the ferry when it is ready to board. While waiting, you can take advantage of the food villages and facilities.

Join the club

P&O Ferries offers 3 distinct extra services, which can be pre-booked or, in the case of the Club Lounge, booked onboard (although it then costs more).

The **Club Lounge** is an exclusive quiet lounge, complete with comfy leather armchairs, where you are greeted with a complimentary glass of champagne and offered tea and coffee, biscuits, fruit and newspapers by its own waiter/waitress service. There is also a business area where laptops can be used.

The **Priorité** service is a pre-booked priority loading system, which allows you to embark early and unload first, which is highly worthwhile when time is of the essence.

These can be combined in a **Club Plus** service, which provides use of the Club Lounge and the priority loading/unloading as well. At the time of writing, the prices were: £12/person each way for the Club Lounge, if booked in advance (£14 if booked onboard); £12/vehicle each way for Priorité; if opting for Club Plus, £12/person each way plus £6/vehicle. For 2 people, Club Plus would be £60 return.

Three main companies operate from this busy cross-Channel hub, all using the well-provisioned Eastern Docks.

BRITTIP
For more info on the port of Dover: 01304 240400, **www.doverport. co.uk**.

P&O Ferries: Dover's biggest and most sophisticated operator, with up to 46 crossings to Calais a day, 364 days a year, they operate the most frequent services on this route and in a high degree of comfort and quality. The crossing time from Dover is 90mins, although you mustn't forget to put your watches forward an hour on arrival in France.

BRITTIP
Visit P&O's website **www.poferries. com** to take advantage of their Best Fare Sailings, which offer cheaper fares the earlier you book.

Once settled aboard, you have a good choice of bars, shops, lounges and cafés in which to while away the time. All P&O Ferries' ships include a Food Court (usually the busiest area on board, especially just after embarkation), the **Costa Coffee** company, **The Bar** and a shop selling sweets and other snacks. **The Brasserie** offers a more upmarket choice for a meal in mid-Channel and, if you have opted for Club Plus when you booked, you also get the benefit of the Club

Lounge and its personalised service, as well as priority embarkation and unloading at the other end.

For the young ones, there are children's entertainers on the 5 Dover–Calais ferries for the school holidays, along with soft play areas, while children eat at half-price in the Food Court. Provisions for the youngest members of the family now extend to free Heinz baby food. There is also a good video games centre, the Megadrome, to keep older children amused.

For shoppers, some of the biggest savings available are on fragrances, at up to 40% off UK high-street prices.

Designer sunglasses at up to 20% cheaper include Gucci, Prada, Ray Ban and Police. Up to 30% can be saved on a wide range of wines and spirits.

BRITTIP
You can save money on P&O Ferries by booking a night crossing. Some onboard services are closed (Club Lounge and The Brasserie, for example) but prices are reduced for these 'Lite Night' crossings.

P&O now has two new vessels operating on this route, *Spirit of Britain* (Jan 2011) and *Spirit of France* (Nov 2011), the largest short-haul ferries ever built at 49,000 tons (replacing the old-faithfuls of *Pride of Dover* and *Pride of Calais*). They offer more capacity, more comfort and more facilities, as well as being the most

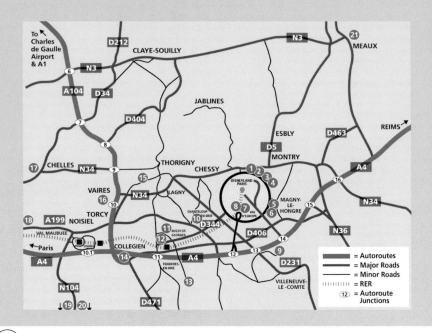

Map labels:
To Charles de Gaulle Airport & A1
CLAYE-SOUILLY — D212 — N3 — 21 MEAUX
6 — N3 — A104 — D34
JABLINES
7 — D404 — ESBLY — D463 — REIMS
8 — D5 — MONTRY
17 CHELLES — N34 — THORIGNY — CHESSY — DISNEYLAND PARIS — A4
15 — 16
VAIRES — 16 — N34 — LAGNY — MAGNY-LE-HONGRE — N34
10 — CHANTELOUP-EN-BRIE — VAL D'EUROPE — 15
18 A199 TORCY NOISIEL — 10 — D344 — D406 — N36
VAL MAUBUEE — BUSSY-ST-GEORGES — 14 — N36
Paris — LOGNES — COLLEGIEN — D231
10.1 — 14 — 11 — A4 — 12 — 13 — 9
FERRIERES-EN-BRIE
N104 — 13 — VILLENEUVE-LE-COMTE — D231
19 20 — D471

Legend:
= Autoroutes
= Major Roads
= Minor Roads
= RER
12 = Autoroute Junctions

44

GETTING THERE

environmentally friendly ferries at sea. 0871 664 2121, **www.poferries.com**.

SeaFrance: This is the only French ferry operator on the Dover–Calais route, offering up to 30 daily crossings, 364 days of the year (not Christmas Day). All of its tourism crossings are now operated by its latest trio of superferries, the award-winning *SeaFrance Berlioz*, *SeaFrance Rodin* and *SeaFrance Molière* (the latter being the longest and arguably most stylish ferry on cross-Channel routes), which cover the journey in a brisk 90 minutes.

SeaFrance Berlioz

The impressive super-ferry fleet provides a wide range of dining and onboard activities. Each ship offers a choice of restaurant areas: **Le Relais**, a self-service restaurant; **Le Parisien**, a French café; **Le Pub**, a traditional bar; and **La Brasserie**, a fine-dining restaurant serving gourmet French cuisine. All three ships feature a well-stocked shop, with major discounts on high street prices and the smart Latitudes observation lounge/bar. There is also an information disk, bureau de change and a Kids' Zone section of fun and activities in 3 areas for children from nursery age to teens (including, of course, the requisite video-game zone!).

BRITTIP

As we go to press, the future of SeaFrance is uncertain so keep up-to-date with developments if you are considering booking with them.

Prices fluctuate depending on the month of travel and early booking is strongly advised, with discounts often available. SeaFrance's website displays prices next to each crossing

Cars Quatres Roues Rallye at Walt Disney Studios

and alternative crossing times, so passengers can see which will suit them best. They also offer 2 types of ticket: *Saver*, their lowest-rate, non-refundable fare, with a £5 booking modification fee and 100% cancellation fee; and *Flexible*, with no modification fees. 0871 22 22 500, **www. seafrance.com**.

DFDS Seaways (formerly Norfolkline): An alternative to the occasionally hectic Calais crossings, with up to 12 sailings a day to Dunkerque, just over 40km/25mls along the French coast from Calais. The crossing time is a slightly long 2hrs but the Dunkerque port facilities are well run, usually congestion free and easy to negotiate. There is a distinctive DFDS travel centre within the Dover Ferry Terminal while, at the Dunkerque Terminal, there is a lounge area with facilities for the disabled and a snack bar, **La Véranda**, offering non-alcoholic drinks and food 9.30am–5.30pm (Sat–Thurs).

DFDS also has a fleet of 3 modern ferries, each of 35,293 tons, and has added significantly to its onboard facilities. They include relaxation areas, video games, a cinema, 2 playrooms for children (the Games Castle and Little Nippers), a full-service restaurant, fast-food restaurant and bistro. Freight drivers also have a separate restaurant and relaxation area. You can upgrade (for £15/person on board or £12 if booked in advance online) to the **First Class Lounge**, which has an exclusive seating area, free internet access and complimentary tea, coffee and soft drinks. All interior facilities are smoke-free but there is an outside deck area for smokers.

For the tourist market, DFDS continues to focus on the needs of the motorist by carrying only cars, caravans and trailers, motorhomes and motorcycles, but no foot passengers. The gift shop (taking advantage of French duty-paid prices) is worth a visit, especially on your return, to grab a last-minute bargain in wines, spirits, beers, tobacco and perfumes.

You are advised to check in an hour before your departure time. From Dunkerque, Marne-la-Vallée is just over 300km/186mls away – follow the signs for the A16, then take the E42 to the A25 all the way to Lille and pick up the A1 to Paris. 0871 574 7235, **www. dfdsseaways.co.uk**.

Thank you ferry much

We asked Britain's leading cruise and ferry website, Seaview (**http://seaview.co.uk**), to pass on their top tips for getting the most out of your cross-Channel journey – at the best price. Here's what they said:

To thwart those gendarmes eager to penalise Brits, drivers would do well to carry an emergency triangle and a high-visibility warning jacket. Above all, do NOT use a radar warning device. You will be fined about €750, lose the device and risk having your licence confiscated

Don't leave your booking until the last minute. Prices rarely improve by waiting.

Don't try to pull a fast one by buying a day-trip ticket when you plan to stay longer. Ferry operators have a knack of finding out and take a very dim view.

Most ferry companies make it easy to book online and offer discounts for doing so.

Booking online has improved enormously in recent years and usually saves money. If you do so, be sure to keep the confirmation e-mail with its unique reference number. Short crossings are often ticketless, so a booking reference is vital. And look after it – you'll have to produce it at the ferry terminal.

Read the reservation details carefully – twice! Mistakes do happen.

Make sure you give the correct details when booking, such as names as they appear on passports, exact length of car, etc. It can save vital minutes at check-in.

If there is a person with disabilities in your party, enquire about priority on-and-off arrangements.

Try to book a sailing time that you can make without having to dash. However, don't panic if you miss it. Nowadays, there's usually room on the next sailing. If you are ahead of schedule, there's a chance you'll be put on an earlier sailing.

If you are taking your dog on holiday, the train is best. Eurotunnel has areas for dogs to excuse themselves before travelling and, unlike the ferry, they have the pleasure of their owners' company on the journey.

If you sail with SeaFrance, go for the new Berlioz or virtually new Rodin, by far the best ships in the fleet.

If you prefer P&O Ferries and can afford the extra, treat yourself to the Club Lounge. It's comfortable, usually quiet, and soft drinks, coffee and tea, etc. are complimentary. You can also pamper yourself with a meal at Langan's Brasserie.

Be aware that, should an emergency arise, Apex bargain tickets are non-refundable, while full-price tickets usually are.

Remember you lose an hour on arrival in France, so take this into account when you are considering sailing times.

Newhaven

Situated between the towns of Brighton and Eastbourne on the Sussex coast is this small, busy port. Newhaven is on the A259 coast road, but is best reached (driving from London) via the M23, A23, A27 (at Brighton) and A26.

Transmanche Ferries: This French company (sister company of LD Lines) is now the only service sailing Newhaven–Dieppe. There are 2 return crossings daily on the *Côte D'Albâtre* and the journey takes 4hrs. Check-in begins 2hrs before sailing and passengers must arrive at least 45mins before departure. 0844 576 8836, **http://transmancheferries.com**.

From Dieppe, it is 257km/160mls to *Disneyland Paris*; follow the N27, A151, A150 and N15 before picking up the A13 and the route from Caen.

Portsmouth

For the closest port to Paris, head for Caen with Brittany Ferries or Le Havre with LD Lines. The city is barely 2hrs from the Normandy ports (see map on page 41) and Portsmouth is more accessible from the Midlands and West Country than Dover or Newhaven. It is, however, a much longer crossing.

Brittany Ferries: Brittany's new high-speed *Normandie Express* can do it in 3¾hrs, but their older classic ferry offers either a 6hr day sailing or 7hrs at night. However, the night crossings have an advantage, arriving in Caen at 6.30am so you can be in *Disneyland Paris* by 9.30am. There are up to 4 sailings a day (one a day with the high-speed ferry, from mid-Mar–mid-Nov), leaving Portsmouth at 7am (high-speed), 7.30am–12.30pm and 10.30–11.30pm, and the port facilities are all well organised.

Normandie Express features a self-service café, a bar, shop and open viewing deck, with reclining seats and a video games room, while the older MV *Normandie* and *Mont St Michel* have the extra facilities of cinemas, children's entertainment, a full-service restaurant, a second bar, wi-fi internet access and a coffee shop, plus 2- and 4-berth cabins.

The Caen terminal is actually located at Ouistreham, the newest ferry port on the Channel, 15km/9mls to the north of Caen (open 6.30am–11pm), and is well designed to provide a smooth return journey, with easy access and good facilities. To reach Paris, simply follow signs to Caen along the D514 and D515, then pick up the city ring road (N814) and go south-east for 3.5km until you hit the A13. Then it is autoroute all the way to Paris (210km/131mls), with around €17 in tolls. Stay on the *périphérique* and skirt the city to the south, then pick up the A4 to *Disneyland Paris*. On the return to Caen/Ouistreham, follow the signs for 'Car Ferry'. 0871 244 0744, **www. brittany-ferries.co.uk**.

LD Lines: They offer 1 sailing a day from Portsmouth to Le Havre (can be 2 per day in summer), from where it is only 200km/124mls to Paris, using the N15, A131 and A13. Departure time is usually 11pm on the high-speed ferry *Norman Spirit*, arriving in Le Havre at 8am. All LD Lines vessels have a bar, restaurant, cinema, wi-fi access and a choice of comfortable lounges. They also dock at the exclusive, modern Citadelle terminal in Le Havre, making for a smooth departure or embarkation. 0844 576 8836, **www. ldlines.com**.

Portsmouth (**http://portsmouth-port. co.uk**) itself is also served by excellent road links, with the port at the base of the M275 having its own exit on to the motorway. It is actually closer to London than either Dover or the Channel Tunnel and is arguably Britain's best-connected ferry port. The Newbury bypass on the A34 has also cut down the journey time from the Midlands, West and North.

Hull

One final possibility for those living in the north who don't fancy the long drive down the M1, M25 and M3 or M2/A2 is to take the **P&O Ferries** overnight route from Hull to Zeebrugge in Belgium. The *Pride of Rotterdam* and *Pride of Hull* are both big, modern propositions (at 60,000 tons apiece), offering 3 categories of cabin as well as a good choice of bars and dining – including the upscale choice of The Brasserie – and excellent children's facilities. It is a 13¾hr ferry journey but then only a 3¼hr drive from Zeebrugge to *Disneyland Paris*, via the N31, A17, A14, A22, D656, A1, A104 and A4 (with €25 in tolls).

Useful websites: To help you with ferry crossings and road access after you arrive, the following are helpful, starting with the essential **www.seaview. co.uk**. Then there's **www.ferrybooker. com** (with more useful info on driving in France, the ports and working out your route). When it comes to driving, **www.autoroutes.fr**, **www.viamichelin.com** and **www.sytadin.fr/** (for Paris traffic reports) are useful and worth checking in advance.

By Eurotunnel

Eurotunnel can get you to Calais fast, conveniently and with a choice of services 24 hours a day. This versatile shuttle service from Folkestone in Kent has up to 4 departures an hour, with a crossing time of just 35 minutes. In fact, it can take just 45mins from the time of loading to driving off at the other end, making it easily the quickest vehicle crossing time of any cross-Channel service. Finding Eurotunnel also couldn't be easier as the terminal is just off Junction 11A on the M20, about a 45min drive from its intersection with the M25, and is well signposted.

BRITTIP
For the latest travel, weather and road news for the area, call Eurotunnel's information line on 0844 335 3535.

After arriving at the Eurotunnel terminal, proceed straight to check-in and quote your booking reference number (or use their self-check-in facility, which you can practise online). You can just arrive on spec, but you will be allocated a space on the next available shuttle, and may have to wait a while. It will also usually be more

Cabin on the **Norman Spirit**

expensive than booking in advance. In busy periods a booking is highly advisable to avoid a wait of more than an hour. You are requested to arrive at least 35mins before your booked departure time. You can stop off in their extremely smart and spacious main terminal building, grab a bite to eat and do a bit of pre-trip shopping. Once checked in, you drive through both British and French passport controls (there are no checks on arrival, as with the ferry). Please note LPG vehicles are NOT allowed on Eurotunnel trains.

Eurotunnel recognises it is not always possible to plan your arrival time accurately. So, if you arrive late but within 2 hours of your booked departure time, they transfer you to a space on the next available shuttle at no extra charge (although this could take a while if it's busy). If you arrive 2–24 hours after your departure time, you will be charged only the difference between the price paid originally and

RER-ing to go

Using the RER system to get to and from *Disneyland Paris* is a doddle. This largely overground train link takes about 35–40mins to get from the resort into central Paris and runs until after midnight. While the trains may not be the cleanest (the graffiti menace has been here with a vengeance!), they run at regular intervals every hour and scrupulously to time. The RER goes underground through central Paris, where it links up with the Métro underground system. You do not need to use the Métro – or the well-organised bus system, which links with both – unless you are on a serious sightseeing tour of the city.

Marne-la-Vallée is at the end of the (Red) Line A4, which runs basically east–west through Paris. Gare du Nord is at a junction of the (Green) Line D, which runs largely north to south and (Blue) Line B, which bisects the city from north-east to south-west, and has the **Charles de Gaulle Airport** at the end of the B3 link (north-east). **Orly Airport** is on a special branch line – the Orlyval – connecting to the Antony station on the (Blue) Line B4.

that applicable to your new departure. If you arrive more than 24 hours late, you will need to buy a new ticket.

BRITTIP
Don't forget the necessary documentation for your vehicle, insurance and any breakdown cover you have for the journey.

For an even quicker and smoother passage, travel **FlexiPlus** and benefit from a priority lane at check-in and a guaranteed space on the next available shuttle. There is also an exclusive lounge (open 6am–10pm) to allow you to freshen up and enjoy the benefits of complimentary refreshments, magazines, newspapers and wi-fi. The extra speed, convenience and service is highly worthwhile, especially on a short trip. For direct access to the lounge, go straight to passport control, then follow the FlexiPlus signs (in Folkestone, keep to the right-hand lane, in Calais, keep left). Stay in the

At the Eurotunnel entrance

respective lane until you reach the Eurotunnel FlexiPlus barrier, then use the PIN number given to you at check-in to gain access to car parking for the lounge. You will also be given a paper hanger at check-in, which you need to display on your rearview mirror. From the lounge, you will be given priority boarding on the next available shuttle. (NB: vehicles over 1.85m in height and motorcycles cannot access the FlexiPlus lounge.)

Once you're ready to board, you just drive straight on to the shuttle where you stay in your car. You can get out to stretch your legs in the carriage (and there are toilets, usually in every third carriage). On arriving at the other end, you drive off (in Calais/Coquelles) practically straight on to the A16 autoroute. From there, you head for

Gare du Nord

the A26 (signposted initially to Calais and then to Saint-Omer, Arras, Reims and Paris) before picking up the A1 at Arras (see map on page 42). On the return journey, you come off the A16 at Junction 13 (look for the signs for Tunnel Sous La Manche). If you have time to spare, you can visit the huge **Cité Europe** shopping mall, which has some 200 shops and offers the usual great deals on things like wine, beer, spirits and food, notably at Tesco Vin Plus. Plus there are clothing stores such as Armand Thierry, H&M, Andiamo, Mango and Zara, as well as other well-known chains like Footlocker, Sephora, Yves Rocher and even a Disney Store.

BRITTIP
Check out **http://day-tripper.net** for more details on Cité Europe, the bargains to be had and an excellent map.

All in all, the Eurotunnel operation really is as simple as it sounds, and the ease with which you are suddenly off and running in France comes as quite a surprise the first time, so don't forget to drive on the right! It is also a relatively cheap option, with Short Stay Saver fares (2–5 days) from £84/car (at 2011 prices) and Standard Fares (more than 5 days) from £106. A 5-Day FlexiPlus costs £149 each way and a Standard FlexiPlus £199 each way (you can also 'mix and match' FlexiPlus and Standard fares).

The other great benefit of Eurotunnel as opposed to the ferries (apart from it suiting more independent-minded travellers) is the fact the shuttle service is rarely affected by the weather and you are certainly not likely to suffer from seasickness! 0844 335 3535, **www.eurotunnel.com**.

BRITTIP
An excellent route-planning facility can be found at **www.eurotunnel. com**. Just type in your route details and you get easy-to-follow instructions to your destination. It even provides the total cost of the tolls en route. Click on 'Passenger Travel,' then 'Travel With Us' and 'Route Planner.'

A Disneyland day-trip?

The high-speed nature and regularity of the Eurostar service means you *could* opt for just a day-trip to *Disneyland Paris*. Taking the 6.52am from London to Paris and RER to the resort would get you to the theme parks by around 11.30am. The direct return service is at 7.37pm from Marne-la-Vallée, arriving back in Ashford at 8.37pm and St Pancras at 9.19pm. But, if that does not suit you, the last train from the Gare du Nord station in Paris to London is usually at 9.13pm, which means you could still have until 7.30pm in the parks before catching the RER service back into Paris.

By rail – Eurostar

The fastest direct route from London to Paris these days is via the smooth Eurostar operation from St Pancras International station. There are up to 18 services a day to the Gare du Nord station in Paris, with a fastest journey time of 2¼hrs (usually quicker than flying when you consider the door-to-door time). You can go to Gare du Nord and then use the RER rail service to get to *Disneyland Paris* (at the Marne-la-Vallée station). But you are much better off waiting for the **daily direct service** – 2hrs 47mins from London to Mickey! This is literally the fast-track service – at up to 300kph/186mph – especially as it's just 2hrs from Ashford International station in Kent. It is a high-speed link with great comfort, style and convenience.

Put aside any preconceptions (and real misgivings) of the British rail system, because this is how modern rail travel *should* be. You are guaranteed a seat (no mean feat for some regional rail services), the trains are clean and comfortable and their time-keeping is second to none in the UK (OK, the latter is not saying a lot, but Eurostar does have an excellent punctuality record). The opening of the final section of the high-speed rail link trimmed almost 30mins off the rather pedestrian journey from London to the tunnel itself, while the whizz through northern France remains a breathtaking experience. The move from Waterloo to St Pancras has also brought a wonderful range of purpose-built facilities to this high-quality experience.

Add to this the excellence of all the other terminal facilities at Ebbsfleet station in Kent (although not on the direct route to *Disneyland Paris*), Ashford, Gare du Nord and Marne-la-Vallée, and you have an operation of the highest order and user-friendliness. For anyone living within 2hrs' drive of Ashford, this is a highly worthwhile alternative to the London station, as the ease and efficiency with which you can park and walk across to your train makes for a hassle-free journey, especially with children.

Eurostar operates a daily service direct to Marne-la-Vallée during school holiday periods, departing St Pancras at 9.44am, arriving in the heart of the Disney Magic at 1.31pm (with the 1hr time change). There are also direct services to Lille, Brussels, Avignon and the French Alps, while connections are possible to more than 100 destinations in France, Belgium, Germany and Holland (NB: there are no Eurostar services on Christmas Day. Sunday train times also vary slightly – consult **www.eurostar.com** for the latest timetables). Outside school holidays, the service does not run on Tues and Sat, but it is still possible to travel direct with one change at Lille or going to Gare du Nord and using the RER line.

If you choose the Gare du Nord route (or are unable to take advantage of the Disney direct service), you should find it relatively easy to transfer to Marne-la-Vallée via the RER train link on Line D (although the trains are seriously crowded in the morning and evening rush hour). Just follow the (Green) signs to Melun. From Gare du Nord, you change trains at Châtelet Les Halles to switch from Line D to Line A for Marne-la-Vallée.

Another alternative (and a worthwhile tip if you miss the direct service) is to take one of the Eurostar trains to Lille and change there for a TGV train to

Marne-la-Vallée (about 65mins). You do not even have to change platforms at Lille, just wait (usually no more than half an hour) for the French high-speed train and you're off to the heart of the Magic once more.

Ticket types: With the Eurostar service to Paris and Lille (or any of their other regular destinations), you have the choice of 3 classes, **Standard**, **Standard Premier** or **Business Premier**. If you are used to using your local train service, Standard will feel like travelling first class – the individual seats are all comfortable, with decent elbow room, carriages are roomy and there is easy access to the 2 buffet cars. With Standard Premier and Business Premier, the service is seriously upgraded.

🇬🇧 **BRITTIP**

A special reduced fare applies for both wheelchair users and a travelling companion on Eurostar – priced at the lowest available Standard fare – and there are toilets and an area adapted especially for wheelchairs in Standard Premier or Business Premier. Blind people travelling with companions also benefit from the same deal.

Standard Premier fares offer a 3-course meal at your (extra-width, reclining) seat and complimentary newspapers and magazines. There is plenty of space if you need to work en route (or keep the kids amused with board games etc.) and uniformed staff are always on hand. Business Premier, as you would expect, is the most expensive and affords complete flexibility for travel any day of the week from London to Paris, as well as other perks like a 10min check-in and exclusive lounge access. However, if you are interested only in the direct service to *Disneyland Paris*, your choice is just Standard or Standard Premier fares. There are always 2 buffet cars per train and a smattering of Disney fun to whet your appetite, with Disney Cast Members onboard to assist with hotel arrangements and provide some entertainment for the

GETTING THERE

children, ensuring your visit gets off to a flying start. Baby-changing facilities and bottle-warming are available, along with activity packs for children if you ask at the terminal. Plenty of ramps, passenger conveyors and lifts are provided as well.

> **BRITTIP**
> Using the RER from Gare du Nord to get to *Disneyland Paris*? Change at Châtelet Les Halles, as you simply need to switch platforms rather than go up and down a potentially confusing set of escalators – the RER signposting takes a bit of getting used to.

On the direct St Pancras–Ashford–Marne-la-Vallée route, Standard fares start from £69 return/adults and £49/children under 12. Standard Premier fares start from £159 and £49 (children under 4 travel free without an assigned seat). Their cheapest fares are also *non-flexible*, which means there are no refunds or exchanges; you need to choose a (more expensive) *semi-flexible* ticket for leeway with exchanges and refunds. With the

London–Paris Standard Premier variety, all trips (except the Weekend Day Return) must include a Sat night stay. But there is NO stay-away condition if tickets are booked more than 21 days in advance.

Eurostar fares compare extremely favourably with airline prices (even the low-cost carriers) and, for the extra convenience of arriving right in the heart of the Disney fun, they take some beating.

> **BRITTIP**
> It is possible to travel one way in Standard Premier and the other in Standard. It is definitely worth considering Standard Premier on the way home to give yourself room to wind down after all that exhausting fun!

Eurostar services: At the main Eurostar **terminals**, you should find everything efficient and easy to use. At London's **St Pancras International** mainline station, the Eurostar services operate on the main level from platforms 5–10. The departure terminal is built into an upper level in

Disneyland Railroad

the old station's undercroft and here you will find the impressive range of purpose-built facilities – shops, cafés and bars, along with a cash machine that dispenses both euros and sterling. There is not much car parking nearby, though, and it's a whopping £36 a day at the NCP station car park.

At **Ashford International**, the main concourse offers a pleasant café, plus shops, currency exchange and left luggage, while passing into the departure lounge gives you more chances to grab a drink or bite to eat, another shop and currency exchange, plus a Eurostar information desk. The multi-storey car park here holds 2,000 cars and parking is £11.50 a day (an alternative, open-air car park is available nearby at £10 a day, although it involves about a 100m/109yd walk to the station). To plan a rail journey to Ashford (or any other UK station), look up details on **www.nationalrail.co.uk** or **www.thetrainline.com**.

If you are returning from **Gare du Nord**, the Eurostar service is upstairs on the first level (it's surprising how many people don't notice this when they arrive), where there is again a good range of cafés and shops once you pass into the departure area. You have to check in at least 30mins before your departure to allow plenty of time for security screening.

BRITTIP
At Ashford International, if you want a drink or snack, go through to the second café as you enter the departure lounge as it is usually less congested.

Marne-la-Vallée is the least exciting of the main Eurostar terminals (but then it can afford to be with its situation). You arrive at the lowest level of the station and take the escalator or lift up to the main concourse. If you are heading straight for the theme parks, there should be a Disney Cast Member to direct you to the nearest exit. If you are heading for your hotel first, go out of the main doors straight ahead of you, and the bus stop for all the Disney hotels (except *Davy Crockett Ranch*,

which does not have a bus service) and those of the 4 Selected Hotels (the Explorers, Vienna International Dream Castle, Vienna International Circus Hotel and Kyriad) are immediately in front of the station.

BRITTIP
If you haven't already bought your RER ticket to get from Gare du Nord to Marne-la-Vallée (which you can do at any Eurostar station), avoid the often crowded main ticket offices on the Paris station concourse. Instead, wait until you reach the last, smaller ticket office just before the entrance to the (Green) Line D of the RER as there is rarely much of a queue there.

If you are staying in a Disney hotel, the Eurostar service includes the considerable bonus of the **Disney Express** baggage arrangement, which enables you to go straight to the theme parks on arrival while your bags are taken to your hotel. This has to be organised before you travel either through your tour operator or at the St Pancras terminal if you have booked Disney accommodation independently (you need to show confirmation of your hotel booking at St Pancras).

Once you have the correct baggage tags (and Disney Cast Members will be on hand to assist and provide the right tags if you have not been sent them), you simply attach them to your luggage and take them to the first-floor *Disney Express* baggage office when you arrive at Marne-la-Vallée.

For our money, this is the most efficient and stress-free form of travel we have encountered, especially in Europe. When travelling with children it provides much to ease parents' minds (as well as the bonus of children's general fascination with trains). The onboard buffet food has improved a lot recently and Eurostar is a completely non-smoking service.

Eurostar also now features **packages** to *Disneyland Paris*, with a full range of Disney hotels and others nearby on the RER line to Marne-la-Vallée. Go to **www.eurostar.com** and click on the *Latest Deals* link, but you must add Disneyland tickets to your booking as they are not included automatically.

By air

If the Eurostar route is the most time-efficient way of getting to the heart of the Magic, where does that leave air travel? Well, if you live anywhere outside the South East, it provides the best alternative, especially using the 2 main Paris airports of Charles de Gaulle and Orly. The proliferation of low-cost airlines in recent years has broadened the choice considerably.

BRITTIP

Several low-cost airlines use Beauvais as their 'Paris' airport, even though it is 64km/39mls *north* of Paris. The airport does provide a shuttle bus to Porte Maillot RER and Métro station in west Paris for €17.50/person. However, the best way to get to *Disneyland Paris* is on the **VEA Navette** shuttle. This runs 3 times a day via Charles de Gaulle airport at €24/person one way and takes 2½hrs.

All the regional airports around the UK have at least one daily service to the French capital and, with the likes of **EasyJet** (Luton, Liverpool, Bristol, Belfast, Glasgow, Edinburgh, Newcastle), **flybe** (Manchester, Birmingham, Cardiff, Exeter, Glasgow, Jersey, Southampton), **Ryanair** (Glasgow Prestwick, Dublin and Shannon to Paris Beauvais), **Jet2. com** (Leeds Bradford) and **bmi baby** (East Midlands) all offering variations on the low-cost alternative, it means your choice of flights has never been

greater. Add the scheduled services of **Air France** (from eight UK airports, including Aberdeen, Bristol and Newcastle) and **British Airways** (up to 10 flights a day from Heathrow) and you have almost 20 regional flight gateways to Paris.

Paris Charles de Gaulle Airport: (CDG) is by far the bigger (and more complex) of the 2 Paris airports (it is the main international terminus, whereas Orly has more domestic flights). Situated some 23km/14mls to the north-east of the city centre, it actually consists of Terminals 1, 2 and 3. Terminal 2 is subdivided into 2A, 2B, 2C, 2D, 2E and 2F, with the RER station (Aéroport Charles-de-Gaulle 2) and TGV station situated between 2C/2D and 2E/2F. From Terminal 1, the nearest RER station (Aéroport Charles-de-Gaulle 1) is located next to Terminal 3. A new Satellite 4 (S4) next to 2E and 2F is due to open in 2012 to handle the giant Airbus 380, while there is also a 2G terminal purely for local traffic.

BRITTIP

It's about a 10min walk from the RER station to the Air France departure gates in Terminal 2F and from the station to Terminals 2A and 2B.

There is also an automated shuttle train that links all 3 main terminals, in a straight line fashion, from Terminal 1 to Parking PR, Terminal 3 (for the RER), Parking PX and Terminal 2 (for the TGV station and second RER stop), then back again. It covers the full 3.5km/2¼mls distance in 8mins and the service runs every 4mins.

VEA Navette: The shuttle offers a direct service from Terminal 2 (from 2E/2F, with a linking shuttle service from all the other terminals) to the hotels of *Disneyland Paris* 8.30am–7.45pm (10pm on Fri) daily, either to the 6 Disney hotels and the Marne-la-Vallée bus station OR (4 times a day) to the 4 partner hotels of the Val de France area (if no direct Val de France service is scheduled, take the Disney hotels service and change at the bus station for the free shuttle bus). It is a fairly plodding coach service, taking a good 45mins to reach the first stop, but it does have the great benefit of being door to door and runs at 20–40min intervals throughout the main part of the day. It costs €18/adult and €13/child aged 3–11 one way (under 3s free). The Shuttle will take a credit card payment, so don't worry if you don't have any euros in hand. 01 53 48 39 53, **www.vea-shuttle.co.uk**.

RER: Alternatively, you can take the RER service on Line B all the way in to Châtelet Les Halles (about 40mins), then change there for Line D to Marne-la-Vallée (another 35–40mins). It is a simple enough route at off-peak times but harder to negotiate with luggage in the morning or evening rush hour. 00 33 1 58 76 45 91, **www.ratp.fr** and click on the UK flag for the English version.

BRITTIP
If you arrive at Terminal G, take the N2 airport shuttle that goes to Terminal 2F for the VEA Navette shuttle.

TGV: Another alternative is to take the TGV train from the airport to Marne-la-Vallée, which can work out slightly cheaper than the VEA shuttle (although services are fewer). There are 9 trains from 6.54–11.43am, then another 8 from 12.58–5.51pm and 8 in the evening from 6.24–9.55pm. At off-peak times the ticket is around €16 one way but it tops €25 at peak times. The big benefit though, is that it takes just 12mins and you can walk out of the station to pick up the shuttle bus to any Disney hotel right outside. For the return journey to the airport there are 11 services from 7.25am–12.27pm, then another 13 from 3.11–10.56pm (be warned – if you miss the Charles de Gaulle stop, you will end up in Lille or even Brussels!).

Taxis: You can also get taxis outside all the terminals, although it will cost at least €90 one-way to any Disney hotel.

Paris Orly Airport: 15km/9mls to the south of the city centre, Orly is divided into Sud (South) and Ouest (West) terminals, and there is a free shuttle

service operating every 5mins or so over the 2min journey between them (from the South terminal, look for Exit K and from the West terminal, go to the departure level and Exit W). With good direct links into the city, Orly makes a reasonable alternative to Charles de Gaulle.

RER: Unfortunately the RER route is a little more complicated (take the airport link to Antony on Line B, then go to Châtelet Les Halles and change to Line A for Marne-la-Vallée). At Orly South, take Exit G on the ground floor (platform 1 to Paris), and at Orly West, also take Exit G.

BRITTIP
For information on both Paris airports – including terminal maps, flight times and services – visit **www.aeroportsdeparis.fr** and click the Union Jack for English text.

VEA Navette: This direct shuttle bus to all the Disney hotels is the best choice (8.30am–7.30pm daily, journey time 45–50mins) for €17/adult, €13/child 3–11 (under 3s free). At Orly South, head for the bus station, platform 2 for the VEA bus and at Orly West, go to Level 0, Gate C.

Taxis: A taxi from Paris Orly to any of the Disney hotels will cost around €50.

Airlines: Then it comes to the airlines themselves.

- **Air France** (**www.airfrance.co.uk**) is the biggest carrier in terms of daily flights, using both main Paris airports. At Charles de Gaulle, their UK destinations fly into Terminal 2E.

- **British Airways** (**www.britishairways.com**) flies to Terminal 2A.

- **flybe** (**www.flybe.com**) and **bmi baby** (**www.bmibaby.com**) both use Terminal 1.

- **EasyJet** (**www.easyjet.com**) operates at Terminal 2B.

- *Jet2.com* (**www.jet2.com**) flies into Terminal 3.

- You could also try **Alitalia** (**www.alitalia.com/gb_en**), which flies

Top 10 romantic options for *Disneyland Paris*

Although it's well known as a family destination, *Disneyland Paris* is also popular for honeymoons, anniversaries and other special couples-only celebrations. Here is our guide to the best things to do when it is just the 2 of you, so you can really make the most of your visit.

1 Stay in one of the Tinker Bell suites at the *Disneyland Hotel*.

2 Or stay in the Roosevelt Suite at *Hotel New York*.

3 Failing either of those, *Newport Bay Club* offers a lovely Honeymoon Suite.

4 Take one of Cityrama's Illuminations evening tours of Paris.

5 Have dinner at the California Grill at the *Disneyland Hotel*.

6 Take an evening stroll around Lake Disney and stop for a drink at the Redwood Bar at *Sequoia Lodge*.

7 Have lunch at the wonderful Blue Lagoon restaurant inside the Pirates of the Caribbean ride at the *Disneyland Park*.

8 Enjoy a drink in the Fantasia Bar at the *Disneyland Hotel*, listening to the relaxing sounds of their pianist.

9 Try the dinner buffet al fresco at the Vienna International Dream Castle Hotel.

10 In winter, stop at *Hotel New York* to watch the ice-skating and grab a mug of hot cocoa from the nearby drinks stall.

GETTING THERE

from Aberdeen, Birmingham, Dublin, Edinburgh, Manchester, Newcastle and Shannon to Terminal 2E and **American Airlines (www. americanairlines.co.uk)**, which flies from Heathrow to 2A.

There are few direct flights to **Orly** from the UK, although **Air France** flies there from London City Airport (to Orly West). **EasyJet** also uses it as a base, but only for operations elsewhere in Europe, not the UK.

Disneyland Hotel

Choosing a tour operator

While it is perfectly possible – and sometimes cheaper – to book a DIY holiday by putting together your own hotel and travel arrangements, the tour operators to *Disneyland Paris* have developed a sophisticated, not to mention exceptionally good value, raft of packages that make booking with them (especially if you book direct) highly worthwhile. Add the number of internet travel companies like **www. ebookers.com** and **www.lastminute.com**, and there is a bewildering variety on offer to choose from.

The first thing to do is shop around and get an idea of the prices for the different types of package. Most tour operators in this market are the big, well-known brands, who feature some of the keenest pricing thanks to their ability to deal in bulk (notably Leger Holidays and Thomas Cook), but several specialists are worth considering.

When it comes to simple price comparisons, it is more the method of travel that makes the main difference, hence a coach-based trip is usually the cheapest, followed by Eurotunnel or ferry self-drive, then Eurostar and finally flying. But there are often special deals to be found – particularly at off-peak times – and it definitely pays to keep your wits about you when looking for a bargain. So you need to know what the general going rate is before you plunge in!

Look for the *Kids Go Free* season (usually Jan–Mar) when under 12s travel, stay and play for free (return travel, hotel accommodation with continental breakfast and park tickets); or *Kids Under 7 Free*, when children aged 4–6 benefit from free accommodation and park tickets. Look out also for periodic **All your meals free** offers, as Disney have used this in recent years to boost quieter times, adding 2 free meal vouchers per person for each night booked (on a minimum 3-day stay).

Here is a look at the main tour operators on the *Disneyland* beat. With all of them, Disney accommodation usually comes with theme park passes for the length of your visit (but check full details before booking).

Harry Shaw: A popular and busy Midlands coach-tour specialist, this company's speciality is 2- and 3-night trips, with either 1 or 2 full days in the theme parks. They feature primarily

Disney accommodation at the *Santa Fe, Cheyenne, Newport Bay* and *Sequoia Lodge* hotels, inclusive of park tickets and breakfast. The 2-day tour picks up during the morning at more than 30 points in the Midlands (including Tamworth, Newport Pagnell and Milton Keynes) and 6 in the South East (including Thurrock, Farthing Corner and Dartford), arriving in *Disneyland Paris* in the evening. You then have a full day in the parks before returning in the afternoon of the third day after more park time (arriving back in the Midlands in the early hours). The 3-night option adds a second full day in the parks before returning on the morning of the fourth day. There are also some tempting packages for special occasions like Christmas, Bonfire Night and New Year. 024 7645 5544, **http://harryshaw.co.uk**.

Transport: Coach via P&O Ferries or Eurotunnel.

Leger Holidays: The biggest coach-tour operator to *Disneyland Paris* (although they also offer all the main package opportunities), Leger have a countrywide network of routes, with more than 490 joining points in England, Scotland and Wales, taking customers to Dover or Folkestone and

Eva and Wall-E

crossing the Channel for the 4hr drive to the resort (with one refreshment stop). They operate a mixture of their own branded coaches plus those of well-known companies from all over the country. All are modern and comfortable, with toilets and drinks facility and they reduce travel hassles to the minimum, which goes down well with families. The 4-day package features 2 full days in the parks, with departure after breakfast on the fourth day, while the 5-day trip offers 2 park days and a full-day Paris tour on the fourth day, with the option to stay in the parks (that day's park admission not included). Leger are the only coach company offering Disney rooms during New Year week, with their 4-day departures having a 2-Day Park Hopper ticket. Arrival time aims to be between 8 and 10pm on the first evening. The return journey usually leaves after breakfast on the last day.

Leger is the only UK tour operator to offer all 4 modes of transport, with increased departures of coach, self-drive, Eurostar and air packages, and a huge choice for all budgets. Included is a range of early booking offers – from room discounts to hotel upgrades and single-parent discounts – to enhance their value-for-money family prices. They also package it extremely well, using their most popular hotel, the 3-star Thomas Cook Explorers Hotel (see page 83), which is wonderfully family-friendly and the only one that will accommodate 6 to a room. The Explorers is Leger's base price accommodation and comes in slightly cheaper than Disney's most budget-orientated offering, the *Hotel Santa Fe*, which is 2-star. They have the option to upgrade to *Disney's Hotel Cheyenne, Sequoia Lodge* or *Newport Bay Club*. The Kids Go Free season (for 3–11s, from Jan–Mar) is available on coach and self-drive options (based on one adult to one child). The self-drive alternative is *Disney's Davy Crockett Ranch*, which offers self-catering accommodation. Their brochures also highlight special events like Bonfire Night, Halloween and Christmas extremely well.

Leger's innovative flight programme features scheduled and low-cost airlines from 15 UK airports, including Birmingham, Manchester, Newcastle, Aberdeen, Glasgow, Belfast and Cardiff. Transfers are provided with all flights, either using the VEA Navette shuttle or a Leger coach.

Summer is easily their busiest period and the 4- and 5-day packages prove immensely popular. The Thomas Cook Explorers Hotel is always tops for demand but Leger have also added the 4-star Vienna International Magic Circus hotel in recent brochures, located just 8mins (by the free shuttle) from the parks. This reflects a demand for quality hotels that are still well priced compared to Disney's 3-star range, with higher standards of service and the bonus of swimming pools.

Leger have a year-round programme to Disney. The majority use P&O Ferries from Dover but some dates are served via Eurotunnel. We describe a typical Leger 5-day break in Chapter 2 (see page 20), which shows how hard it is to fit everything in! 0844 686 2323, www. gotothemagic.co.uk.

Transport: Coach via P&O Ferries or Eurotunnel; Eurostar; self-drive with P&O Ferries or Eurotunnel; flights (Air France, BA and various low-cost carriers).

Newmarket: A specialist tour operator you won't find in any travel agency, their Magical Breaks packages appear in many local and national newspapers, plus a range of direct-sell holidays by coach or car. From Aberdeen to Plymouth, you are likely to see their newspaper-endorsed reader offers and usually at eye-catching prices (even for Eurostar packages). They offer mainly off-site hotels (hence the budget-orientated operation) with reliable coach services (most of which use P&O Ferries from Dover). Their Paris expertise dates back to the opening of *Euro Disney*, hence they have a knowledgeable staff (including their own in-resort reps), and also do big business with special interest groups and schools. With their coach tours (the vast majority), they have some 500 pick-up points all over the

UK and the coach is your mode of transport throughout the trip at the off-site hotels, which tend to be in the greater Paris area (usually of the Campanile, Ibis, Novotel standard – a basic but comfortable 2- and 3-star). The only drawback is you're restricted to the coach's one trip to and from the hotel (you have to make your own way back if you want to return from the parks earlier). Occasionally, they do use Disney hotels, which provides greater convenience.

All are on a bed and (continental) breakfast basis, and they feature either 3- or 4-day trips. On coach tours, the 3-day trips feature a 1-Day ticket to the *Disneyland Park* (you arrive mid-evening on the first day, have one full day there, then return early afternoon on the third day), while the 4-day version has a 2-Day Hopper ticket (as you have 2 full days for the theme parks, before the final day return; Scottish departures leave earlier on the final day). They also offer a good range of Disney breaks for specific events such as Christmas, New Year, Bonfire Night and Halloween. 0844 391 2190, **www.newmarketholidays.co.uk**.

Transport: Coach or self-drive via P&O Ferries or Eurotunnel.

Other operators: There are other regional companies who all feature *Disneyland Paris*, including: **Applebys** of Lincolnshire, part of the Bowen Travel Group (0845 330 3747, **www.coachholidays.com**), who feature coach tours of three and four days, some using P&O ferries from Hull to Zeebrugge; Yorkshire's **Gold Crest Holidays** (01943 433457, **http://gold-crest.com**), with 3-, 4- and 5-day coach tours staying at a standard off-site hotel; York-based **Superbreak** (0871 221 3344, **www.superbreak.com**); and Middlesbrough-based **Siesta International Holidays** (0845 271 2443, **www.siestaholidays.co.uk**), with 3-night coach-tours staying at Disney hotels.

Finally, to use some of the best online search engines (that seek out deals and special offers from a wide range of tour operators) for flights or holidays, try any of: **www.lastminute.com**, **www.expedia.co.uk**, **www.travelocity.co.uk**, **www.opodo.co.uk**, or **www.ebookers.com**.

Book direct

Of course, you can always book directly with Disney if you have an idea of what you want to do. The resort offers a full range of packages with all the usual methods of transport and they even feature a good range of off-site accommodation, with 7 hotels in Val d'Europe and Val de France, including the handy Adagio Aparthotel, with rooms for up to 7. Disney's brochure is worth getting just for all the lavish photography and large-scale maps, and they highlight all the extras, free nights and Kids Go Free deals. The pricing system and dizzying array of supplements for the different forms of transport can take some deciphering, but basically every possible permutation is open to you.

The brochure is designed so you begin by choosing your dates, then your accommodation (inclusive of breakfast, local taxes and park tickets); if you want to add a Meal Plan; then your transport option to get there (by train, self-drive or flying); and finally, in the Pricing section, how long you want to stay (1–4 nights, with additional night pricing). You can also select any additional features such as character meals, shows, excursions or even birthday celebrations, plus seasonal events like Halloween parties and Christmas/New Year dining. Hotline 08448 008 111, or visit **www.disneylandparis.co.uk**.

Transport: Eurostar; flights (Air France, British Airways or flybe.com); self-drive via Eurotunnel or P&O Ferries.

But wait, before you can make a fully informed choice, you need to have a good idea of the array of accommodation that awaits you, both in the form of the Disney resorts themselves and the usually cheaper alternatives for staying off-site. So, read on and we will reveal all about how to choose your hotel…

4 Staying There

or Making Sense of the Hotel Choice

When it comes to where to stay in and around *Disneyland Paris,* you will not be surprised to know there is a bewildering variety. Disney alone has 6 contrasting hotels on site, while their *Davy Crockett Ranch,* about 15mins away, offers an alternative for those with a car. There are another 8 hotels 'near the Magic', and several dozen more within a 15–25min drive.

The key is the combination of location and price. All Disney resorts offer the convenience of being just minutes from the theme parks, but they do tend to be on the expensive side. If you stay on-site you won't need any other transport. But you can also get away without a car elsewhere, as the easy-to-use RER rail line makes staying in places like Bussy-St-Georges, Noisiel or even Bercy, towards the centre of Paris, perfectly viable.

The section on the tour operators in the previous chapter shows the great range of packages on offer. Many feature off-site hotels, as the demand for Disney hotels is high and they are at virtually 100% capacity in peak periods. The area along the RER corridor makes a handy base for

The pool at Thomas Cook Explorers Hotel

tackling Disney (and Paris, for that matter), and the general standard of hotels is sound if unspectacular. Their star-rating system is pretty accurate and virtually every hotel works on a bed and breakfast basis (a continental breakfast with cereal, pastries, cold meats, cheese and tea/coffee. The Vienna International Dream Castle and Magic Circus Hotels are rarities in providing a full breakfast). It is advisable to stay off-site during the summer when Disney's prices are at their highest, while the price difference between on- and off-site properties is less in the winter.

◀▶ **BRIT**TIP
The quoted price rates of hotels in France are always per *room* and not per *person*.

Off-site: Staying off-site can actually provide you with more flexibility if you want to use the hotel just as a base and not part of the holiday itself (Disney hotels all play a role in the holiday experience). You'll have more incentive to get out and about if you stay off-site (see map on page 85) and it's convenient for seeing more of Paris, while many hotels offer 'extra night free' deals.

You should certainly check in advance, however, whether or not you'll need a car. If you are not close to an RER station – or the hotel does not have a shuttle service to the nearest station – you will struggle without your own transport.

Disney hotels

When it comes to getting the very best from your trip, you can't beat the full and all-encompassing experience of staying **on-site** (see map on pages 72). The majority of Brits choose this option; yet, curiously, only a small percentage of other nationalities do, so Disney hotels often have a high percentage of British guests. Just the simple fact of being able to walk into the parks in the morning, through *Disney Village*, is one of the great pleasures of staying here. Even from

Extra Magic Hours Rides

The **Extra Magic Hours** perk for Disney hotel guests (and those at the Disney-owned Hotel L'Élysée, and Dream Annual Pass holders) is great if you have specific rides you'd like to do without the queues of later in the day. Here's what is usually open for these extra 1–2 hours in the morning (no rides are guaranteed, though):

Disneyland Park Rides: *Fantasyland* – Le Carrousel de Lancelot, Peter Pan's Flight, Dumbo, Mad Hatter's Tea Cups; *Discoveryland* – Buzz Lightyear Laser Blast; Space Mountain: Mission 2. **Restaurants:** Au Chalet de la Marionnette (only with breakfast reservation voucher).

Extra Magic Hours at the *Walt Disney Studios* are rare but, if they do occur, the following are likely to be the early birds' opening list: Crush's Coaster, The Twilight Zone Tower of Terror, Rock 'n' Roller Coaster starring Aerosmith, RC Racer, Toy Soldiers Parachute Drop, Slinky Dog Zigzag Spin.

Disney's Hotel Santa Fe, the furthest of the 6 on-site resorts, it is no more than a 20min stroll and, on a sunny morning, a delightful one. The old estate agent adage of 'location, location, location' is just as true here.

◀▶ **BRIT**TIP
France is now officially a public **No Smoking** zone. All public places have been declared smoke-free, which means restaurants, bars, museums AND the theme parks are off limits to smokers. However, the smoking ban is not rigidly enforced in the parks while not all hotels are fully smoke-free. Apart from at Disney hotels (and a few others), you usually still need to specify a non-smoking room.

Extra Magic Hours: There are other benefits to staying *chez* Mickey for the duration of your visit, most notably the Extra Magic Hours perk. This allows guests staying at the 7 Disney hotels and the Hotel L'Élysée in Val d'Europe (plus Dream Annual Passport holders) to enjoy specific attractions in Fantasyland and Discoveryland at the *Disneyland Park* on certain dates, 1–2 hours before park opening. On Extra

Magic mornings, follow the signs for 'Extra Magic Hour' or 'Disney Hotel Guests' to bypass the regular queue. Just show your Disney Hotel EasyPass (which you collect when you check in). On rare occasions Extra Magic Hours can occur at the *Walt Disney Studios* but there are no Extra Magic evenings as there are at *Walt Disney World*.

Character interaction: This is another important perk, especially for families, at all 6 hotels in the morning and evening. At least one character will always be 'on parade' in the hotel foyer and kids are virtually guaranteed to get their autograph books off to a flying start.

Service and hospitality: This adds significantly to everyone's enjoyment, while all Disney resort guests get their own **ID Card** to use as a charge card in both parks and at *Disney Village* (apart from the Rainforest Café, Planet Hollywood, McDonald's and Starbuck's).

Resort guests also benefit from **free parking** at the hotels, theme parks and *Disney Village*; the free **shuttle bus service**; and a whole range of **recreational activities**, from swimming and tennis to outdoor playgrounds, video games and even ice-skating (outside *Disney's Hotel New York*, but open to all Disney hotel guests for a small fee). The 2 tennis courts at *Disney's Hotel New York* are available to all Disney hotel guests (there is a small fee for ball and racket hire), on production of your Disney resort ID card.

There is a **shopping service** for hotel guests, whereby you can have anything you buy in one of the theme parks delivered to the Disney shop in your hotel, for collection from 8pm that day. Each hotel also organises regular **children's activities** and all have Disney TV and a computer games console in their play area. For bookings, call 08705 030303, or visit **www.disneylandparis.co.uk**.

Character breakfast: Finally, and highly importantly for those with children, you can book a character breakfast at one of 2 locations – the Inventions restaurant for guests at the *Disneyland Hotel* or Café Mickey in *Disney Village*. These feature an American buffet breakfast with breads, pastries, scrambled eggs, ham, sausages, cereals, fruit juices and hot drinks, and are priced at €17/adult and €12/child (3–11) as it counts as a supplement against the normal hotel breakfast. They are available for non-Disney hotel guests, but the prices are €24 and €16.50.

BRITTIP — The character dining options can be booked through your hotel concierge in the foyer (see Brit Tip on page 67), and it is advisable to do this as soon as you check in.

Good Morning Fantasyland: An additional (non-character) feature at peak times for guests at *Disney's Newport Bay Club, Sequoia Lodge, Hotel Cheyenne* and *Hotel Santa Fe* offers the option of entering the *Disneyland Park* an hour early and boarding the Disneyland Railroad train (or just walking) to Fantasyland, where a basic continental breakfast is served in Au Chalet de la Marionette.

BRITTIP — Although there is no extra charge for the Good Morning Fantasyland breakfast, you need to specify whether you would like to do it when you book your package, as it is likely to be fully subscribed when you check in.

Park Hopper: In nearly all cases, when booking a Disney hotel or one of Disney's partner hotels, you are obliged to accept a Park Hopper Ticket for the duration of your stay as part of the package (or a 3-Day ticket if you opt for the minimum 2-night/3-day package), which obviously suits most people as it keeps you up and running in the theme parks from first minute to last. However, it may not be suitable if you plan on some non-Disney sightseeing as well, so you need to weigh up whether an off-site hotel

The Half-Board Option

One extra possibility for all Disney resort guests is the **Half Board Meal Plan** – a series of pre-paid meal vouchers that can be used in a wide variety of Disney restaurants for a saving of up to 10% off menu prices. Designed to encourage guests to try more than just the counter-service dining options, it has proved highly popular but it takes a bit of explaining and you need to be aware of your voucher use to get full value for money.

To start with, you MUST purchase the vouchers prior to arrival for all members of your party and for each night of your stay. Each adult voucher is valid for a starter, main course and dessert *or* an All-You-Can-Eat Buffet, plus one soft drink or mineral water. Children's vouchers include a main course and dessert *or* an All-you-Can-Eat Buffet, plus one soft drink. Prices also depend on dates of arrival and it is not available on December 24 or 31.

There are 3 basic Plans that provide different levels of dining choice, getting more expensive each time. The **Half Board Standard** meal plan is designed for guests staying at the *Hotel Santa Fe, Hotel Cheyenne* and *Davy Crockett Ranch*, including the restaurants at those hotels plus 6 in the parks and 2 in *Disney Village*. It costs £21–25/adult and £9–11/child (3–11) per night. The **Half Board Plus** is designed for guests staying at *Hotel New York, Newport Bay Club* and *Sequoia Lodge*, so it includes their restaurants, 8 in the parks and 5 more in *Disney Village* at £26–31/adult and £11–13/child per night. The **Half Board Premium** is designed for anyone staying at the *Disneyland Hotel* or *Hotel New York* as it includes the restaurants at both hotels, all those in the Standard and Plus plans, as well as the big Princess character meal in the *Disneyland Park* and Buffalo Bill's Wild West Show. This costs £43–51/adult and £17–20/child per night.

You can **upgrade** the Standard or Plus vouchers to **Plus** or **Premium** on any night (at the specific restaurants only), simply by exchanging your voucher for its face value when you dine. Or you can combine 2 Half Board Plus vouchers for the Grand Princess character lunch or dinner at Auberge du Cendrillon in the *Disneyland Park*.

You can book vouchers up to 3 months in advance on 08705 03 03 03 and they can be used for lunch or dinner.

The restaurants

Half-Board Standard entitles guests to eat at: La Cantina (*Hotel Santa Fe*), Chuck Wagon Café (*Hotel Cheyenne*), Crockett's Tavern (*Davy Crockett Ranch*), Silver Spur Steakhouse, The Lucky Nugget Saloon, Cowboy Cookout Barbecue, Agrabah Café and Plaza Gardens Restaurant (*Disneyland Park*), Restaurant des Stars (*Walt Disney Studios*), Annette's Diner and La Grange at Billy Bob's (Disney Village).

Half Board Plus includes the above, plus: Hunter's Grill and Beaver Creek Tavern (*Sequoia Lodge*), Cape Cod and Yacht Club (*Newport Bay Club*), Parkside Diner and Manhattan (*Hotel New York*), Blue Lagoon and Walt's – An American Restaurant (*Disneyland Park*), The Steakhouse (*Disney Village*).

Premium includes the above, plus: California Grill and Inventions (*Disneyland Hotel*), Auberge du Cendrillon (*Disneyland Park*), Café Mickey and Buffalo Bill's Wild West Show (*Disney Village*).

The pros and cons

With the vouchers, you can budget for meals in advance, avoid having to carry too much cash and not be tempted to try too many restaurants. You also save up to 10% on the full menu prices.

Disney benefit because you will probably eat in a table service or buffet restaurant more often that you would do otherwise. It is also *essential* to book your restaurants in advance to avoid queuing or, more importantly, not being able to get in. This means being more organised than just deciding to eat as you go along. Having to have the vouchers for every day CAN still work out quite expensive – staying for 3 nights at the Newport Bay Club with Plus vouchers would cost a family of 4 (with children under 12) £222–252, and they will still need to fund another meal at some point during the day (this is Half Board, not Full Board, remember). A typical counter service meal is around £32 for that same family of 4 (£96 over those same 3 days), so this is not a cheap option. Vouchers cannot be used at McDonald's,

Starbucks, Planet Hollywood, Rainforest Café, Earl of Sandwich or King Ludwig's Castle, and they are NOT valid December 24 or 31. Some restaurants can also be closed from time to time.

NB: You receive the Half Board vouchers when you check in to your Disney hotel but they do NOT guarantee a table reservation. Reservations must still be made separately. See your hotel concierge desk on arrival or call the Dining Reservation Service (in France) on 01 60 30 40 50 or from the UK on 00 33 1 60 30 40 50 (listen for the English option). Premium vouchers can be used at the second sitting of Buffalo Bill's only. Present your vouchers when you are ready to pay. The Dining Plans should be avoided if you have an Annual or Shareholders pass. You save only UP TO 10% for the set option (with any extras, like second drinks, at full cost). With an Annual pass, you automatically save 10% while a Shareholders card saves 15% on your complete meal, including any extra drinks.

might be a better option. The main exception to the Disney hotel rule is if you are an Annual Passport holder, in which case you can book just bed and breakfast packages through the central reservations office on 00 33 1 60 30 60 69 from the UK.

BRITTIP
If you are on the Plus or Premium **Dining Plans**, you will need to make sure you dine in one of the top restaurants each day to get full value for your vouchers.

Rooms: Most will accommodate a family of 4 comfortably, but you are limited for choice with 5 or more (although some rooms can accommodate a cot if required). Basically, you have only 4 choices in this instance: *Disney's Davy Crockett Ranch*, where the cabins can house up to 6 (but you must have your own transport); 2 connecting rooms in one of the 6 hotels; the family rooms in the (expensive) *Disneyland Hotel*, which can sleep 5; or one of the 15 family rooms, which can accommodate up to 6, at *Newport Bay Club*, although these rooms are more expensive and are at a premium, so you'd need to book early.

Looking outside the resort, the Pierre & Vacances Residence Val d'Europe is an ultra-smart apartment block in the town which can accommodate up to 7, while the Thomas Cook Explorers Hotel can take family groups of up to

Newport Bay Club

10 and the Adagio City Aparthotel, also in Val d'Europe, can take up to 9).

Rooms for guests with disabilities are available in all 6 Disney hotels, but not *Davy Crockett Ranch*.

All rooms feature a phone, international TV channels and radio, and a shower/bath. *Disney's Hotel Cheyenne, Hotel Santa Fe* and *Davy Crockett Ranch* do NOT have air-conditioning (although the former 2 have ceiling fans), while only the *Disneyland Hotel* and *Hotel New York* have hairdryers fitted as standard in the bathrooms (the others have hairdryers available on request). *The Disneyland Hotel, Hotel New York* and *Newport Bay Club* all have mini-bars, as does *Sequoia Lodge* in its Montana rooms only, while the former trio also have room safes. All Disney hotels now feature ONLY non-smoking rooms, hence it should not be necessary to request one, and all have a left-luggage service, with the exception of *Davy Crockett Ranch*.

Other details: When checking in, you will be given your park tickets, any vouchers for various options you might have booked (for meals or Buffalo Bill's Wild West Show), park maps, an information guide to the hotel (these are well written and highly collectable), a *Disney Village* programme and your Resort ID card, while children also get a name badge to wear (if they wish!).

BRITTIP
If you arrive at *Hotel New York* between noon and 2pm, have lunch there before heading off to the parks; you will get served much quicker.

Each resort hotel should be able to supply a cot on request and all feature **children's menus** in their main restaurants. **Room service** is available at the *Disneyland Hotel, Hotel New York* and the Admiral's Floor of *Newport Bay Club*. There is no official **babysitting** service for any hotel, although there is a private firm who can arrange in-room babysitting for you via the front desk.

STAYING THERE

Check-in time is 3pm (rooms are occasionally available from 1pm) but you can take advantage of the left-luggage provision if you want to head straight for the parks. Check-out is 11am.

BRITTIP
If you have booked Eurostar's Disney Express service (see page 54), you simply leave your bags with the porters at your hotel when you check out, and they will be transferred for you to collect at the Disney Express office at the Marne-la-Vallée station. The standard Hotel Baggage transfer to the station costs €10–11 one way.

Suites: Finally, almost the ultimate perk of staying onsite comes if you opt for one of the suites at the *Disneyland Hotel, Hotel New York, Sequoia Lodge* or *Newport Bay Club*. All guests at these accommodations receive **VIP FastPasses** providing all-day front-of-line access to all the rides that have the FastPass system (see page 105). All guests at the *Disneyland Hotel* also receive one free FastPass per day, for use on any FP ride of their choice.

Disadvantages: The pros of staying on-site are substantial, but what of the cons? Well, the price difference is the obvious issue. You can save 20–30% by opting for one of the smaller hotels nearby, while the 7 official nearby hotels (4 in the **Val de France** area) also represent significant savings while offering much of the convenience, facilities and service. In fact, we rate the Vienna International Dream Castle and Thomas Cook Explorers Hotels as possibly the best all-round value.

Breakfast at the Disney resorts can be slightly chaotic at peak periods. You are allocated a set time-slot, which can be anywhere from 7–10am, OR you can queue up for the next available table (by showing your hotel card) when you are ready for breakfast, both of which can be a bit of a bun-fight when it's busy. Some check-in staff do not tell guests of the queue-up option but it's often better than sticking to the pre-set time (especially if it's too early for you). If you're looking to be in the parks by 9am, you may struggle to get through

Princess for a day!

Young girls wishing to have the full princess touch should head for the *Disneyland Hotel* where, on the first floor landing, there is a special 'Princess for a day' parlour, offering different packages of dresses and make-up and a range of accessories sure to please any princess-in-waiting! The packages go from €40 (for hair and make-up) and €60 (adding a tiara and photo), to The Princesse Luxe at €130 (adding a wand and a dress) and the Princesse Prestige for €160 (adding a figurine). There is also a Princesse Luxe Tiana option (make-up, hairstyle, tiara, photo, bag and dress) and Princesse Luxe Ariel package (make-up, hairstyle, photo, bunch of flowers, boa and dress) both for €135.

breakfast in time, unless you have the 7.30am time-slot (not everyone's idea of a holiday rise-and-shine!). The off-site hotels are less frenetic (with the possible exception of the busy Thomas Cook Explorers Hotel).

Those in the Val de France area benefit from a beautiful countryside location, with a large lake that backs on to the 4 hotels, providing a pleasant way to unwind after the parks. However, the (free) shuttle bus service can be a bit of a trial at peak times (half an hour before park opening and at park closing). It calls at all 4 hotels in turn, which means either an uncomfortable 10–15min ride or, occasionally, having to wait for another bus if the first is full.

Having underlined the price differential, Disney's 6 hotels (amounting to 5,200 rooms, plus the 535 cabins of *Davy Crockett Ranch*) do offer a range of prices to suit most pockets, from the budget *Hotel Santa Fe* to the opulent *Disneyland Hotel*.

We at the *Brit Guide* have our own ratings system for the hotels, too, allocating €s in the following price ranges:

€€€€€	=	More than €150/night
€€€€	=	€100–150/night
€€€	=	€75–100/night
€€	=	€50–75/night
€	=	Less than €50/night

We also award C ratings out of 5 for the facilities at each property. A CCCCC hotel should have all the creature comforts you can think of, including a swimming pool and a choice of restaurants, while a CC would be of a more basic type. Here are Disney's magnificent 7 in detail.

◄► BRITTIP
Each Disney hotel has a Concierge desk in the foyer for booking meals and shows in any of the hotels, parks or *Disney Village*. Try to plan day by day and visit the desk first thing in the morning to book, especially at peak times. If you can book for your whole stay straight away, you will be one step ahead of the masses.

Disneyland Hotel

The resort's signature hotel, right at the entrance to the *Disneyland Park* (and otherwise known as the Pink Palace), is a massive mock-Victorian edifice featuring the most comfortable and spacious rooms, sumptuous decor and one of the best restaurants in the area. The Disney theming is discreet (you have to look closely at the wallpaper to realise the Mickey subtlety) and there is some elegant furniture sprinkled around (witness the 4 classic grandfather clocks along one corridor that display the times at each of the Disney resorts around the world – they also play Disney tunes on the hour and half-hour!).

Rooms and suites: Standard rooms feature either a king-size bed and a fold-out or 2 doubles, plus a highly elaborate TV/video cabinet with mini-bar, and all have the high ceilings reminiscent of Victorian buildings. However, there is a supplement for a Standard room with a park view.

Castle Club: The top 2 floors feature this exclusive club, with a private lift (straight to the theme park!) and reception desk, a lounge bar for breakfast, afternoon tea and light refreshments, plus a fabulous view over the *Disneyland Park*. There are spacious Junior Suites (58m^2/624ft^2 as opposed to the 34m^2/366ft^2 of

STAYING THERE

Disneyland Hotel

Join the club!

The Empire State Club at Hotel New York is a concierge-level option for guests that adds some tempting privileges (like the Castle Club level at the Disneyland Hotel and Admiral's Floor at Newport Bay Club). The 34 top-floor rooms and suites all have their own check-in, an exclusive lounge (with complimentary refreshments) and a buffet breakfast with characters every day. The rooms are also furnished in a more luxurious style, with upgraded amenities. More importantly, the Club gives all its guests a valuable VIP FastPass (see page 106) for the duration of stay, all for around £26–41 extra per person per day.

standard rooms), plus 4 Tinker Bell Suites (69m²/743ft m²) with a lounge and a separate walk-in shower as well as a bath. In addition there are 3 one-off suites of truly exceptional order – Walt's Apartment, the Cinderella Vice-Presidential Suite and the Sleeping Beauty Presidential Suite. One great perk for all Suite guests is a **VIP FastPass** valid all day long on all park FastPass attractions for the duration of stay.

68

STAYING THERE

BRITTIP

If you find *Disney Village* too frenetic in the evening, head for the City Bar at nearby *Hotel New York*, which offers the perfect surroundings for relaxing and enjoying a drink.

Shopping and dining: From the 3-storey lobby right through to the Celestia Spa, the period theming is impressive. There is a **Galerie Mickey** selling souvenirs and travel essentials,

---

Panoramagique provides a bird's eye view of Hotel New York and Lake Disney

Hotel New York

the main bar area **Café Fantasia** (with inventive decor geared to the film of the same name) as well as 2 restaurants. **Inventions** is themed on the great technical creations of the 20th century and offers an excellent dinner buffet, in addition to character breakfasts. The **California Grill** is the hotel's fine-dining option and the quality on offer is superb, with a conservatory-style motif and an open kitchen at one end. At the other end, a lounge affords more great views of the theme park. It is important, though, to book ahead for these two restaurants as, even with their higher price tag, both are popular and can be fully booked, especially during high season.

Facilities: The indoor pool area is equally smart, with a medium-sized pool, Jacuzzi, gym and massage treatment rooms, as well as a sauna, steam room and solarium. The inevitable video games room is fully geared up for kids of the requisite age, while the Club Minnie activity centre includes TV, video and computer games. The only thing it doesn't have is an outdoor play area, but then the *Disneyland Park* is right on the doorstep! The Celestia Spa offers a

fabulous array of spa, massage and beauty treatments, including couples treatments, and adds the ultimate relaxation after the parks. Call 01 60 45 66 05 to book, or 6605 from a Disney hotel phone. Prices vary from €65 for a back rub to €350 for a full 3-hour package.

In all, there are 496 rooms, plus 18 suites, and it really is the pinnacle of the on-site accommodation. **Official rating ****; our rating €€€€€, CCCCC.**

Disneyland Hotel

Disney's Hotel New York

Welcome to the Big Apple! While this is a Disney hotel, it is wonderfully themed in its own right, with an art deco 1930s' view of New York that extends from the massive 'tower block' façade to individual touches in the rooms and background jazz in the lobby and bar area. There is little overt Mickey-ness about it, but lots of grand style and clever imagery, with the bonus of rooms with a fabulous view over Lake Disney. It also has, we reckon, the most amazing suite of them all, the 2-storey Presidential Suite, with floor-to-ceiling windows, a living room complete with piano and a dining room for up to 10 guests. The upstairs double bedroom has a separate lounge and Jacuzzi.

BRITTIP
Hotel New York is a product of American architect Michael Graves, who also designed the Swan and Dolphin Resorts in *Walt Disney World* in Florida. So, if you enjoy the fun-style architecture of those, this should appeal to you, too.

Rooms and suites: There are 565 rooms in all, including 27 spacious suites. Most standard rooms (31m²/334ft²) have lovely rosewood cabinets and sleep 4 comfortably, while others offer just one king-size bed. The Resort Suites (56m²/603ft² (on the corner of each floor) have masses of space for a family of 4, with a separate bedroom and living room. There is a beautiful Honeymoon Suite (62m²/667ft²) as well.

Dining: The hotel features 2 restaurants, the intimate, formal **Manhattan Restaurant** and the more relaxed, cosmopolitan style of the **Parkside Diner**, as well as a delightfully elegant bar. The same breakfast buffet is served in each.

BRITTIP
The elegant and comfortable Manhattan Restaurant in the *Hotel New York* is an oft-overlooked but worthwhile venue for a special dinner, with a terrific Italian-tinged menu.

Facilities: There's a hair salon (the only one on-site), boutique and well-stocked gift shop, 2 outdoor tennis courts (small fee for racket and ball hire) and an ice-skating rink (an eye-catching facility in winter).

For kids, there is the indoor **Roger Rabbit Corner**, with themed activities at different times of the day, and the ubiquitous video games room, plus daily appearances of Disney characters in the main hall each morning. The one drawback here is that the hotel is also a big convention facility, and it can draw a sizeable business crowd at times.

BRITTIP
Big fan of Mickey Mouse and want to see him without the hour queue in the park? *Hotel New York* is the place to be as Mickey is available for pictures and autograph-signing at his special photo-op just past the shop. Even during high season, waits are rarely longer then 10mins.

A bonus with *Hotel New York* is the excellent swimming pool complex (the New York Athletic Club), which is among the best of the on-site hotels. The extremely large pool has both an indoor and outdoor aspect, while there is also a Jacuzzi, sauna, steam room and a good-sized gymnasium, plus a pleasant outdoor terrace. After the *Disneyland Hotel*, it is also the closest to the theme parks, situated at the opposite end of *Disney Village*, just a 10min stroll from the parks.

The (winter) **ice rink** at the back of the hotel (facing Lake Disney) offers skates to rent for a small fee. In summer months, this space offers other entertainment such as go-karts and giant-sized, zip-up beach balls for children to play in.

While it may be a touch too formal for some tastes (mainly due to the conference aspect), *Hotel New York* has an exciting feel, especially for young adults and teenagers, and is in a perfect situation looking over Lake Disney but still within easy reach of *Disney Village* and the parks. **Official rating ****; our rating €€€€, CCCCC.**

STAYING THERE

Disney's Newport Bay Club

Keeping with the American theme, *Newport Bay Club* has a New England seaside resort feel, with the largest spread of rooms of any hotel in Europe. It may not appeal quite so much to children (it has the most 'grown-up' style), but it is well equipped to cater for all the family. However, the sheer size of the hotel (1,080 rooms, plus 13 suites) means the foyer can get terribly congested, especially from 9–10am when people are checking out.

Rooms and suites: There is a separate reception desk for the **Admiral's Club**, which covers the lake side of the top 2 floors for wonderful views and offers a more personal level of service, plus room service and a quieter, more relaxed atmosphere (quite a bonus when the hotel is full). The majority of the spacious, 2-room suites ($55m^2/592ft^2$) are at this level, with the unusual octagonal Honeymoon Suite ($45m^2/484ft^2$) being stunningly romantic. The main suites also feature lovely colonial-style furniture and extra nautical touches. Standard rooms ($27m^2/290ft^2$) continue the refreshing blue and white colour scheme of the rest of the hotel and all include mini-bars and room safes.

Dining and shopping: The 2 restaurants are semi-formal – the **Cape Cod** serves a big selection of different foods buffet style, including a handy all-you-can-eat dinner option. The **Yacht Club** specialises in fish, seafood and grilled meats, plus a handful of Asian-influenced dishes. There are 2 set menus as well as a tempting à la carte selection (try the Surf & Turf option with grilled fillet of beef and grilled lobster half) as well as a vegetarian option. Children can choose between a set menu or the Little Sailors Menu, a buffet-style option. You are allocated either one for breakfast when you check in (if the hotel is full; if not, the Cape Cod is used on its own), but the breakfast offerings are the same in both. There are 2 fine bars, **Fisherman's Wharf**, which opens from the foyer and also offers a range of snacks during the day, and the more nautically themed **Captain's Quarters** piano bar, that both look out over Lake Disney. The large **Bay Boutique** offers a good selection of Disney merchandise and travel essentials.

Facilities: It has 2 excellent pools (a large one outdoors and an elaborate one, with a pirate ship centrepiece, inside), a Jacuzzi, steam bath and fitness room, an outdoor play area, the usual video games arcade and a **Children's Corner** play area with organised activities on certain days. There is also a convention centre here, but the business aspect is less intrusive than at *Hotel New York*.

> **BRITTIP**
> Hairdryers and irons are available free on request from the front desk at most Disney hotels, subject to availability and sometimes a deposit, except for the *Disneyland Hotel* and *Hotel New York*, where they are provided in the rooms. Some rooms in *Newport Bay Club* and *Sequoia Lodge* will also have them.

Newport Bay Club is at the furthest end of Lake Disney, so it is a good 15mins to the theme parks (although you can also use the free bus service). But, on a pleasant morning, there is not a more delightful walk anywhere in the Ile de France. **Official rating ***; our rating €€€, CCCC.**

Disney's Sequoia Lodge

If you like to be surrounded by gardens and greenery, head straight for *Sequoia Lodge*. Here you will be transported to one of the great American national parks. The main aspect of the hotel is a touch flat and monolithic but the interior and landscaping are breathtaking, with a fabulous use of stone and hundreds of imported trees and bushes for an authentic feel. A 2011 refurbishment added some neat Bambi theming in the rooms, along with new flatscreen TVs and internet access in all the rooms.

For the ideal warming winter retreat, the **Redwood Bar and Lounge** has

Disneyland Paris Hotels

DISNEYLAND PARIS HOTELS

1   Disney's Hotel Cheyenne
2   Disney's Hotel Santa Fe
3   Disney's Sequoia Lodge
4   Disney's Davy Crockett Ranch
5   Disney's Newport Bay Club
6   Lake Disney
7   Disney's Hotel New York
8   RER/TGV/bus station
9   Disneyland Hotel
10 *Disneyland Park*
11 *Walt Disney Studios*
12 Vinci Car Park
13 Disney Village

Newport Bay Club

a massive open fireplace and cosy furniture. The low, sloping, beamed ceiling and flagstone floor of the lobby set the scene for an outdoor adventure with all the comforts of a luxury resort (well above its 3-star rating, in our opinion). The judicious use of dark woods adds to the rugged feel and, when the weather is good, there is a lovely terrace overlooking Lake Disney where you can sit with a drink. The Lodge underwent a big refurbishment in 2011, with all the rooms refreshed and updated, along with attention to the exterior and grounds. This hotel is now the perfect choice for a fresh and enhanced Disney hotel experience.

BRITTIP

Not sure of where to stay at Christmas? *Sequoia Lodge* is the perfect choice as, during winter, it takes on an enchanted atmosphere with all the festive decorations.

Rooms and suites: The 1,011 rooms (including 16 suites) are split between the huge main building and 5 lodges spread throughout the gardens.

Standard rooms (22m²/237ft²) have either a lakeside or gardens/car park view, large windows and a few extra themed touches like rocking chairs and rustic light fittings, which combine well with the dark wood furniture and dark bedspreads and curtains to provide that American backwoods ambience.

Hotel Cheyenne

The cabin lodges offer exactly the same room space and facilities as the main building (Montana) rooms, apart from a mini-bar (so they are slightly cheaper). A lakeside view carries a supplement but is well worthwhile (and should be requested when you make your booking). The spacious 2-room suites (55m²/592ft²) all have a lake view, and the Honeymoon Suite features an open-plan arrangement with no door between the bedroom and living room.

Dining and shopping: There are 2 mouth-watering diners, the **Beaver Creek Tavern** and **Hunter's Grill**. The former is the more family-orientated option, with a varied menu to suit those with a big appetite. It offers a big starters buffet and an outstanding dessert buffet, while main courses are à la carte and range from €18.50–31. There is also a set 3-course option. Within the restaurant is a kids' area with a TV showing Disney cartoons. The Hunter's Grill continues the outdoors theme in magnificent style, with a huntin', shootin', fishin' motif that boasts a feature kitchen serving up a fabulous international buffet. Neither restaurant is open for lunch.

The gift shop, **The Northwest Passage**, sells a standard range of toiletries, snacks, drinks and souvenirs.

Facilities: The **Little Prairie** is the kids' corner, with a TV and video, games station, and Disney characters appear daily, mostly near the shop area. There is the usual video games room, plus an outdoor play area, with slides and a sandpit, set among some beautiful gardens, full of unique (for Western Europe) foliage, a waterfall and even a mock beaver dam. Stroll the paths along the 'Rio Grande' and you come to the hotel's pool lodge, an indoor/outdoor facility that features a waterslide, freeform leisure pool (great for kids), large Jacuzzi, sauna, steam room and gymnasium.

At a first look, *Sequoia Lodge* may seem more of an adult environment, but children usually love the 'outdoorsy' feel and the great extras of the pool,

gardens and play area make it a great family base. In fact, you may have trouble persuading the kids to leave when the characters are in residence! It takes 10–15mins to walk into the theme parks, or you can take the free 5-min shuttle bus ride. **Official rating ***; our rating €€€, CCCC½.**

Disney's Hotel Cheyenne

Howdy partners, welcome to the Wild West – or Disney's version of it at least (a lot safer and more comfortable!). This imaginative hotel is usually a huge hit with children and is therefore a popular family choice (although it can be a little raucous at times when the kids re-enact Custer's Last Stand at regular intervals, armed with rifles and bows and arrows from the hotel shop!). The theming is comprehensive, from the wonderful period-style entrance lobby (complete with 2 bronze horse and rider statues) to the rooms and their rustic, kid-friendly bunk-beds. It is also quite extensive, as all the rooms are low-rise (no more than 2 storeys) to give the feel of a Western town.

The level of creature comforts is not quite the same as elsewhere – no swimming pool or air-conditioning, no luggage delivery to the rooms and only a self-service restaurant. But, there are some significant extras aimed at the kids – optional pony rides (spring and summer, for a small fee) and a Fort Apache outdoor play area, plus the Nevada games room. There is also one of the nicest photo opportunities locations of all the resorts. In front of the main entrance of the main building stands a post wagon where Pluto usually comes to meet and greet his fans. Other characters can appear too.

The lobby is themed like a Goldrush-era claims office, with a Land Claims desk instead of a reception area, a huge stone fireplace and a mock hotel entrance at the opposite end of the vaulted-ceiling foyer. The lobby also has a kiddie corner (with organised colouring and drawing on certain days) that boasts mini-saddles instead of chairs! Of course, there is the usual video games room.

Davy Crockett's Adventure

This is an adjacent public forest park with tree-top adventure trails for all ages from 8 up, offering 3 hours of challenging tree-climbing, rope bridges, giant swings, obstacle courses and the feature Tarzan Tree Jump. Look up more on page 182 or (in French only) on **www.aventure-aventure.com**.

Step out of the main building and you are in a true cowboy town, with raised, boarded sidewalks, dirt streets and blocks of hotel rooms all disguised as various buildings, such as the Guest House, Blacksmith and Sheriff's Office.

Rooms: The 14 blocks are each named after a famous character like Doc Holliday, Jesse James, Calamity Jane and Running Bear. Blocks 17–19 (they are actually numbered from 10–25, omitting 13), Sitting Bull, Wyatt Earp and Billy The Kid, are closest to the main building and the bus stop for the free shuttle to the theme parks and *Disney Village*. There are 1,000 identical rooms (all 21m²/226ft²) spread out through the 14 blocks, which have internal access only and most with a double bed and 2 bunks.

The in-room theming is more limited and the bathrooms slightly more spartan compared to the other resorts, but then it is designed for more budget-conscious visitors (no air-conditioning, just ceiling fans).

Dining and shopping: Western paraphernalia abounds and the theming continues into the bar and restaurant areas, with saloon-style doors, wooden tables, chairs, balustrades and ceiling beams. The **Red Garter Saloon** features live country music in the evening and has an outdoor terrace. The 750-seat **Chuck Wagon**, which also has its own **Saddle Bar** and wagon play area, is a cafeteria-style eaterie dressed up like a Texan pioneer marketplace. It serves a good mixture of international dishes, from barbecue-smoked chicken and beef to salads, pasta, risottos and

fresh wok-fried Chinese specialities. There is also a set-meal choice and a children's buffet. **The General Store** is the standard gift shop.

BRITTIP

If the bus queues are too long when you want to return to *Hotel Cheyenne*, take the short cut back in around 10mins. Walk out past the train station, cross the bridge to the main road, turn right and you can enter the hotel's main gate (along a walkway) from the car park. You may need to show your hotel ID.

Facilities: As well as the kid-friendly options, the 2 guest launderettes are free to use, although you need to buy washing powder from the General Store. Kettles can also be provided for in-room use with a small deposit.

The regular shuttle bus to the theme parks, *Disney Village* and RER station takes about 5min (queues permitting) or you can walk it (in 15–20mins) along a pathway under the main road and past Hotel New York. **Official rating **; our rating €€, CCC½.**

Disney's Hotel Santa Fe

Right at the budget end of the 6-hotel spectrum is this extensive *pueblo*-style resort decked out in best American South West fashion, with Native American, Spanish and Mexican cultures providing the decorative motif, and a giant billboard from the Pixar film *Cars* (like a drive-in movie screen) welcoming you 'into town'. In truth, this is a glorified motel, but that doesn't stop it being fun for kids, reasonable value for money and still well situated to enjoy all the Disney magic. It gets extremely busy in high season (breakfast sittings are pre-allocated from 7–10.30am) and is popular with coach operators, so it gets congested in the morning with large numbers of guests arriving and departing at the same time.

On first impressions, the hotel looks rather dreary with its collection of square, concrete blocks up to 5 storeys high, but the Imagineers have added

Hotel Cheyenne

a few fanciful touches, even if the original 'volcano' is now a derelict grey hulk. There are 4 'trails' through the resort (corresponding to the 4 different room sections – Artefacts, Water, Monuments and Legends), each with their own symbols and icons scattered around – from rusting desert 'vehicles' to outlandish meteorites, water trails, a geyser and even a crashed flying saucer!

The smattering of desert scenery is also quite eye-catching, but much of the resort is still in need of a major overhaul, despite a 2011 refurbishment that added more *Cars*-themed touches to the rooms. If you are just looking for a place to sleep with all the Disney advantages, though, this should fit the bill. The main facilities are in the reception building, while the 1,000 rooms are spread out over 41 blocks surrounded by small car parks, so if you are driving, this is the only hotel where you can more or less park outside your room.

BRITTIP

You need to request a room with bunk-beds when booking at *Hotel Santa Fe* if that is what your children want (usually a lot more comfortable for children aged 6-plus).

Rooms: The identical rooms ($21m^2/226ft^2$) are cheerfully decorated – enjoying new *Cars* bedspreads and artwork – if rather sparse by comparison with the other hotels, but many also come with bunk-beds instead of 2 double beds. As with all Disney accommodation, they can house a family of 4 (or 4 plus one in a cot), although they are a bit short of drawer space. There is no in-room air-conditioning, just a ceiling fan.

STAYING THERE

Hotel Santa Fe

Red Garter Saloon at Disney's Hotel Cheyenne

As at *Hotel Cheyenne*, breakfast at *Hotel Santa Fe* is the basic continental kind – cereal, croissants, pastries, juice, tea/coffee – but you can pay a supplement to add bacon, eggs and fresh fruit.

Dining and shopping: The 700-seat **La Cantina** serves up a Tex-Mex dinner buffet (6–10.30pm) in a food-court-style servery for a set fee, either with or without a drink. Imaginative touches have food served from the back of a flat-bed truck and drinks dispensed from 'petrol pumps' – worth highlighting as so many people miss them in their rush to get to the parks. Next door to La Cantina is the **Rio Grande Bar**, with live entertainment and karaoke on certain evenings. **The Trading Post** is the Disney gift shop, with a good range of souvenirs, snacks, drinks and basic toiletries.

Facilities: The children's corner, with organised colouring and drawing activities (in the evenings), is in La Cantina, with a computer console and Disney TV. A video games room is available for the kids, plus an outdoor playground, the Totem Circle, which is handy if they have any energy left

at the end of the day! Back in the lobby, characters meet 'n' greet in the morning, which is the ideal way to start the day if you have young autograph hunters. The hotel is adjacent to *Hotel Cheyenne*, so it is perfectly permissible to pop 'next door' to enjoy some of the facilities there too, notably, the Fort Apache play area for kids, the pony rides and the Red Garter Saloon.

Disney's Davy Crockett Ranch

> **BRITTIP**
> The petrol station next door to *Hotel Santa Fe* is one of the few places on-site where you can buy fresh milk and other handy groceries.

The hotel is a good 20–25min walk from the parks, but once again, if the weather is fine, it is a lovely way to start the day as you stroll alongside the 'Rio Grande' and up by *Hotel New York*, around Lake Disney and through *Disney Village*. Alternatively, the shuttle bus takes about 10mins and, while there is usually quite a queue in the morning, they run several buses at once on this route (as they do at all the bigger hotels). **Official rating **; our rating €€, CCC.**

Disney's Davy Crockett Ranch

If you drive to *Disneyland Paris* and are happy to use your car to get to the parks every day, staying at *Davy Crockett Ranch* is possibly the best value way to enjoy all the fun and still have a taste of Disney imagination in your accommodation. Here, in 'trapper country', are 595 cabins with 1 or 2 bedrooms accommodating up to 6 (sadly, the campgrounds and caravan sites are no longer available).

Set in 57ha/140 acres of pretty woodland about a 15min drive from the theme parks (where parking is free with your resort ID card), you do get the feeling of being out in the wilds (see map on page 85). The woods are dotted with imaginative touches such as Native American tepees, while all the main services and facilities are located in a wonderfully fun cowboy 'village' at the heart of the ranch, where you will find a host of activities and amenities.

The site is completely secured against non-visitor traffic. You check in at the reception area at the main entrance, much as you would for a hotel, and they provide you with your keys, the all-important Disney resort ID cards and the security code to access the

STAYING THERE

site, which you punch in at the gate just past reception. Then, when you depart, you just drop the keys off in a deposit box, so you need not go back into reception.

Rooms: Eight circular 'trails' house all the accommodation. Each trail has its own take-away 'cottage', where breakfast is served (7–11am) for you to take back to your cabin, caravan or tent. The 1-bedroom cabins (all 36m²/388ft²) feature a spacious lounge with TV, a kitchen with 2 hot-plates, dishwasher, fridge, microwave, kettle, coffee machine and all the necessary cutlery, crockery and cooking utensils. There is also a breakfast bar area. The bathroom (fully stocked with towels) includes the toilet but the 2 are separate in the 2-bed cabins. Some have a pull-down double bed in the lounge, others a convertible sofa, while the bedroom has a double bed and 2 bunks. Outside, they all have their own barbecue and picnic bench, plus parking.

> **BRITTIP**
> The ranch's 2-bedroom cabins are all newer than the 1-bed ones, and come at a slight premium. They also go quickly, so it's best to book early.

The 2-bed cabins (39m²/420ft²) have the 2 bunk-beds in their own room, giving mum and dad a little privacy. The living quarters are arranged slightly differently and the general fixtures and fittings are a bit smarter. The difference in price is minimal, so these are the better option.

Dining and shopping: The 'village' is actually a fully fledged resort in its own right, centred on the Trading Post and **Crockett's Tavern**, a log-cabin restaurant serving lunch (12.30–2.30pm) and dinner (6–10.30pm), with a take-away service, too. The buffet-style servery offers up a good variety of dishes, from salad, fish and chips, roast chicken and pasta to entrecôte steak and even a vegetarian meal, while there is a choice of 4 kids' meals. Across the street is the authentic (if rather small) **Saloon** (5pm–midnight)

Our top tips

Having stayed at all the hotels at different times, we are happy to pass on our Top 10 of *Disneyland Paris* places to stay, based on what we feel is the best combination of quality, service and value for money.

1   Vienna International Dream Castle Hotel
2   Thomas Cook Explorers Hotel
3   *The Disneyland Hotel*
4   *Disney's Hotel New York*
5   Vienna International Magic Circus Hotel
6   *Disney's Sequoia Lodge*
7   *Disney's Newport Bay Club*
8   Hotel l'Elysée, Val d'Europe
9   Hotel Kyriad at *Disneyland Paris*
10 *Disney's Hotel Cheyenne*

We are confident this selection will provide a memorable experience (which is not to say others won't, just that these represent the best of the options at or near the parks). Adagio Aparthotel in Val d'Europe is a surprisingly good choice for larger groups (up to 7).

serving beer, wine and cocktails, with live entertainment and karaoke at peak times, plus outdoor seating and a large-screen TV in summer. The **Alamo Trading Post** is the gift shop and grocery store (8am–11pm).

BRITTIP
It is advisable, especially in summer when the resort can hold almost 4,000 people, to book a table for dinner at Crockett's Tavern. Lunch is rarely over-subscribed.

Facilities: Bowie's Bike Barn, the resort's information centre (8am–6pm, 8am–10pm seasonally) also houses the children's activity corner, with a computer play station, video console and colouring sets for kids, all set up around a large table with clever mini-saddles to sit on. Disney characters make an appearance every evening, while there is grown-up entertainment too, with themed evenings, line dancing and discos, plus organised sports, from jogging and aerobics to *petanque* and archery.

The **Lucky Raccoon** video games room adds that essential amenity for kids, and they are then spoiled for choice with the likes of horse and pony rides (ages 4–11, for a fee), Davy's Farm (a petting zoo with reindeer, goats, sheep, rabbits, birds and ducks), an outdoor play and climbing area, table tennis, volleyball, basketball, archery and mini-golf. There are 2 free-to-use indoor tennis courts (one of which is used alternately for archery, table tennis and volleyball in winter) and a nature park with the Indian Meadows village and walking trails.

BRITTIP
The reindeer 'work' in Disney's Christmas Parade at the *Disneyland Park*, but they get 10 months off, which they spend at the ranch!

Cycling is another activity for children and adults, with a huge range of bikes and quadri-cycles (Surrey bikes) for hire, to be used on the cycle trails throughout the resort and woods. The final outstanding element of the resort is the **Blue Springs Pool**, an extensive indoor water park (8.30am–10pm) with a semi-circular paddling pool for toddlers, a large, free-form leisure pool that has a waterfall, long water-slide, fountains, squirt pond and a huge Jacuzzi. You can rent towels for a small fee. Under 12s must be

View from the Disneyland Hotel

STAYING THERE

accompanied by an adult at all times in the pool area. It is an exceptional facility and you may struggle to get the kids out, even with the lure of the theme parks!

BRITTIP

The pool at the *Davy Crockett Ranch* is good enough to be worth driving back for during busy park hours. Crowded parks often mean a largely empty pool (but do check operation hours of the pool during your stay).

The Alamo Trading Post

The Ranch is about 3km/2mls off Exit 13 of the A4 autoroute. To get to the parks, simply come out of the property, take the second exit from the roundabout (signposted A4 Reims) and continue along the A4 to Exit 14 for 'Les Parcs Disneyland'. **Official rating **; our rating €€, CCCC.**

BRITTIP

To call any of Disney's hotels, simply dial the main switchboard – 00 33 1 64 74 40 00 from the UK, or 01 64 74 40 00 in France – and ask for the hotel you require.

Beyond Disney

Once you move beyond Disney for your choice of accommodation, things become simpler. There are few grand themed hotels (the Magic Circus, Dream Castle and Thomas Cook Explorers Hotel at Val de France are the only exceptions) and no great variation in style or facilities (almost all are 2- or 3-star). Rooms tend to be small but comfortable and the majority will provide a good, basic continental breakfast. We have toured the Seine-

et-Marne region extensively and have been impressed by the generally high standard of cleanliness and friendliness.

Many hotels in the immediate vicinity of Marne-la-Vallée are modern and pleasant, while all hotels are inspected regularly to ensure they conform to their star rating. Quite a few have swimming pools, but you need to decide if you are likely to use a pool after a long day at the parks to make it worthwhile paying extra.

We have subdivided the off-site hotels into those that are Near the Magic (including the sub-region of Val de France), those that are a short drive away, and hotel chains that have accommodation in Paris itself (which is not necessarily a bad idea if you want to see a lot of the city, as it is only 35–40mins from *Disneyland Paris* by RER).

Near the Magic

When it comes to hotels that are within a figurative stone's throw of the theme parks, there are 8 contrasting choices in the Val d'Europe area. These include 4 in an associated development just

Dream Castle Hotel

off the main ring road (which Disney refers to as its Selected Hotels). One of these, the Thomas Cook Explorers Hotel, was built with the UK market in mind, while all usually host a high percentage of British guests.

Adagio Aparthotel Val d'Europe: Opened in 2003, this stylish apartment complex has a good array of flexible accommodation that makes it an ideal base for a longer stay in the region. With 290 apartments and studios, sleeping 2–7, this is a modern and well-furnished offering. All

Adagio Aparthotel Val d'Europe

feature a fully equipped kitchenette (cooking hob, fridge, microwave and dishwasher), a living room and either a 1- or 2-bedroom option. The studios offer living/sleeping space for up to 3, while the largest apartments can sleep 3 in the living room and 4 in the 2 bedrooms. All have a bathroom and the larger ones have a shower room, too. There is no daily maid service, however, and linen service only every 7 days.

The resort-style set-up offers a launderette, indoor car park (for a fee), luggage room, small gym and an outdoor heated swimming pool open May–Sep. A separate charge (on check-in) is made for TV, wi-fi and phone use and there is also a charge for their 'baby kit' (cot and high chair). Good location for the shops and hypermarket of Val d'Europe itself. There is a free daily shuttle to the parks. 00 33 1 60 42 82 82 (in France) or 01 55 26 32 00 (UK only), **www. accorhotels.com**. **Official rating ***; our rating €€€, CC.**

Hotel l'Elysée: At the heart of the Val d'Europe development, and therefore just a 5min RER ride to *Disneyland Paris*, this rather chic 3-star property opened in July 2002. It features a grand reception lobby and underground parking and has a quiet, relaxing ambience, which is a nice contrast after the hurly-burly of the parks. The 152 rooms all accommodate 4, in a double bed and 2 single sofa beds (made up ready for you), while there are 4 spacious junior suites and 5 rooms adapted for the disabled (2 persons maximum). The rooms all have a mini-bar and safe and the marbled bathrooms are extremely smart. Cots are available on request, but they can't add up to a fifth person. However, there are inter-connecting rooms for larger families.

The hotel has a left-luggage room, free shuttle to the theme parks, a video games room for kids, an elegant bar and a high-quality restaurant and bar, the **Pop Art** (with a pleasant outdoor terrace in summer), while 24hr room service is also available. An extra bonus is the fact the hotel benefits from the **Extra Magic Hours** programme, providing access to the *Disneyland Park* 2 hours before official opening time. The last train from Marne-la-Vallée back to Val d'Europe is around midnight each day if you need to use the RER line. 00 33 1 64 63 33 33, **www. hotelelysee.com**. **Official rating ***; our rating €€€€, CCC.**

BRITTIP

Anyone visiting Val d'Europe for some shopping or a meal should consider dinner at the Hotel l'Elysée's **Pop Art restaurant**, where the French chef provides an excellent menu featuring local produce.

Hotel Ibis Marne La Vallée Val d'Europe: A member of the budget Ibis chain, this is right in the middle of Val d'Europe and just a short walk from the RER station. With 100 air-conditioned rooms (4 of them with disabled access), it offers a sound choice in an ideal 'near the Magic' location. With an all-you-can-eat breakfast buffet you won't start the day hungry and the Ibis chain also feature 'anytime snacks,' available 24/7 from the bar or reception, just to make sure! The hotel is fully wi-fi accessible and, while the facilities are fairly simple – just the Tuscan-themed Pasta & Cie Café (open 7–10.30pm, not weekends) and a bar – it is hard to fault their eager-to-please attitude. It is just a 5min walk from the Val d'Europe shopping centre, with its cafés and restaurants, and has its own car park. 00 33 1 60 36 20 06, **www. ibishotel.com**. **Official rating **; our rating €€€, CC.**

Radisson Blu Hotel at *Disneyland Paris*: This smart property in the Radisson group stands right on the edge of the Golf Disneyland complex in Magny-le-Hongre, with impressive views over the 9-hole courses. The hotel has 250 fully air-conditioned rooms, including 20 suites and 139 family rooms (with convertible sofa-beds) for up to 4 people, some of which are inter-connecting. All have flatscreen TVs and tea and coffee-

STAYING THERE

making facilities. It is set up, to a large extent, as a convention hotel with excellent business facilities, so you can expect a busy but elegant style. But there is also plenty to attract the Disney holidaymaker. There are 2 restaurants – the casual **Restaurant Birdie** for breakfast and the gourmet dining of **Pamplemousse Restaurant** – as well as the **Chardon Bar** (also serving snacks) and a Wellness & Fitness Centre, including a swimming pool, fully equipped gym and a state-of-the-art spa. Free wi-fi is available throughout the hotel. 00 33 1 60 43 64 00, **www.radissonblu.com/golfresort-paris**. **Official rating****; our rating €€€€, CCCC.**

BRITTIP
The shuttle bus serves all 4 Val de France hotels and runs every 15mins (5–10mins at park opening and closing times). It operates 6.30am–11.30pm Sep–Jun and 6.30am–12am Jul–Aug, and stops at each in turn (Explorers, Kyriad, Magic Circus, Dream Castle). However, during busy mornings, 2 separate buses are used to get guests to the park, one for the Explorers and Kyriad and a second for Magic Circus and Dream Castle.

Val de France

This region consists solely of 4 neighbouring hotels that are well worth considering. Disney counts them as official partner hotels, tour operators call them 'Near the Magic' and they can be found just off the Boulevard de l'Europe, about a 10min drive from the Marne-la-Vallée station hub for drop-off to the parks and *Disney Village* (with a regular free shuttle bus service). It is possible to walk from here, but it takes a good half an hour.

Thomas Cook Explorers Hotel: This highly imaginative 390-room hotel – one of the real highlights of this area – is run by tour operator Thomas Cook and used by a variety of UK companies, notably coach-tour specialists Leger Holidays. It is designed with British visitors in mind, with more than 30% of guests usually from the UK, hence there are some smart touches for families. It was the first fully themed off-site hotel (followed by the Magic Circus and Dream Castle) and offers both extra-spacious rooms (with families of 6–10 in mind) and superb children's facilities, although only a handful of rooms have air-conditioning. It is much the same price to eat and drink here as in the parks or *Disney Village*, however, and their fine-dining restaurant can be a touch expensive.

BRITTIP
There is a €2 charge for a pool towel at the Explorers, but guests can keep these towels for the entire time they are booked into the hotel. It does also get rather busy in late afternoon.

Designed like a grand French manor – the preserve of mythical explorer Sir Archibald de Bacle (ouch!) and his various 'discoveries' – it is a fun and spacious creation, from the busy lobby area (complete with a Kids' Corner with mini-cinema and 2 rides, plus a novel fountain) to the buffet-style restaurant with its outdoor terrace (wonderful on a sunny morning). Walk through the lobby and you have a great view over

Holiday ownership

Inevitably, the explosion in tourist interest in the area has created the opportunity to 'buy' a piece of the holiday dream and there are several timeshare companies who would love you to sign on the dotted line. However, the only one we believe carries the right seal of approval is the extensive **Marriott's Village d'Ile de France** property, less than 2km/1ml from *Disneyland Paris* in the village of Bailly-Romainvilliers. It opened in 2003 and consists of 190 2- and 3-bed townhouses with around 117m²/1,260ft² of living space and full air-conditioning. The Marriott Vacation Club has genuine international bona fides and strong Disney ties, so you can be sure of getting a quality product, with excellent back-up at a good price.

The Village has access to 3 nearby 18-hole golf courses, plus its own impressive array of facilities, including 2 swimming pools (one indoor lap pool and one outdoors), children's pool, whirlpool, health club (featuring a gym and aerobics room, sauna and steam room), children's facilities (games room, activity centre and outdoor playground), a bar/restaurant featuring local cuisine, a lobby lounge and a convenience store and deli (the Market Place, with a full array of fresh produce, wines and spirits, plus other essentials and even branded apparel). There is also 24hr security and full reception services, and a regular shuttle bus to the parks.

The 2-storey townhouses offer some of the most upmarket accommodation in the region, with a king-size bed in the main bedroom, fully equipped kitchen (including microwave and dishwasher), spacious living room (with satellite colour TV, DVD player and stereo), utility room with washer/dryer, an individual terrace and TV in each bedroom.

With Marriott Vacation Club, you purchase weeks within a particular season and you are free to reserve weeks within that season. You may change dates within your purchased time period from year to year (and there are then more than 50 Vacation Club resorts worldwide you can exchange weeks for). 020 3027 3891 from the UK, 00 33 1 60 42 90 00 in France, **www.marriottvacationclub.co.uk**.

the **Tropical Atrium** at the heart of the hotel, which is also home to the **Secret Lagoon Swimming Pool**, a 20m/66ft heated indoor pool with a small but fabulous waterpark 'aqua-play' area. The wreck of the *Seven Seas Raider* pirate ship is beached at one end of the lagoon, allowing kids the chance to explore the decks and passageways or take to the water-slide. A second, more elaborate, dragon-themed water-slide provides guaranteed fun for kids of all ages. The pool is open 8am–11pm.

The **Plantation Restaurant** is the main diner, offering breakfast (7–10.30am) and dinner (6–10pm). The plentiful continental-style buffet breakfast offers a good selection for all the family (or you can choose a cooked breakfast for a few extra euros), while dinner is an elaborate all-you-can-eat buffet (salad bar, cooked meats, grills, fish, pasta, vegetables and rice) including soft drinks, at €22.50/adult (€29.50 with wine or beer) and €12/child. The salads and desserts are especially good.

Thomas Cook Explorers Hotel

BRITTIP
Like the Disney hotels, you are given a time-slot for breakfast each day. You collect these from reception when you check in and it is advisable to pick your times for your whole stay as the best ones go quickly.

For more informal dining there is **Marco's Pizza Parlour** where you can

Off-site Hotels

1 Thomas Cook Explorer's Hotel
2 Vienna International Dream Castle Hotel
3 Vienna International Magic Circus Hotel
4 Hotel Kyriad at *Disneyland Paris*
5 Radisson Blu Hotel at *Disneyland Paris*
6 Marriott's Village d'Ile de France
7 Adagio City Aparthotel Val d'Europe
8 Hotel l'Elysée
9 *Disney's Davy Crockett Ranch*
10 Chanteloup Hotel
11 Best Western Golf Hotel
12 Antipodes Resort Marne-la-Vallée
13 Tulip Inn
14 Novotel Collégien
15 Comfort Inn Langny-sur-Marne
16 Parc de la Colline
17 Kyriad Chelles
18 Novotel Atria Marne-la-Vallée
19 Hotel Abbaye du Golf
20 Hotel Saphir
21 Camping Le Parc

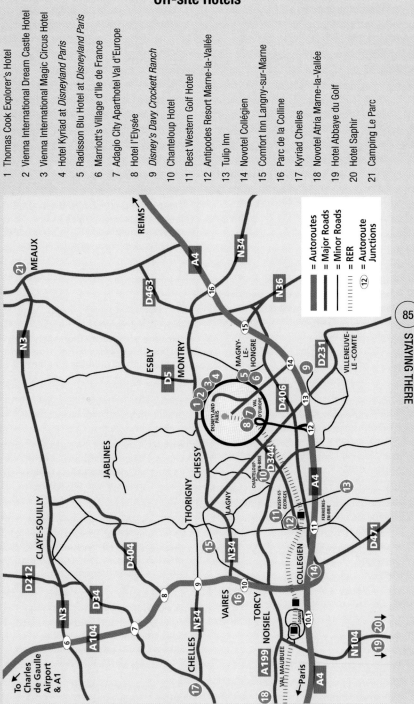

order a take-away if you prefer and **Traders Café Bar** for snacks and drinks (both 5–11pm). The **Brioche Doree** kiosk (8am–5pm) offers an elevated view of the Atrium and the chance to sip a speciality tea or coffee and grab a pastry or sandwich. You will also find 3 **internet** terminals here (although there is free wi-fi in the rooms). **The Captain's Library** (6–10pm) is a themed full-service restaurant, once again offering children's meals, and with a small play area to keep them amused while mum and dad finish dinner. While it is a touch expensive for an off-site restaurant (featuring salads, chicken, salmon, mixed grills and mussels, plus a range of kids meals), the food is excellent for what is, in theory, a 3-star hotel.

Finally, **Smugglers Tavern** (5pm–12am) is the hotel's main pub-style bar. There are pool tables and dartboards, a big-screen TV for sports events, and snacks are available here, too. It is highly popular most evenings (you might want to request a room in a different block to the Tavern if you are early-to-bed types).

Traders Café is also brilliantly designed for parents to be able to sit back and watch their offspring expend some energy in **Scally Wagg's Jungle Adventures**, a big indoor soft-play area (in 2 sections, for 2–4s and 5–12s), with all the requisite ladders, ropes, slides and ball pools, while the Seven Seas Raider is also nearby. Then there is a 2-part arcade/games room, children's fitness machines and **Harry's Action Zone** for older kids, with the usual (noisy!) video games.

BRITTIP
The Thomas Cook Explorers' room configurations are the most family-friendly of any hotel here. The use of the 'bunk cabins' and single beds (instead of 2 doubles) give them huge flexibility, especially with older children.

The room choice is definitely a cut above the usual accommodation. Standard rooms, called Crew rooms, feature a double bed and 2 singles,

with a bath, shower and separate toilet (a useful idea), as well as flat screen TVs with interactive satellite television programming, pay-per-view programmes and films, room safe, hairdryer and ceiling fan (but no air-conditioning), plus tea- and coffee-making facilities. Each Crew room can be connected to a 'bunk cabin' for 2 children. Extended families or groups can take 2 interconnecting Crew rooms with the bunk cabin in between and sleep up to 10 (the bunk cabin doors can be closed).

There are 7 Captain's Suites sleeping up to 6 in 2 bedrooms, plus 3 imaginative Themed Suites (Planet Hollywood, Jungle and Sweets), which have superbly equipped kids' quarters (you may struggle to get your youngsters out of these!). All 10 suites have a lake view and air-conditioning for the hot summer months.

An additional suite on the top floor is classified as an executive room, and features a plasma TV. There is even a selection of executive rooms especially for business travellers, which include a complimentary mini-bar, double bed and sofa bed, a work desk and a coffee table. Finally, 9 rooms are fitted out for guests with disabilities (arguably the best of their kind in the whole area).

Additional features include free parking at the hotel, the parks and *Disney Village*, picnic lunches (with 24 hours advance notice), currency exchange facilities, an outdoor kids' playground, a Disney store, a concierge and information desk. The Explorers is a non-smoking hotel, apart from areas such as Smugglers Tavern terrace outside. The hotel can also be booked on a half-board or a full-board option (with a small saving per person). Full board gives the option to enjoy dinner in a restaurant at *Disney Village* (Planet Hollywood, Rainforest Café or King Ludwig's Castle). The hotel is situated just across the resort-encircling Boulevard de l'Europe from the Hotel Santa Fe and is the first of the 4 hotels of the Val de France district. 00 33 1 60 42 60 60, **www.explorershotels.com**. **Official rating ***; our rating €€€€, CCCC½.**

STAYING THERE

Hotel Kyriad at *Disneyland Paris*: Next door to the Magic Circus is the flagship hotel of the budget Louvre Hotels group. With a lovely country house style, it is an excellent option for those who want to watch the pennies but still get a taste of the Magic. The 300 airy, clean rooms are all air-conditioned, which is a bonus at this end of the scale, and also come with tea- and coffee-making facilities, hairdryer and room safe.

The standard room features a double bed and 2 bunks, while the twin room can be either 2 singles or a double bed. No room can accommodate more than 4, but there are various connecting rooms, bringing the number up to 6 or 8. The rest of the hotel is equally straightforward, with one restaurant – the country-style **Le Marche Gourmand**, with mixed salads, pate and cooked meats, plus a pasta buffet and home-made pizza – and 2 bars in a friendly, relaxing ambience, including a delightful outdoor terrace. The small children's play area in the lobby can get quite crowded in the morning. Although it is French owned and run, up to 40% of guests can be British at peak times and the overall feel is fresh and cosmopolitan. 00 33 1 60 43 61 61, **www.disneylandparis.kyriad.fr. Official rating **; our rating €€€, CC½** .

> ◄█► **BRITTIP**
> Don't overlook the value of the Magic Circus and Dream Castle's family rooms and Kid Suites. They have bags of kiddie appeal and you may have difficulty getting your offspring out of the room because of 'their' area!

Vienna International Magic Circus Hotel: If you prefer a more upmarket touch, look no further than one of our favourites in the Seine-et-Marne region (formerly the Holiday Inn and heavily renovated in 2009). Designed in French manorial style with an extensive and stylish circus-themed flavour, this is a cut above the usual tourist fare and scores high marks for families, too. It is also a rarity in being completely non-smoking. At once both chic and cheerful, the 396-room hotel comes as a refreshing change from the usual identikit design and styling, with bright, fresh colouring to go with the imaginative circus theme. It should appeal to all ages and boasts the extra flair and service touches you would expect from a 4-star property, such as 24-hour room service, wi-fi and a business centre.

The Standard rooms (some interconnecting) feature a double bed; Family rooms have a curtained-off section (like a circus big top) with bunk-beds and a separate TV/games console for the kids; Kid Suites have children's areas built into them in a more elaborate fashion; and a handful of Executive rooms feature a more upmarket and businesslike touch. The one-off Tower Suite sleeps 4 in amazing spaciousness. There are also 9 rooms for disabled guests. All rooms come with a main TV with international channels and internet access, plus room safe, hairdryer and tea- and coffee-making facilities (although there is a charge for tea and coffee refills).

Even the bathroom amenities (L'Occitane) are a cut above. They are also fully air-conditioned. The hotel offers a sophisticated indoor leisure pool (with toddler area), smart fitness club and an extensive outdoor playground in the park-like gardens for the young 'uns, where they can burn off any excess energy.

The main restaurant, **L'Etoile**, serves a pleasing mix of traditional French and international cuisine, while their buffet breakfast (7–11am, with an extensive array of cereals plus hot and cold dishes) is possibly the best in the area – including Disney's hotels – and there is no pre-set time allocation. The inner courtyard features an adjoining terrace to the restaurant and, for breakfast, this makes a wonderful start to the day if the weather permits. There is the inevitable Disney Store and an excellent bar/lounge, **Bar des Artistes**, which also serves a good array of family-orientated snacks (salads, sandwiches, omelettes, baguettes) for lunch and dinner.

Hotel Kyriad

BRITTIP

If the parks are especially hectic or you just want a quiet break for lunch, head back to the Magic Circus and take advantage of their relaxed and friendly service in Bar des Artistes or L'Etoile restaurant.

The hotel has its own bureau de change, and the overall value for money here is top notch. As with the other hotels of Val de France, the VEA Navette airport shuttle for both airports calls 4 times a day and is available without reservation. 00 33 1 64 63 37 37, **www.magiccircus-hotel.com**. **Official rating ****; our rating €€€€, CCCC.**

STAYING THERE

Vienna International Dream Castle Hotel: This wonderful option opened in 2004 and is now part of the Vienna International group, who specialise in independent hotels across Europe. Having stayed here several times, we have no hesitation in pronouncing it our favourite hotel in the area, and the addition in 2009 of the dramatic Royal Suite gives it an extra helping of upmarket style easily equal to any of Disney's grander touches.

Next door to the Thomas Cook Explorers Hotel and similarly on the free shuttle route to the parks, the 397-room property (250 family rooms, 43 'Double Queen' rooms, 76 'King' rooms, including 10 fitted for disabled guests, 27 Baron von Munchhausen and Rapunzel suites, and the Royal Suite, which sleeps up to 7 in regal fashion) exhibits a beautiful castle style, from the elegant lobby, complete with twin 'thrones', a sword-in-the-stone replica and suits of armour, to the well-fitted rooms (many of which feature curtained-off bunk-beds, a great family touch). All rooms have tea and coffee-makers, mini-fridge and wired internet. There is a neat children's play area in the lobby, complete with ball pool, plus pool tables.

The Sans Souci restaurant at the Vienna International Dream Castle Hotel

Vienna International Dream Castle Hotel

The restaurant choice is impressive, with the more standard offerings of **Sans Souci** (check out its excellent buffet breakfast – a big rival to its neighbour's!), augmented by the expansive style of **The Musketeer's**, which features a spectacular themed buffet each evening (the desserts alone are worth stopping in for). There is also a charming outdoor terrace that makes a lovely setting for dinner on a summer evening. Both restaurants serve breakfast at busy periods, meaning there are no frustrating queues in the morning, as there are at some hotels.

BRITTIP
We rate the Excalibur Bar at the Dream Castle one of the most enjoyable places to relax with a drink or 2, and at a good price – their alcohol tariff is often notably less than bars in the *Disney Village*.

Their regular rate also includes a full American-style buffet breakfast (quite a rarity) and, as Vienna International set great store by the quality of their cuisine, it is a real highlight. The fully themed **Excalibur Bar** (11am–midnight) is a great place to enjoy a drink after a day in the parks and also serves light lunches and snacks.

Other notable features of the Dream Castle include a fun swimming pool

Hotel Abbaye du Golf

with a Jacuzzi, smart fitness facilities, video arcade and a garden overlooking the lake, which backs on to the other hotels in Val de France. They also have an array of their own characters, or 'mascots', to keep children entertained in the lobby and at mealtimes. The hotel even boasts an indulgent **Spa**, with sauna, steam bath, Jacuzzi and solarium, and a range of Thai and Californian massages, manicures, epilation, facials and other beauty treatments – a blissful tonic after a day pounding the parks! 00 33 1 64 17 90 00 from the UK, **www.dreamcastle-hotel. com**. **Official rating ****; our rating €€€€–€€€€€, CCCC.**

A short drive from the Magic

Hôtel Abbaye du Golf: A little way to the south, in the older confines of the town of Lésigny, this 12th-century former monastery has been tastefully converted to hold 47 immaculate rooms and a wonderful brasserie restaurant. The hotel is right on the edge of a beautiful golf course yet under half an hour's drive from the theme parks. It makes a great base for exploring some of the other villages in this area but note that it is some way off the RER routes.

Family rooms offer an extra bed or bunks for children, and all feature satellite TV, wi-fi, mini-bar and hairdryer, while the superb traditional-style restaurant has a children's menu. To get there, take Exit 18 off the N104, then continue south on the Avenue des Hyveneaux and turn left after 1km/½ml at the signpost for Golf du Réveillon. 00 33 1 60 02 25 26 from the UK, **www.parisgolfhotel.com**. **Official rating ***; our rating €€€, CC½.**

Antipodes Resort Marne La Vallee: The former upmarket Best Western in Bussy-St-Georges is now an independent hotel but still offers some classic features, albeit in a more formal, business-like manner, with 120 spacious rooms sleeping 2, 3 or 4. Free in-room wi-fi and marble bathrooms are notable highlights, along with an

excellent seafood-style restaurant, Les Sens De L'Art, and bar, plus an inclusive buffet breakfast and even an outdoor swimming pool. The hotel hosts a lot of business conferences, which can make it busy during week-day mornings, but it is only a 5min walk from the RER station and a 10–15min drive to the theme parks. To get there, take Exit 11 off the A4 and follow the signs to Bussy-St-Georges, go straight across 2 roundabouts and it is immediately on your right. Call 00 33 1 64 76 06 06, **www.antipodes-hotels. com**. **Official rating ****; our rating €€€€, CCC.**

Chanteloup Hotel: Tucked away in the pretty little village of Chanteloup-en-Brie, just to the west of Val d'Europe, is this small, family-run hotel. With just 64 small but smart rooms, each with a double bed and 2 fold-up bunks, plus a fitness centre, Jacuzzi and sauna, this is an ideal retreat after a day of frenetic theme-parking. It has a pleasant restaurant and a little foyer bar, and that's about it for the creature comforts, although there is a daily shuttle bus to Disney for a set fee (must be reserved at reception). To reach the hotel, turn off the A4 at Exit 13 and take the D231 past Val d'Europe for 4.5km/3mls, then turn left into Chanteloup-en-Brie. 00 33 1 64 30 00 00, **www.chanteloup-hotel.fr**. **Official rating **; our rating €€€, CC.**

Best Western Golf Hotel: On the rural side of Bussy-St-Georges is this distinctly countrified hotel, with a genuinely welcoming aspect, set on the edge of a golf course and with obvious benefits for the sporting fraternity. However, you don't need to like golf to stay here! The 93 light, airy, non-smoking rooms cater comfortably for most tastes, with a double bed and a large sofa-bed. All were extensively refurbished in 2011. Mini-bars and hairdryers are standard, as is internet access, and there is also plenty of storage space.

The cosy restaurant (closed at weekends) has big picture windows and an outdoor terrace, while there is a children's play area to the side and a large green for kids to expend any remaining energy on. The outdoor heated pool is open May–mid-Sep, and there are 2 private tennis courts for guests. There is a small lobby bar where you can have a quiet drink.

Given the surrounding greenery you could easily think you were a million miles from the hectic Disney whirl, but you are only 10–15mins walk from the RER station or 5mins on their free shuttle bus (on request). To get to the hotel, take exit 11 off the A4 and follow signposts to Bussy-St-Georges, cross the Place du Clos-St-Georges, then turn right at Boulevard du Golf and the hotel is on the left. 00 33 1 64 66 30 30, **www.golf-hotel.fr. Official rating ***; our rating €€€, CCC.**

Novotel Collégien: Slightly off the beaten track lies this smart hotel in the business-like Novotel chain. Just south of the A4 and the town of Collégien, it is tucked away on a mini-industrial estate but has some surprisingly family-friendly touches, with video games and an indoor play area. There is an outdoor pool (mid-Apr–end Sep) and an extremely pleasant bar and lounge area (open until midnight). The Novotel Café serves a balanced, contemporary cuisine, is open midday–2.30pm and 7–10.30pm.

The 195 rooms (with one floor designated non-smoking) are all brightly furnished and feature a double bed and a fold-out sofa that will sleep 2 (smallish) children. Each room has a mini-bar, wi-fi access and TV with English channels and pay-per-view films. There are 2 pairs of connecting rooms and 6 adapted for guests with disabilities. Usefully, the toilet is separate from the bathroom.

A busy convention hotel for much of the year, it is given over completely to the tourism business in July and at weekends. You can find it just past the junction of the A104 and A4; heading south (to Croissy-Beaubourg), turn left off the D471, straight over at the traffic lights and it is on the right. You really do need a car here as it is 3km/2mls from the nearest RER station. There is a

free, secure parking area. 00 33 1 64 80 53 53, **www.novotel.com. Official rating ***; our rating €€€€, CCC.**

Hotel Saphir: This one-off property, just to the south in Pontault-Combault, has 179 exceedingly smart rooms for 2–4, with the family rooms consisting of a double bed plus a single or a double sofa bed. While not the prettiest of hotels, it maintains a high standard of interior decor and service. The heated indoor pool is an excellent (and rare) amenity, along with a sauna and fitness centre for an additional charge. The 2 restaurants (including the art deco Le Canadel) are both family-friendly and well priced, and there is a pleasant bar, l'Ecrin. It can be found just off the N104 travelling south at Exit 15, about 20mins drive from *Disneyland Paris*. 00 33 1 64 43 45 47, **www.saphir-hotel.fr. Official rating ***; our rating €€€, CCC.**

Tulip Inn: Opposite the RER station in Bussy-St-Georges (2 stops from Marne-la-Vallée) is this smart hotel. It has 87 non-smoking rooms, all with high-speed wi-fi and air-conditioning. The brightly decorated rooms come with a king-size bed, 2 singles, or a double and 2 singles for a family of 4. The hotel's facilities include restaurant L'Olivier for breakfast daily, lunch (mid-day–1.30pm, not weekends) and dinner (7–9pm), with French specialities, pizza and pasta, and the Cotton Bar for drinks and snacks in a relaxed setting. There is also a variety of shops and cafés within a short walking distance. There is a fee for the car park. 00 33 1 64 66 11 11, **www. tulipinnmarnelavallee.com. Official rating ***; our rating €€€, CC½.**

Camping
With the ease in which you can drive down to this region of France, it makes sense to look at camping alternatives.

Camping Les Etangs Fleuris: This campsite near the village of **Touquin** (13km/8mls south of Coulommiers) is worth highlighting in particular. It is a wonderfully rural and secluded site with 170 pitches and a host of

La Croix du Vieux Pont

STAYING THERE

clean, modern facilities, including an excellent pool (with a separate pool for children), a games room, bar and take-away, plus showers, toilets and a launderette. Their sporting activities include table tennis, mini-golf, *petanque* and fishing, plus horse-riding and nature walks nearby. The site also offers 2 types of 2-bed mobile homes. It is about 45mins from *Disneyland Paris* and an easy drive along the D231. Canvas Holidays package the site with either a Channel crossing or flights to Beauvais or Charles de Gaulle, plus theme park tickets. 0845 268 0827, **www.canvasholidays.com**.

Camping Le Parc: Another site in the Seine-et-Marne region, this is 20km/12mls from *Disneyland Paris* in

Novotel Collégien

10ha/25 acres of woodland just outside the town of Villevaudé to the north-east (near Meaux). With an impressive array of 330 tent, camper van and caravan pitches, plus mobile homes sleeping 2–8, it has a bar–restaurant, launderette, TV room and facilities for volleyball, table-tennis and petanque, plus a great playground for kids. There is wi-fi and a daily shuttle (for a fee) to *Disneyland Paris*. 00 33 1 60 26 20 79, www.campingleparc.fr.

Le Parc de la Colline: Even closer, near Torcy to the west, this has a mixture of mobile homes and chalets for up to 7 people as well as campsites, all with electric hook-ups. They even have their own shuttle bus to the Torcy RER station (for €7/adults and €3/ child return). 00 33 1 60 05 42 32, **www. camping-de-la-colline.com**.

La Croix du Vieux Pont: For those looking to explore more of northern France, this popular and extremely well-appointed site at Berny-Rivière (near Soissons, about 80km/50mls north of *Disneyland Paris*) comes highly recommended. Set in 34ha/84 acres along the River Aisne, with 3 swimming pools, bar, restaurant and tennis court, plus a good range of mobile homes, pitches and apartments sleeping 2–10, as well as facilities for the disabled. You will find it featured by British tour operators such as Haven, Keycamp and Canvas Holidays. 00 33 3 23 55 50 02, **www.la-croix-du-vieux-point.com**.

Gîtes and Clévacances

Two other notable local forms of accommodation are the individual B&B style of the Gîtes de France, with more than 200 *gîtes* and 132 guest rooms in the Seine-et-Marne region, and the newer Clévacances, or town centre holiday homes.

Gîtes de France: Generally speaking, the village style offers charming,

Hotel Kyriad Chelles

rural tastes of the local area and its people, with anything from 2–10 rooms available to guests who enjoy becoming 'part of the family'. With so many to choose from throughout France they have become a mini-industry and you can obtain a full guide to the area's *gîtes* from the Comité Departemental du Tourisme de Seine-et-Marne at 11 Rue Royale, 77300 Fontainebleau, France, 00 33

Comfort Inn Lagny-sur-Marne

1 60 39 60 39, **www.tourisme77.fr**. Log on to **www.gites-seine-et-marne.com** for more info about *gîtes*.

Clévacances: These are apartments, flats or suburban detached houses to let when not in use by their owners – from fully furnished weekly rentals to guest rooms. Prices are about €300–500/week and they can be found throughout the Seine-et-Marne region, many close to *Disneyland Paris*, including in Bussy St Georges, Bailly-Romainvilliers and Favieres. Reservations are usually handled directly with the owners and they are categorised for comfort by a number of 'keys' from 1 to 5. To get a free booklet or request more information, contact Clévacances Seine-et-Marne, 11 Rue Royale, 77300 Fontainebleau, France, 00 33 1 60 39 60 39, or look up **www.clevacances.com/EN**.

Clévacances

Hotel chains

Several French hotel chains offer good, cheap, basic accommodation for those on a budget both in Paris itself and the Marne-la-Vallée area. Most are in the 1- and 2-star categories but a few offer a greater level of creature comforts.

Formule 1: Basic, motel-type chain that keeps things pretty much cheap and cheerful (okay, forget about the cheerful bit). Built in boxy, prefab units, they are accommodation only (apart from a basic continental breakfast) but they are almost invariably the cheapest, with many in the Ile de France region. They are surprisingly high-tech, with automated check-in and clean but small rooms. However, rooms do not have a shower or WC, just a washbasin. Instead, there are communal facilities on each floor. Part of the huge Accor hotel group, this is not the ideal place for families because their service is so limited (and most rooms sleep only 3) but for couples on a budget, they might be worth considering. 00 33 892 685 685, **www.hotelformule1.com. Our rating €, C.**

Etap: Similar to Formule 1 (and also with a lot of hotels in the region), but better, with an in-room shower and WC. Their new 'cocoon-design' rooms are quite chic, if still fairly basic, but include wi-fi and a surprisingly good unlimited breakfast buffet. Rooms still accommodate only 3 at most. Non-smoking rooms are also available. 0871 702 9469 in the UK, **www.etaphotel.com. Our rating €, C.**

Campanile: This fairly basic motel-style chain has upgraded its offering significantly in recent times with its Next Generation upgrades now offering high-quality bedding, free wi-fi, a welcoming lounge-bar and chic, stylish restaurants. They are still pretty uniform but are ideal for those on a budget, offer plenty of rooms for guests with disabilities and usually serve a good buffet breakfast. Rooms are small but clean and comfortable and they rate officially as 2-star but provide a few more thoughtful touches, such

as in-room tea- and coffee-making facilities and smart-phone charging technology, making them a worthwhile choice. Rooms usually sleep only 3 and you need to reserve a child's fold-out bed in advance. 0033 1 64 62 59 70, **www.campanile.fr. Our rating €, CC.**

Kyriad: There are a lot more variations within this generally 2-star chain (also part of Louvre Hotels and a half-step up from Campanile) but it is still a basic family-orientated hotel. They have decent rooms that comfortably sleep 3 and some that accommodate 4 (1 double bed, 2 singles). Some hotels include mini-bars and hairdryers and provide pleasant individual touches such as a welcome snack tray and wi-fi. Their excellent-value restaurants all have children's menus. 00 33 1 64 62 59 70 from the UK, **www.kyriad.com. Our rating €–€€, CC.**

The Hotel Kyriad at *Disneyland Paris* has already been noted (see page 87), but another to look out for is the **Kyriad Chelles**, a friendly 2-star property in the town of Chelles just 20mins drive from the theme parks (00 33 1 60 08 54 27). The **Kyriad Prestige** version adds more upmarket touches like fitness facilities and saunas, more spacious, air-conditioned rooms and the signature La Rose des Vents restaurant. **www.kyriadprestige.com. Our rating €€, CCC.**

Comfort Inn: A similar quality and style to the Kyriad and Campanile chains, the Comfort Inn hotels (part of the Choice Hotels International group) are mainly found in central Paris and offer an excellent-value selection. Their city location means there is quite a difference in the style of each property but the basic standard remains sound. 0800 44 44 44 in the UK, 0800 91 24 24 in France, **www.choicehotels.com. Our rating €€, CCC.**

There are some 36 Paris Comfort Inns, with the closest to *Disneyland Paris* being the 56-room **Comfort Inn Lagny-sur-Marne**, a good 15mins away. However, it is still a good choice, easily accessed via A104 and A4. Lunch and dinner are available Mon–Fri at the on-site Casa Flavio, with drinks at the hotel bar. Babysitting, car hire service and guest laundry are available for an additional fee. There are also rooms for the disabled. 00 33 1 64 30 44 88 from the UK. The Choice Hotels group also has 38 of their more upmarket **Quality Hotel** properties in the Paris area, with an official 3-star rating and some elegant touches.

Ibis: A more upmarket 2-star choice (in the Accor group), this chain is functionally comfortable in general, with standard rooms (international satellite TV is a bonus, as is in-room internet connection) that sleeps 3 (with an extra fold-out bed) and compact bathrooms. All have a restaurant, bar and snacks available 24 hours a day (part of their commitment to a more personal service), with an outstanding self-service breakfast buffet from 6.30–10am and a drinks and pastries service from 4–6am and 10am–noon. The restaurant choice varies from hotel to hotel. There are 46 Ibis hotels in the Paris region, including 4 in Marne-la-Vallée (see also page 82). 0892 68 66 86 in the UK, **www.ibishotel.com**. **Our rating €€–€€€, CC.**

Mercure: This member of the Accor group has a 2-tier quality system, the basic 3-star Hotel Mercure and the more distinctive MGallery, with enhanced levels of service and comfort. Most rooms accommodate 3, with some family rooms for 4, all have mini-bars and hairdryers. Non-smoking and rooms for the disabled are also available. They also specialise in weekend breaks, and most of their 41 hotels are in central Paris, with the 192-room **Mercure Noisy Le Grand** (free parking, non-smoking rooms, wi-fi and a nice restaurant, Les Meteors, open for dinner Mon–Fri) the nearest to *Disneyland Paris* and close to the RER station. 0870 609 0965 in the UK, **www.mercure.com**. **Our rating €€€–€€€€, CCC.**

Novotel: More of a business hotel in the past (and another member of the Accor group), they are increasingly looking to attract a family market, with 'Kids Eat Free' deals and other special offers from time to time, Also full of mod cons to suit tourist tastes, this modern chain offers fresh, spacious and comfortable rooms (sleeping up to 4), chic restaurants and bars, and extras like satellite TV, wi-fi, mini-bars and room service. Most feature outdoor swimming pools (although they close from the early autumn to the end of spring) and conference/meeting facilities. While they can be busy during the week, they often offer great weekend breaks when they are quieter. 0870 609 0962 in the UK, **www.novotel.com**. **Our rating €€€€, CCC.**

In addition to the Novotel Collégien (see page 90), look out for the large **Novotel Marne-la-Vallée Noisy**, in Noisy Le Grand, just 11km/6¾mls from *Disneyland Paris*. It features 144 rooms (112 non-smoking and 5 disabled-accessible), a smart bar-restaurant, wi-fi and a nice heated outdoor swimming pool in the summer. 00 33 1 48 15 60 60.

Sofitel: The premium brand in the Accor group, each hotel is individual, but all with a deluxe style in both the sumptuous rooms and the excellent restaurants, with the latter featuring some of the best cuisine in Paris. The full range of mod cons and facilities are accompanied by efficient, courteous service. However, the handful of Sofitel hotels (6 of them) in the Ile de France are either in central Paris, Versailles or by Charles de Gaulle Airport, hence their price reflects their location and upmarket nature. 0870 609 0964 in the UK, **www.sofitel.com**. **Our rating €€€€€, CCCC.**

Well, that's about all the essential accommodation info you need for now. Having dealt with the preliminaries, it is finally time to … hit the theme parks!

5 Welcome to the Parks

or Here's Where the Fun Really Starts!

Okay, it's finally time to deal with the main business of being in *Disneyland Paris* – the theme parks themselves. There is a lot to take on board – the *Disneyland Park* alone boasts some 48 attractions on its 57 ha/140 acres, and there is something for all tastes and ages. The *Walt Disney Studios* provides even more, having added a whole new area in 2010 – and there are plans for even more.

In all, there is at least 3 days' worth of pure adventure-mania spread between the parks, and you need to have a pretty good idea of what's in store to get the most out of it and ensure you don't waste too much energy in the process! It is easy to get sidetracked by some of the clever details or minor attractions and miss out on some big-time thrills, while equally, there is a genuine treasure trove of small-scale Disneyana that it would be sad to overlook. Therefore, the following chapters will provide all you need to know to draw up your own plan of campaign for visiting each one.

If you have never visited a Disney theme park before, it is probably fair to start by reminding you this is not a comparable experience to a day at any other European park. That is not to denigrate the likes of Alton Towers (which is pretty sizeable), Thorpe Park or Chessington World of Adventures. All have some wonderful rides and

Welcome to Disneyland

offer good value for money. It is just that Disney builds and creates with a detail and a sense of wonder and fantasy no one else can match. These are 'theme' parks in the true sense of the words.

You enter a truly magical world when you pass through the gates reading 'Le Parc Disneyland'. And, for the duration of your stay, you will be beguiled by a realm that offers the most enchanting and thrilling range of attractions anywhere on earth.

Anyone who has already been to the parks in Orlando or California will have a good idea of what to expect. However, while the *Disneyland Park* bears a strong resemblance to both, a lot of the essential detail and many of the attractions are different. When the Walt Disney Company set out to build their European resort experience, they wanted to update, enhance and improve, go back to the Imagineering drawing board if you like, cherry-picking the best features of their parks and re-inventing them in a dramatic new setting.

The Paris version is, to our eyes, a more refined and artistic interpretation. The Imagineers were well aware they were building for a European market and have tried to tailor their designs in a less overtly American way, even though much of the fundamental magic inherent in the parks is quintessentially American. There is a greater awareness of Disney's European heritage here (Walt himself spent a good deal of time in France as a young man and his family traced their lineage back to French ancestors) and of the need to tell the stories in a way that makes sense to an audience consisting primarily of French, British, German, Dutch, Belgian, Spanish and Italian visitors (and they are never just 'rides' in a Disney park – everything has to tell a story and add to the theme).

Therefore, the multi-lingual nature of the resort is a key component of the overall feel and style of what's in store. Some of the design influences of the various nations are also evident in the theme parks themselves (the Sleeping Beauty Castle in the *Disneyland Park* is partly modelled on stunning Mont Saint-Michel in Normandy, for example).

BRITTIP

It pays to arrive a little early for the opening time at each park to put yourself in front of the crowds for the first couple of hours and enjoy some of the rides that attract serious queues later on.

The language challenge

The need to think in several languages provided the Imagineers with additional challenges, demanding subtitles, translations and extra soundtracks. While this adds a unique feel to familiar attractions ('it's a small world' or The Adventures of Snow White, for example), it does irk a small minority of English-speaking visitors – although we have yet to meet any children who didn't enjoy their ride on Pinocchio's Fantastic Journey simply because the commentary happened to be in French!

In our view, we always need to remember we Brits are the visitors, and it pays to try to remember those few words of French we learned at school. At the end of the day, the resort is trying to appeal to the widest possible audience and, by and large, they succeed with extraordinarily cosmopolitan ability.

Set menus

A point worth highlighting for anyone unfamiliar with continental restaurant culture is the usual provision of a fixed-price menu (*prix fixe*) alongside the à la carte choice. Even at the standard counter-service burger-and-chips type diners, there is a set menu, usually consisting of a main course (burger, salad, pizza or pasta), a choice of dessert and a soft drink. At the full-service restaurants, the cheaper the set menu (starter, main course and dessert), the more limited the choice.

For both parks, we provide an at-a-glance guide (on pages 110 and 146)

Top 10 attractions

Here, purely for fun, is what we rate as our top 10 attractions, first for the *Disneyland Park*:

1 Pirates of the Caribbean

2 Space Mountain: Mission 2

3 Big Thunder Mountain Railroad

4 Phantom Manor

5 Indiana Jones and the Temple of Peril

6 Fantillusion Parade

7 Disney's Magic Parade

8 Star Tours

9 Peter Pan's Flight

10 Buzz Lightyear's Laser Blast

And for the *Walt Disney Studios*:

1 Twilight Zone Tower of Terror

2 Cinémagique

3 Moteurs…Action! Stunt Show Spectacular

4 Rock 'n' Roller Coaster starring Aerosmith

5 Crush's Coaster

6 Disney's Stars 'n' Motor Cars Parade

7 RC Racer

8 Armageddon: Special Effects

9 Animagique

10 Toy Soldiers Parachute Drop

that gives you some idea of what to expect to pay for food and souvenirs. Costs can quickly mount up if you buy numerous snacks – a small mineral water costs around €2.60, a 25cl beer is €3.90, soft drinks variously €2.60–3.50, a large portion of chips is €2.99, sweet treats start at €2.50 and pastries are €3.50. Kids' meals, which consist of a main course, such as chicken nuggets or pizza, chips, a small drink and a 'surprise' toy, start at €5.70. This should help you work out the kind of real cost you are looking at for a day in the parks (you can also check the latest exchange rate at **www.xe.com**).

Many outlets can provide something for the veggie appetite as the full-service restaurants all offer at least one vegetarian main course and good salads are not hard to find. They will also do their best to accommodate requests from guests who have particular dietary requirements, including food allergies, so don't be afraid to ask. Unlike the versions of the *Magic Kingdom* in America, this resort does serve alcohol, but it is not cheap. A 33cl beer in one of the full-service restaurants can be €4.60–7, while a bottle of wine can vary from €17–60.

◄ ► BRITTIP

If you fancy a beer at one of the counter-service restaurants around the theme parks, the best value is to choose the set meal option with beer instead of soft drink and you will save a little on ordering it as an extra.

Disney has also moved to make some of their food offerings – especially kids' meals – a touch healthier by introducing more vegetables and fruit. Ask for these options when you order.

Character dining

Whether you are travelling as a family, a couple or on your own, some of the most magical memories can be made when you have a meal with Mickey and Co. Meeting the characters in a more intimate setting, with no long queues to navigate, is a real treat, with one-on-one interaction that is second to none. Watching Pluto cuddling the children, seeing dad's reaction when Cinderella passes by or capturing Prince Charming kissing mum's hand are moments to be treasured for a lifetime.

Characters circulate inside the restaurant, stopping at each table for play time and family photos (don't approach them at other tables – they will come to you!). The amount of time available to each group is dependent upon how busy the restaurant is (so book off-hours, when things are quieter). Don't forget to bring your autograph book and a fat pen, which is easier for the characters to hold. Some children may initially be put off by the size of some characters (who appear huge to little guests!) so you may want to see how your children react to them

The 20th Anniversary Celebrations – And Beyond!

Disney constantly looks at new ways to engage repeat visitors and provide additional experiences, so there is a constant flow of live entertainment and other changes, updates and refurbishments. In 2011, they brought us **Mickey's Magical Moments**, where characters were the centre of attention. In the *Disneyland Park* that meant a new show, Mickey's Magical Celebration, on the Central Plaza stage in front of the Sleeping Beauty Castle; the Princesses got a new meet 'n' greet location in Fantasyland; in Adventureland, children were invited to dance and sing along with Peter Pan in Following The Leader and meet Baloo, King Louie and Timon in Rhythms Of The Jungle; and Disney's Dance Express added more song and dance fun with Minnie, Goofy and Co, while more characters than ever before showed up around the park. **Captain EO** also returned in Discoveryland, replacing the 'Honey I Shrunk the Audience' attraction.

The **20th Anniversary** of *Disneyland Paris* from April 1, 2012, will see more changes, with 2 stunning new elements and a novel way to meet the head Mouse himself. **Disney Dreams!** will be a fabulous special effects show on and around the Castle each night, using water effects, fireworks and lasers. **Disney Magic On Parade** takes over as the daily parade, utilising new floats, characters and music for yet another original Disney experience. **Meet Mickey Mouse** will then be a special photographic meet-and-greet in an elaborate theatre backdrop that promises a magical touch for all visitors. **Main Street USA Celebrates** is then an elaborate make over for the park's entry section, with an array of colourful lighting and other effects that really come into their own after dark. Plus there will be full refurbishments of classic rides like Phantom Manor, Pirates of the Caribbean and Big Thunder Mountain Railroad.

The *Walt Disney Studios* is also developing apace. Recent additions are the **Toy Story Playland** area, with 3 new rides – RC Racer, Toy Soldiers Parachute Drop and Slinky Dog Zigzag Spin – while *Cars* star Lightning McQueen is now a part of the Moteurs…Action! Stunt Show. And there's more on the horizon, the **Ratatouille** ride that will use dramatic new technology. The indoor journey into the Parisian realm of Remy the rat from the film *Ratatouille* will link new 3-D film with a revolutionary trackless ride system and over-sized animatronics for a truly novel experience in 2013/14.

Be sure to check the News pages of the www.dlp.info website for even more updates.

in the parks (from a 'safe' distance) before booking a meal.

Character meals can be booked as an add-on option to your package, when booking a room at a Disney resort, at City Hall or Studios Services or by calling the Reservation Hotline (from the UK) 00 33 1 60 30 40 50.

Enjoying the parks

Meals with the characters

Disneyland Park: **Cowboy Cookout Barbecue**, at the far end of Frontierland, Woody and Mickey are bringing their friends for a set Tasty Cowboy Chow buffet starting at €26 adults and €13 children. Late afternoon, a Tea Party with the Disney characters is organised at €19 per person for the Pastry Buffet.

Auberge de Cendrillon (with Disney Princes and Princesses, plus Suzy and Perla, Cinderella's mice) offers a set-price lunch or dinner featuring a non-alcoholic cocktail for adults (soft drink for children), starter, main course and Cinderella Delight dessert at €60 adult, €25 ages 3–11s.

Disney Village: Character Breakfast at **Café Mickey**, where characters will include at least 4 of Mickey, Minnie, Goofy, Pluto, Captain Hook, Tigger and Eeyore. It serves a buffet of breads, cereals, scrambled eggs, pastries, fruit juice and hot drinks in 2 sittings at 7.30 and 9.30am (€18 adult, €12 ages 3–11 if you are staying at a Disney hotel, except *Disneyland Hotel*; €23 and €15 if you are staying at a non-Disney hotel. NB: guests at Hotel l'Elysée, Adagio Aparthotel Val d'Europe and Radisson Blu Hotel, second sitting only). **Café Mickey** also serves lunch and dinner continuously from noon–11pm, with the same line-up of characters present 12.15–3pm and 6–10pm. With the characters here most of the day, you will usually benefit from some of the best character interaction at Café Mickey, which the kids will love.

Disneyland Hotel: Inventions Restaurant has a character breakfast featuring selected characters from Mickey, Minnie, Goofy, Pluto, Tigger and Pinocchio – exclusively for hotel guests. But the character buffet dinner (with some of Minnie, Mickey, Goofy, Pluto, Chip 'n' Dale and Geppetto) is open to the general public. Breakfast is a buffet with breads, hot meats, scrambled eggs, baked beans, potato, fruit and yoghurts, plus hot and cold drinks. Dinner includes seafood, cold meats, salads, carved roast, desserts and more (€59 adult, €29 ages 7–11, €18 3–6). Arrive at Inventions early for their dinner and you will benefit from some of the best character interaction, as it is seldom busy early on.

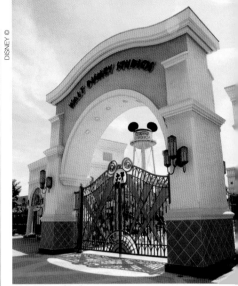

DISNEY ©

Walt Disney Studios

Ticket types

Moving along to more practical matters, you need to work out what type of ticket you should buy to make the most of your stay.

Park Hopper Tickets: These are usually included with most packages that provide your accommodation, for the length of your stay (almost always with the Disney resorts, and with many of the non-Disney hotels nearby). That means you can enjoy both parks from the minute you arrive until the time

WELCOME TO THE PARKS

A meal with Chip 'n' Dale

you leave. It obviously provides the peace of mind and convenience of knowing you do not need to worry about the logistics of which park to visit when, as you can hop between parks at any time. However, there is a range of ticket types, including annual ones, which are worth considering if you are staying off-site or visit regularly.

1-Day Ticket: This provides admission to either the *Disneyland Park* or the *Walt Disney Studios* for a full day's fun (up to 11pm at peak periods). You may exit and re-enter the same park as many times as you wish throughout the day.

1/2/3/4/5-Day Park Hopper: This great-value ticket provides 1, 2, 3, 4 or 5 full days at the 2 parks, offering total freedom of movement between them on each day. The days do NOT need to be consecutive, which is invaluable if you are staying off-site and visiting other attractions over, say, a week. Park Hopper tickets are also valid for a year from the date of purchase (but not if they are part of a package).

Classic Annual Passport: This option might be the cheapest but isn't the easiest to use as there are many black-out dates, especially during weekends. It gives a 5% discount on extra-ticket events like Halloween, plus restaurants and boutiques. Add €30 for the 'free parking' option. The pass will grant access for roughly 275 days during the year but precise planning is important to avoid being at the park on one of the days the ticket is not valid.

Fantasy Annual Passport: This provides entry to both parks, plus useful extras like free parking, free magazine, access to the official website with special offers and invites to special occasions (like new attraction previews), plus 20% off special event tickets (like the Halloween party), 10% off at Disney restaurants and shops and 15% off tickets for Buffalo Bill's Wild West Show. There is 20% hotel discount on certain dates during the year while families who need 5 or more passes get a 20% discount. However,

there ARE still a handful of blackout days when the Passport is not valid for admission. For dates, see this website **http://idf-offres.disneylandparis. fr/passeport-annuel/index.xhtml** (for some reason they give info in French only). In case you do need a ticket on one of the blackout dates, Fantasy Passport holder can buy one at 50% discount. Invite a friend to the park and buy a ticket for them at a 10% discount.

BRITTIP
You can save money if you are tempted to buy an Annual Passport after your first day visit, as the cost of a single day will be deducted from the cost of the Annual Passport. Visit the Annual Passport office at either park before you leave.

Dream Annual Passport: This version offers unlimited year-round access to both parks, access to Fantasyland in the *Disneyland Park* an hour before official opening and preferential rates on Disney hotel rooms at certain times, plus a number of exclusive extras, discounts and events especially for Dream Passport holders. The bonuses include 20% off in most shops, 10% off in restaurants and bars, 15% off tickets for Buffalo Bill's Wild West Show, 50% off special event tickets like Halloween Party Night, up to 40% hotel discount on certain dates during the year, a free aperitif at table-service restaurants, free parking for the theme parks or at *Disney Village* for only €2 a day, free pushchair and wheelchair hire in the parks, free luggage storage, free magazine, priority information and reservation hotline, access to the official website with special offers and info and invitations to special occasions at the resort. Families who need 5 or more Annual passes get a 20% discount. Invite a friend to the park and buy an extra ticket at a 20% discount.

BRITTIP
If one family member buys the Dream Annual Passport, the whole party can still benefit from the many discounts at the shops and restaurants.

Rides for wimps!

For those who are reluctant to hurl themselves on to the fastest rides, here (by special request!) is a guide to a walk on the 'mild side' with Disney. None of these will upset even the most sensitive of stomachs (although, with the exception of The Twilight Zone Tower of Terror, Crush's Coaster, Space Mountain, Indiana Jones, Mad Hatter's Tea Cups, RC Racer and the Rock 'n' Roller Coaster, there are few rides designed to be really dynamic):

1 Disneyland Railroad

2 'it's a small world'

3 Le Pays des Contes de Fées

4 Le Carrousel de Lancelot

5 Peter Pan's Flight

6 Flying Carpets Over Agrabah

7 Casey Junior

8 Autopia

9 Thunder Mesa Riverboats

10 Dumbo the Flying Elephant

There is a substantial difference in price between the three Annual Passports (see at-a-glance guides on pages 110 and 146), but you can save a good deal over a year if you visit more than once, and the savings against the multi-day Hoppers should also be obvious. There is a fourth Annual pass (the Francilien), but that's for the locals only. When buying an AP, make sure to check you will be able to use it on the dates you are likely to visit or make sure you are able to plan around the blackout dates.

BRITTIP

All shareholders of Euro Disney SCA (the holding company that runs the resort) benefit from a range of hotel, park, shop and restaurant discounts similar to those of the Dream Annual Passport holders.

Where to buy tickets

So, where can you buy your tickets, apart from joining the long early-morning queues at the ticket booths at the entrance to both parks?

- Call the UK booking line on 08448 008 111.

- Call the 7-days-a-week French centre on 00 33 1 60 30 60 30.

- Visit any Disney Store in Britain or on the Champs-Elysées in Paris; any FNAC store in Paris; or the Virgin Megastore on the Champs-Elysées.

- Go to the main RATP ticket offices on the Métro or RER.

- Go to any Travelex Foreign Exchange Bureau (notably at the Eurotunnel terminal in Folkestone and at Portsmouth ferry terminal).

- Buy on board P&O Ferries on Dover–Calais routes.

- Buy from Eurotunnel themselves; or the Eurostar ticket desks at the London St Pancras terminal or Ashford stations.

BRITTIP

It is usually worth buying your tickets as far in advance as possible to avoid the usual annual price increase (usually in late autumn/early winter).

In addition to your travel agent and all branches of Thomas Cook, who should all be able to sell the official **1-, 2-, 3-, 4- and 5-Day Hopper Tickets**, specialist ticket broker **Attraction Tickets Direct** often have some great offers (4 days for the price of 3, 15% off 1-Day tickets, etc) that are worth looking up. They provide actual tickets, not vouchers, have free delivery within 7 days and their brochure is free on request. 0800 975 0002, **www.attraction-tickets-direct.co.uk**.

BRITTIP

Attraction Tickets Direct have some handy **discussion forums** on their website and we have been known to make an appearance there from time to time, so drop in and ask us a question or tell us your *Disneyland Paris* stories!

Once you have your tickets, you can avoid the first bugbear of visiting

Casey Jnr.

either park – the ticket booths. These are located prominently outside both parks but, however many windows are open, there is nearly always a slow-moving queue. If you can avoid them, you'll be ahead of the crowd.

The final thing to remember before we get to the theme parks proper is you can always escape the crowds – especially in the *Walt Disney Studios* – during the day by stepping out into *Disney Village* for a while. If the theme parks are heaving, the *Village* and the hotels will be a lot quieter. The great accessibility and convenience of the whole resort means it IS possible to find places without queues to enjoy a meal, a drink or just recharge the batteries (and, at peak periods, you WILL need a breather at times) before you charge back into the hectic whirl.

BRITTIP
If you don't have a ticket when you arrive and need to visit the ticket booths, the queues to the far right or far left are often the shortest.

Disney has an App for that

iPhone users can gain a valuable advantage in their park-going with the latest App for their mobile device. Simply go to the iTunes store and download the free *Disneyland Paris* App, and you will have instant advice on park hours, queue times, navigation, park info, ride descriptions, special offers and pure Disney fun.

Ratings

All the rides and shows are judged on a unique *Brit Guide* rating system that

Dumbo the Flying Elephant in Fantasyland

splits them into Thrill rides and Scenic rides. Thrill rides earn T ratings out of 5 (hence a TTTTT is as exciting as it gets) and Scenic rides get A ratings out of 5 (an AA ride is likely to be over-cute and missable). Obviously, it is a matter of opinion to a certain extent but you can be sure:

- T or A is not worth your time;

- TT or AA is worth seeing only if there isn't a queue;

- TTT or AAA should be seen if you have time, but you won't miss much if you don't;

- TTTT or AAAA ride is a big-time attraction that should be high on your list;

- TTTTT or AAAAA should not be missed!

The latter will have the longest queues, so plan your visit around these rides.

FastPass

Disney has a unique FastPass (FP) system for some of its most popular shows and rides and it is worth taking advantage of it in the parks.

Here's how the FastPass works: at all attractions with the FastPass service (which is FREE – many people don't realise this), there are a series of kiosks next to the main entrance. Slide your park entrance ticket through a

Sleeping Beauty Castle

kiosk and it immediately spits out a separate slip with a time 'window' during which you should return to the separate FastPass queue (usually at least 1 hour later, occasionally 4 or more). When your 'window' is open, simply return to the FastPass queue and enjoy the attraction with only a short wait. You can get a FastPass every 2hrs, or once you have used it; e.g. if

A character breakfast wth Mickey

you get a FastPass for Space Mountain at 9am with a return time of 1–2pm, you can get another FastPass at 11am. NB: You need FastPass tickets for ALL members of your group. You can also use a FastPass at ANY time after the allotted return period, not just during the 'window' specified. But you can't use it before.

BRITTIP
Some rides DO run out of FastPasses before the end of the day, so it is advisable to grab one for the likes of Peter Pan's Flight and Big Thunder Mountain BEFORE early afternoon.

VIP FastPass: For €60 per person, per day, you can now buy a special pass that gives access to the FastPass rides all day. Every person in the party will need their own VIP FastPass, though, which makes it an expensive experience. However, once you have it, you can enter any of the FastPass attractions as often as you want that day. These tickets can be bought only at the *Disneyland Hotel*. With the VIP FastPass, you go straight to the FastPass queue without having to use the kiosks. A special perk for Disney Hotel suite guests includes a **VIP FastPass** at no extra cost.

BRITTIP
If you have young children, put a note in their pocket with details of their name, your mobile phone number, hotel, etc. Cast Members are trained to take lost children to the Meeting Place and the provision of a note makes their job easier. You can also ask for a Disney-style name tag for children at City Hall or Guest Services.

Restrictions

Height: Some rides are restricted to children over a certain height and are not advisable for people with back, neck or heart problems or for pregnant women. Where this is the case, we have noted 'Restrictions: 1.32m/4ft 3in' and so on. Height restrictions (which are strictly enforced) are based on the average 5-year-old being 1.02m/3ft 3in

tall, 6s being 1.1m/3ft 6in and 9s being 1.32m/4ft 3in.

Health: Those with neck or back problems and expectant mothers, are advised to avoid: Space Mountain: Mission 2, Star Tours, Indiana Jones and the Temple of Peril, Big Thunder Mountain Railroad and Mad Hatter's Tea Cups at the *Disneyland Park* and The Twilight Zone Tower of Terror, Crush's Coaster, RC Racer and Rock 'n' Roller Coaster at the *Walt Disney Studios*.

Baby extras

The baby switch: If you have small children, but don't want to leave them while you have a ride, you DON'T have to queue twice. Ask a Cast Member at the entrance of an attraction about Baby Switch, and they will tell you the arrangements for that ride or show. Usually it means the first adult following the normal queue line while the other (with child) waits in a designated area. The first adult rides the attraction and then you do the switch without having to queue a second time.

BRITTIP
Many children also get a big thrill from collecting autographs from the various Disney characters they meet, and nearly all the hotels and shops sell some great autograph books.

Baby Care Centre: You'll find this in the *Disneyland Park* next door to the Plaza Gardens Restaurant at the top of Main Street USA on the right, where there are nappy-changing facilities and a feeding room, with baby food (and nappies) on sale. At the *Walt Disney Studios* the Baby Care Centre is behind the Studio Services in the Front Lot, just inside the entrance on the right-hand side.

BRITTIP
Kids, try to find the thickest pen you can, or buy a thick pen, for collecting autographs. Most of the characters find it a struggle to write with normal-size pens in their great big hands.

Pin trading & Vinylmation

In addition to collecting souvenirs, you will probably also encounter the pin-trading phenomenon at some stage of your Disney adventure. This is hard to explain to the uninitiated as it has no real parallel in British culture. It is a particularly American idea and involves collecting – and trading – the many dozens of different enamel brooches you can buy in almost every shop. They vary from €5.90–25 (with special sets going for €50 or more), and serious collectors carry them on lanyards around their neck, eagerly looking to barter and swap with other members of this not-so-secret society. Disney Cast Members also join in by displaying lanyards with pins to swap, and they are duty-bound to swap for anything they may be displaying. Children particularly appreciate this opportunity for a sure thing, and Cast Members are usually gracious about waiting for youngsters to make a decision.

Disney also organises pin events, mostly at the hotels but some special events take place in the parks, too. During these events, special pins – available only during these events – are offered to collectors. Those pins are limited and usually sell out during the events. Hotel events are a separate-ticket event, while park events are free (just a park ticket is needed).

In the *Disneyland Park*, enthusiasts will find special trading boards at a Pin Cart at the end of Main Street USA, in The Emporium shop and sometimes at a cart in Fantasyland between Le Carrousel de Lancelot and restaurant Au Chalet de La Marionette. Cast Members will also usually give you the option to trade up to 2 from your pins with the pins already on the board (but the pin you trade cannot be on the board already). During busy and sunny weekends, collectors often come into the park to show off their collections on the terrace at the end of Main Street USA (behind the pin cart). Even if you don't collect, it's a great extra feature in the park worth a quick peek. NB: Collectors cannot sell their pins inside the park, only trading is allowed.

Vinylmation: This new craze is another big hit with Disney collectors. These are fun Mickey-shaped vinyl figurines with a twist. Each one carries different painted decorations inspired by a Disney idea, park attraction or something completely different. Regular-size figures are sealed in a box, so you don't know what you are getting until after you have bought it. Figures are normally part of a set that has 1 limited 'chaser' figure (one more difficult to get, with an unknown decorative look). *Disneyland Paris* has dedicated sales locations in the *Disneyland Park*, *Walt Disney Studios* and the *Disney Village*. Vinylmations are also traded in the park.

The Meeting Place for Lost Children: These are in the same place in both parks, with their own Disney staff.

Match the ages: If you have children of wide-ranging ages, check out the special section at the end of each park chapter to see which rides and attractions appeal most to which age groups. It is important in a resort of this size to concentrate on those areas that have the most appeal for YOU and, while it is not possible to be 100% accurate, the advice here is tried and tested, so you can get a pretty good idea of what is most likely to be popular with your family!

Park etiquette

Some final words of warning. Picnics are NOT allowed inside the parks (although you can take bottles of water) but there is a picnic area outside at the exit of the moving walkway from the main car park.

BRITTIP

Losing a child in the park crowds is a scary thought, but parents shouldn't worry as Disney Cast Members are all trained for this eventuality and will drop whatever they are doing to follow their lost-child procedure and ensure that parents and child are reunited.

Appropriate clothing must be worn in the parks – which means shirt and shoes – at all times. No bare chests – even for women! Smoking, eating, drinking, flash photography and video lighting are not permitted on rides, during shows or in queues.

So what are we waiting for? First stop, the *Disneyland Park* …

The Disneyland Park

or To All Who Come to this Happy Place, Welcome

It makes sense to start by taking an in-depth look at the original development here at *Disneyland Paris*, the first Disney park in Europe, which opened in April 1992. Although it is comparable to the Magic Kingdom in *Walt Disney World* (America's biggest tourist attraction), be prepared for some surprises in scale and content. The *Disneyland Park* is bigger by some 17ha/42 acres than its Orlando counterpart and, while there are fewer attractions, the Paris version is more elaborate and involving.

The attractions range from the twee and fairly ordinary (Mad Hatter's Tea Cups and Autopia) to the wonderfully inventive (Phantom Manor and Pirates of the Caribbean) and on to the downright thrilling (Space Mountain and Indiana Jones and the Temple of Peril). The all-encompassing theming covers the Wild West (Frontierland), dark jungles and pirate caverns (Adventureland), film and storybook fantasy (Fantasyland) and a kind of retro future world (Discoveryland), possibly the most imaginative of all. There is at least one (depending on the time of year) unmissable daily parade and a range of other live theatrical productions that all carry the

Parades are popular with all the family

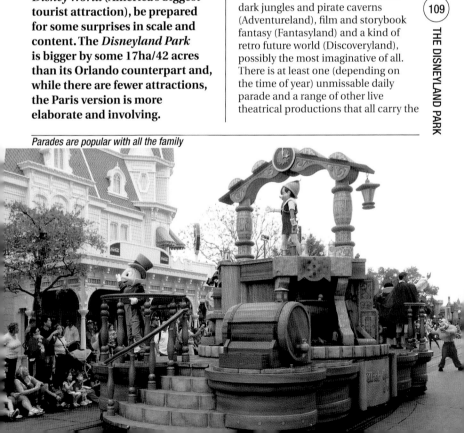

Disney hallmark of captivating family entertainment. Put simply, there's plenty to make you go 'Wow!' plus a lot that will raise a big smile.

BRITTIP

Take advantage of Disney's free package pick-up service if you do a lot of shopping. When you pay, ask for the items to be sent to The Disney Store in the Disney Village for you to collect after 6pm. If you are staying in a Disney hotel, your shopping can be delivered to your hotel's Disney Store for collection after 8pm.

Prepare to be completely immersed in a convincing world of make-believe, where every tiny detail – from the uniforms of the Cast Members to the clever signage – conforms to that land's theme. But, be aware of some fairly blatant attempts to lighten your wallet, notably at the many gift shops, especially after the rides. There are literally thousands of types of merchandise and, although much of it costs less than €20, it can quickly add up if you have children of the large-eyed variety!

Another slight negative to be aware of is the quality (or lack of it) of much of the counter-service dining. With only a couple of notable exceptions, the fare is neither terribly imaginative nor particularly cheap (around €10 a head, even for the most basic meal). In the course of 3 days, that can be almost €190 just in meals for a family of 4,

THE DISNEYLAND PARK

Disneyland Park at a glance

Location	Off Exit 14 of the A4 autoroute, proceed to the clearly signed car park; or turn right out of the Marne-la-Vallée RER and TGV station; or through the *Disney Village* if staying at a resort hotel
Size	57ha/140 acres in 5 'lands'
Hours	10am–6 or 7pm autumn and winter weekdays; 10am–8, 9 or 10pm spring, plus autumn and winter weekends, half-term holidays; 9 or 10am–10pm Christmas and New Year (until 1am New Year's Eve); 9am–11pm summer holidays (mid-Jul–Aug)
Admission	Under 3 free; 3–11 €51 (1-Day/1-park Ticket), €62, €109, €130, €151 (1-, 2- 3- and 4-Day Park Hopper), adults (12+) €57 (1-Day/1-park Ticket), €69, €122, €151, €179 (1-, 2- 3- and 4-Day Park Hopper); Annual Passports (per person): Fantasy €139, Dream €199, Classic €99. NB: All prices subject to annual increase; see **www.disneylandparis.co.uk**.
Parking	€15
Pushchairs	€7.50 (Pushchair shop to right of main entrance, just under railway arch)
Wheelchairs	€7.50 (Pushchair shop)
Top Attractions	Space Mountain: Mission 2, Star Tours, Peter Pan's Flight, Dumbo the Flying Elephant, Big Thunder Mountain Railroad, Buzz Lightyear's Laser Blast
Don't Miss	Disney's Magic On Parade, Disney Dreams fireworks show, Fantillusion parade (summer and Christmas seasons only), Tarzan Encounter, 'it's a small world', La Tanière du Dragon
Hidden Costs	**Meals** Burger, chips and coke €9.95–€11.95; 3-course meal at Blue Lagoon €27 (€14.10 for children); beer 33cl €3.95 Kids' meal €5.70 (at all counter-service restaurants) **T-shirts** €10–35 **Souvenirs** €2.50–37,500 **Sundries** Kids' autograph book €4.90 and €9.90; Space Mountain ride photos €12, 19, 20, poster size €21

eating twice a day at counter-service restaurants (although the new **Half Board Meal Plan** can save up to 10% off these costs if you are a Disney hotel guest – see page 64). Conversely, the handful of full-service restaurants DO offer fabulous food – but at a price. Have lunch at our favourite, the Blue Lagoon, and you could easily be over €100 lighter with 4 to feed. A cheaper alternative is to stock up at breakfast, keep going with snacks from the many hot dog, popcorn, doughnut and drinks wagons around the park and have your main meal in *Disney Village* or at the hotel in the evening (where buffet options can be better value).

Some attractions can also close before the official park closing time. For example, Les Mystères du Nautilus can shut up shop as early as 6pm, some Adventureland attractions occasionally close early and either all or at least part of Fantasyland and even Discoveryland shut early in high season to prepare for the firework show.

BRITTIP
For a simple plan of campaign, shop in the afternoon, ride the attractions in the evening! Most people do it the other way round and encounter the longest queues that way.

Pace yourself

The final piece of advice before we send you off on the great *Disneyland Park* adventure is to pace yourself. It is easy to try to do too much and end up a frazzled wreck by mid-afternoon! In summer, when the crowds are at their peak and the temperature can top 30ºC/86ºF, it can be a particularly tough business negotiating the rides, the long queues and the demands of tramping from one side of the park to the other in the name of entertainment. This is when you will most feel the benefit of a **solid plan**, booking your mealtimes in advance and giving yourselves a rest at strategic moments, whether it be finding a quiet corner for a drink or visiting a show

that provides a welcome sit-down, preferably in the air-conditioned cool.

When it comes to eating, be aware that inclement weather quickly causes long queues to pile up in the restaurants, even in *Disney Village*. If you can pre-empt that sudden rain squall by getting to a café first, you will be well placed to watch the rush come in when the deluge starts. Equally, if you have brought some good **rain gear** with you, it is a great time to enjoy some of the rides while the majority seek shelter.

BRITTIP
Caught in a rain shower without a jacket? Not to worry – all Disney shops will bring out cheap, plastic rain-gear as fast as they can, so you won't have to endure the wet weather too long.

You will also need to **drink** a lot of water during the summer. The physical demands of the parks will quickly creep up on you unless you remember to rehydrate at regular intervals. It is, sadly, an all-too-common feature in mid-afternoon to see or hear grizzly children, often being berated by parents for not enjoying themselves (!), when all everyone needs is to just sit down for a few minutes, recharge the batteries and drink some water.

BRITTIP
Save euros by bringing a bottle of water with you and refilling it from the many drinking fountains around.

Most children get a huge energy charge from being in the theme parks and the adrenalin keeps them going long after they should have keeled over. But that excited state can run out at a moment's notice and turn to angst if they are not regularly fed and watered – and it is easy to overlook the latter with so much going on. In summer, it is advisable to carry a good **sunscreen** and use it liberally while you are queuing to prevent an unhealthy dose of the sun, which also exacerbates the tiredness factor – your biggest enemy.

Boardwalk Candy Palace in Main Street USA

Grand entry

You actually enter 'Le Parc Disneyland' underneath the *Disneyland Hotel*, the rather fanciful conglomeration of buildings known as the Pink Palace. You pass some extremely pleasant gardens (the whimsical Fantasia Gardens, with character-shaped topiaries) and the inevitable fountains and ponds (good photo spot) before entering the main entrance plaza.

BRITTIP
If you want a real budget option for lunch, nip out of the parks to the RER station of Marne-la-Vallée and grab a baguette, sandwich or Croque Monsieur at the station café. The beer alone is €2 cheaper!

Entering the park

The ticket booths are to the right of the entrance passage, but hopefully you already have your tickets and can head straight to the turnstiles. If you need Guest Relations or Left Luggage, bear to the right of the main hotel building and they are in front of you. Be aware there is quite a walk from the main car park to the theme parks, even with the moving walkways. You should allow at least 10mins to get there and pushchairs are a real boon if you have little ones.

BRITTIP
Long queues at the turnstiles under the hotel? Walk to the right of the hotel and check the side entrance to the park. Most of the lines here are shorter and you'll be in the park a little quicker to enjoy the magic.

Main Street USA

Once through the turnstiles, you enter a plaza in front of the main Disneyland Railroad station.

Town Square: Walk under the station and you are in the main entrance to *Disneyland Park* proper and the lower portion of the first 'land', Main Street USA. This is a grand, turn-of-the-century version of small-town America, with an eye-catching array of

DISNEYLAND PARK

Main Street, USA
1 Main Street USA Railroad Station
2 Town Square
3 Disneyland City Hall
4 Main Street Transportation Company Vehicles
5 Liberty Arcade
6 Discovery Arcade
7 Central Plaza

Frontierland
8 Fort Comstock
9 Phantom Manor
10 Thunder Mesa Riverboat Landing
11 Rustler Roundup Shootin' Gallery
12 Big Thunder Mountain
13 Pocahontas Indian Village
14 River Rogue Keelboats
15 Woody's Round-Up
16 Chaparral Theatre
17 Frontierland Railroad Station

Adventureland
18 Indiana Jones and the Temple of Peril
19 Adventure Isle
20 La Cabane des Robinson
21 Skull Rock
22 Pirates' Beach
23 Pirates of the Caribbean
24 Passage Enchanté d'Aladdin

Fantasyland
25 Sleeping Beauty Castle

26 Le Carrousel de Lancelot
27 The Adventures of Snow White
28 Pinocchio's Fantastic Journey
29 Dumbo the Flying Elephant
30 Peter Pan's Flight
31 Meet Mickey Mouse
32 Fantasyland Railroad Station
33 Alice's Curious Labyrinth
34 Le Pays des Contes de Fées
35 Casey Jr – le Petit Train du Cirque
36 Mad Hatter's Tea Cups
37 'it's a small world'
38 Royal Castle Stage
39 Princess Pavilion

Discoveryland
40 Space Mountain: Mission 2
41 Les Mysteres du Nautilus
42 Orbitron – Machines Volantes
43 Star Tours
44 Discoveryland Railroad Station
45 Captain EO
46 Autopia
47 Buzz Lightyear's Laser Blast
48 Videopolis/Cinéma Mickey
49 Arcades Alpha & Beta

Character Meet 'n' greet

Disney seems to have been making an extra effort in recent years to ensure guests get to meet as many of the characters as possible. Not only do we get to see many of the classic characters, the new stars are joining them, too. In fact, you could easily plan a whole day around meeting the characters!

Meet Mickey Mouse: This all-new experience, for the 20th Anniversary Celebrations, features everyone's favourite mouse in a special location at the former Fantasy Festival Stage in Fantasyland. Here, guests can meet Mickey in an elaborate back-stage setting for photos and autographs.

Aladdin: He can usually be found in Adventureland by Le Passage Enchanté d'Aladdin.

Alice in Wonderland: Characters wait near Alice's Curious Labyrinth.

Captain Jack Sparrow: Pirates fans should find their favourite captain in Adventureland, near the Blue Lagoon restaurant.

Disney princesses: Girls love to meet some of the princesses, and it's a royal invitation, too, at their all-new location next to 'it's a small world' in Fantasyland, while Rapunzel, Disney's 10th princess, will meet you near Dumbo, the Flying Elephant but expect a long queue.

Disney villains: Watch out for the bad guys appearing around Fantasyland.

Lion King: Characters meet by the Hakuna Matata restaurant.

Star Wars: Notables appear on allocated times near Star Tours in Discoveryland, but only during the summer season rush. Give Darth Vader some respect – or he might use The Force on you!

Winnie the Pooh: At the end of Main Street USA near Casey's Corner, you'll find Pooh and friends. Be prepared for some long queues when your children want to visit this popular bear.

Disney Dance Express: Another favourite for up-close encounters with the characters (usually Minnie, Goofy, Pluto, Donald, Daisy and Chip 'n' Dale), it makes its way from the back of Fantasyland (next to 'it's a small world') and stops in front of the Castle Theatre Stage, to mingle and have fun with park guests.

THE DISNEYLAND PARK

shop and office façades all built in epic detail. It is not so much a thoroughfare as a living museum to generations of genuine Americana and it offers a fabulous glimpse into an idealised past of the US.

Sleeping Beauty Castle: Here you will get your first look at the most-photographed edifice in the whole resort, Le Château de la Belle au Bois Dormant, to use its full French title.

> **BRITTIP**
> Video camera battery running down? Visit City Hall and they will recharge it for you there and then.

Disneyland City Hall: This guest [rela]tions office is to your left, where [you c]an pick up park maps (if you [haven't] already got one at your hotel or [in an]y cubicles underneath the [sta]tion), book meals at any [restaura]nts or just ask any park-

> **BRITTIP**
> Can't find the characters? Look for the small daily programme insert in your park map to find where they are and at what time. Want to check a character not on the list? Go to City Hall and they will tell you let you know if they are likely to be out and about. City Hall is your best friend for a variety of queries – from the location of baby facilities to meal bookings.

Main Street Transportation Company: On your right is where several vintage and horse-drawn vehicles can take you along Main Street USA to the Central Plaza, the theme park's hub, from which radiate the other 4 'lands'. If you have time (or children), it is quite fun to take one of the horse-drawn trams or vintage cars (including a police paddy-wagon), but it's quicker to walk (especially if you use either of the covered arcades that run alongside Main Street USA).

Disneyland Railroad: One of the most eye-catching features of Main Street is the railroad station, well positioned to catch the unsuspecting visitor (there are 4 stations in all; Adventureland is the only 'land' without a railroad stop.) The Victorian-style station provides an elevated view down Main Street USA, but the signature steam train ride, which circles the whole park and includes a clever 'Grand Canyon' scene en route to Frontierland and a glimpse inside Pirates of the Caribbean, has long, slow-moving queues for much of the day. Be aware some stations may be used for offloading only during non-peak seasons. AAA

BRITTIP

The Disneyland Railroad is a relaxing ride when many of the others are showing long queues but DON'T join it at Main Street where most people usually get on. Instead, try the stations at Frontierland or Fantasyland for a shorter wait.

Information Board: At the top of Main Street USA on the right-hand side (just after the Gibson Girl Ice Cream Parlour) is a handy board that displays the waiting times at the attractions. Late arrivals should take note of this to get an idea of where to head first (and where to avoid for a while until the queues die down). If you missed taking a map on entry, here is another chance. A Cast Member with a cart full of park maps will be near the Board.

Central Plaza Stage: Located at the end of Main Street on the central hub just in front of the castle, this stage is used for shows and also hides some of the light effects used during the nightly fireworks. Mickey shows off his talents (along with the Genie from Aladdin, the Blue Fairy and Merlin) during Mickey's Magical Celebration, a journey from mere mouse to master magician for everyone's favourite character. New shows are created especially for this stage on a regular basis. NB: It seems likely this stage will be rebuilt as part of the 20th Anniversary Celebrations for the new Disney Dreams! special effects show.

BRITTIP

Main Street USA is full of clever Disney memorabilia – look for photos of Walt and wife Lilly in Lilly's Boutique; the two murals of other Emporium shops in the Emporium; and the plates set into the street that bear the legend 'Elias Disney Constructions'. Many of the windows also bear witness to Disney Imagineers and VIPs down the years.

Other entertainment: Running several times a day, from Fantasyland to the Castle Theatre Stage, is the **Disney Dance Express**. The latest incarnation of a train used for many years, it carries a collection of well-known characters, plus singers and dancers, who alight at the Stage to perform a short show. Minnie, Donald and Goofy all take turns at entertaining, while children are allowed to join in during the dancing fun. Once the show is over, the characters take time to mingle with guests, take photos and sign children's autograph books. Don't miss the beautiful decoration on the train, especially Wall-E, who sits on top of the first wagon behind the locomotive.

At **Halloween**, Main Street USA is transformed into **Spooky Street**, with a major pumpkin-inspired makeover and some wonderfully clever visual touches. A giant pumpkin also appears in front of the Castle, with free face-painting for children under 11.

BRITTIP

Halloween is one of the most popular periods at the Disneyland Park, and you can expect some of the longest queues during the school half-term break and weekends in October.

Liberty and Discovery Arcades: As an alternative to walking up the middle of Main Street USA, pick one of the arcades at either side (Liberty on the left and Discovery on the right) and wander right through away from most of the crowds. The Liberty Arcade features a clever tableau about immigrants arriving in New York (in French), while the Discovery Arcade

Town Square

is decorated with some clever period detail, which is worth a look later on.

BRITTIP

Need to stay dry? Both Liberty and Discovery Arcades are fully covered and provide back-door access to most of the shops and cafés along Main Street USA. Very popular in winter!

Shopping: Main Street USA is basically the park's principal shopping area, with a range of stores (including the gargantuan **Emporium**, which stocks just about every kind of souvenir known to mouse-kind!). In all, there are 12 cunningly arranged shops along this 100m/109yd boulevard and it is worthwhile returning in the afternoon

when the rides are busiest to check out some of the amazing detail here.

You should definitely go to the **Emporium** and **Lilly's Boutique** (glass and porcelain), as well as **The Storybook Store** (books, stationery, CD and audio cassettes), **Harrington's Fine China & Porcelain** (china, crystal and glass giftware), **Disney Clothiers Ltd** (adult and children's apparel) and **Main Street Motors** (more clothing).

If you need any photographic equipment, **Town Square Photography** should be able to help (although beware the prices – it is cheaper to bring basics like film, batteries and flashcards with you).

BRITTIP

Looking for hard-to-find, limited edition pins for your collection? Try Town Square Photography, a less obvious location for pin trading fans to round out their collections.

Also here is **Dapper Dan's Hair Cuts**, an atmospheric vintage barber's with the kind of furnishings you would usually find only in an antique shop (or an apothecary's). You can stop for a haircut or shave if the mood takes you, but the shop isn't open on a regular basis, so it is advisable to check upon arrival if this appeals to you. Reservations requested.

Among the many clever shop facades in Main Street USA is this tribute to the Wright Bros.

Disneyland Park

Dining: You can also find 10 different snack bars and restaurants here to provide everything from breakfast, to a gourmet lunch, afternoon tea and evening dessert. Pick of the bunch is **Walt's – An American Restaurant**, which offers an elegant lunch and dinner (set menus €27.50–39 for adults, €15 for children; Express Meal 'Rhapsody' €19.99; birthday cakes available for €25). This fabulous diner, designed like a 1900s hotel, is a tribute to Walt Disney himself, his ideas and creations, featuring a wealth of personal detail, photos and memorabilia (12–4pm daily). All rooms are decorated in one of the 5 main land themes – either Main Street USA, Adventureland, a Gothic Fantasyland, an elegant Frontierland or the most beautiful room of them all, the Discoveryland Nautilus room. Reservations are an absolute must, especially during high season.

BRITTIP

As an example of the Imagineers' art, listen carefully outside Victoria's Home-Style Restaurant and you will catch the distinct sounds of someone using the bathroom in the 'guesthouse' above!

At the top of Main Street USA, the **Plaza Gardens Restaurant** (11.30am–10.30pm, depending on park opening hours) offers an excellent series of all-you-can-eat buffets for lunch and dinner in a plush, conservatory-style setting. The buffet is €23.70 adults with no drink or €26.20 with, and €11.30 children, including one drink, and consists of a huge cold spread – salads, meats, bread and fruit – and an array of hot dishes – casseroles, pasta, roast beef, sausages, hot dogs and several types of vegetable and rice – plus a mouth-watering selection of desserts.

Otherwise, your eateries are mainly of the counter-snack kind, with the **Market House Deli** (sandwiches, salads and desserts), **Casey's Corner** (all manner of hot dogs, chicken nuggets, and soft drinks), **Victoria's Home-Style Restaurant** (sandwiches,

Dapper Dan's

Seasonal magic

Halloween is one of the resort's most popular events and Halloween weekend is always packed. The whole month of October is dedicated to the festival, with some of the nicest decorations. The Disney villains love this celebration and will want to share it with you during the day, too! Maleficent hosts **Disney's Maleficious Halloween Party**. She is still angry at not being invited to the christening of Aurora and is seeking revenge with the help of her fellow villains. Look out for a 'sinfully delicious shower of treats' as the show's highlight. Mickey has his own show, **Mickey's Halloween Treat in the Street**, bringing his friends, Minnie, Goofy and Donald to a party on the Castle Theatre stage. Another sweet ending with even more candy.

For those willing to pay a bit extra, **Mickey's Not-So-Scary Halloween Party** is held each Friday evening after regular park closing, with an extra party on October 31. Tickets are limited and it is highly advisable to pre-book. Tickets cost €25–35 and the evening includes exclusive shows, Trick and Treats, street entertainment and more villains than ever before. On October 31, guests also get a special Fantillusion Parade and Sound and Light Show with Sleeping Beauty Castle as the backdrop.

Disney's Enchanted Christmas starts in early November and ends after the first Sunday of January, giving plenty of opportunity to visit the park at the most magical time of year. It can be cold, with *real* snow, but just in case the natural variety does not turn up, Disney ensures its own 'snowfall' on Main Street every day. Other great special events include the appearance of **Santa Claus** and a beautiful giant **Christmas Tree**. The park is beautifully decorated for the festive season, with an extra Christmas show and a **Christmas Parade** where Santa will appear in his sleigh, pulled by his reindeer.

Christmas Eve and **New Year's Eve** are celebrated throughout the resort restaurants with special menus. Many hotels will offer a special dinner, as well as Walt's, Blue Lagoon, Plaza Gardens and Auberge de Cendrillon in the *Disneyland Park*. Those come at a premium price but advance booking is still necessary.

pizza and salads), **The Coffee Grinder** (coffee, tea and cakes), **The Ice Cream Company** (hosted by Nestlé), **The Cookie Kitchen** and **Cable Car Bake Shop** (2 sides of the same breakfast-orientated servery, with some delicious pastries and cookies) and the **Gibson Girl Ice Cream Parlour** (a full range of ice cream delights). Bear in mind not all of these are likely to be open at any one time (apart from weekends in high season).

Halloween fun

Disneyland Paris regulars will recall when Frontierland used to be completely made over as 'Halloweenland' for the whole of October, giving a wonderfully spooky extra touch to places like Phantom Manor and Fort Comstock. That changed in 2011 with a new emphasis on **Main Street USA** but, happily, with a lot of the clever decorations and artful Halloween touches kept on and embellished throughout this area.

Pumpkins, lanterns and other suitably seasonal effects abound and children (under 12) can get in the 'spirit' with the Halloween Face Painting Workshop in the Castle Plaza (with choices like Witch Pink and Pumpkin Orange!) and an equally fun Hair-Dressing Workshop – for that truly 'hair-raising' look! The daily **Disney Dreams On Parade** cavalcade also has a Halloween makeover for the period, adding another must-see element to the month's festivities.

BRITTIP

A separate night-time Halloween Party event on 31 Oct is not widely publicised in the UK, so it is worth seeking out if you are visiting at that time. The party runs 8.30pm–1am (€35/person, under 3s free; call 00 33 1 60 30 60 53 to order tickets in advance). Tickets to this event tend to sell out well in advance.

Mickey's Not So Scary Halloween Party returns on select nights in Oct, 8–11pm, with a family-friendly atmosphere even the youngest guests will enjoy. Young 'uns can dress up in their Halloween costumes for tricks and treats with Mickey, his Friends and the Disney villains, and the party offers a rare chance to capture some unique and memorable photos of the characters in their costumes. Many attractions remain open during the party, too (€25/person, under 3s free). And, even if you do not have a ticket for the special night events, you can still enjoy a lot of the decoration and theming during the day.

Rope drop

If you arrive before the official opening time (either 9 or 10am), Main Street USA is not the place to linger as most of the crowd will flock to the **Central Plaza** in front of the Castle. This is REALLY where the action starts for a full day in the park, so don't be fooled into thinking they have opened early by letting you into Main Street USA. You need to have already planned your campaign from here to get a head start on the masses.

BRITTIP
If you are among the first to reach Central Plaza and you manage to get to the main rides first, you will enjoy the *Disneyland Park* at its best – with short or non-existent queues at the most popular attractions.

Where to wait: Depending on which of the 'lands' appeals to you most, head in one of the 4 directions and wait for the opening-hour 'rope drop' by the Cast Members at each entrance.

If you fancy the appeal of cowboy country and the lure of a thrill ride like Big Thunder Mountain or the scary fun of Phantom Manor, head up Liberty Arcade and, at the top, wait to turn left into Frontierland.

For the mysteries of Adventureland (including the wonderful Pirates of the Caribbean ride and Indiana Jones), move into Central Plaza and wait at its entrance on the left.

Those with children in tow, who will demand rides in the company of all their favourite characters like Dumbo, Peter Pan and the Mad Hatter, should

wait in front of the Castle for the chance to get into Fantasyland first.

Or, if the appeal of big thrill rides like Space Mountain: Mission 2 (an indoor, looping roller-coaster) and Star Tours (a brilliant simulator space ride) is top of your 'To Do' list, then turn right in the middle of Central Plaza and await rope drop for Discoveryland.

Once the ropes go down, the early-morning crowds will move (quickly!) in one of the four directions, so keep your wits about you. Study the park map for where you want to go and benefit from a first hour or so without lengthy queuing.

BRITTIP
A perk with the Dream Annual Passport is entry to Fantasyland and Discoveryland 1–2 hours before they officially open. The Dumbo and Peter Pan rides often start half an hour early, so you can have a turn on the most popular rides without queuing.

Timing your meals: It also pays (royally so in peak periods) to avoid main meal times if you want to eat without more queues and frenzy. In *Disneyland Paris* people tend to pack out the counter-service cafés rather than the handful of full-service, sit-down restaurants. This means noon–2.30pm is a seriously bad time (unless it is an extremely quiet period of the year) to head for places like the Fuente del Oro Restaurante, Pizzeria Bella Notte, or any of the other 14 counter-service diners. Try to have a snack before midday or look to eat in mid-afternoon and you will also benefit from slightly shorter ride queues during lunchtime.

BRITTIP
Park too busy? Don't forget it is relatively easy to head back out to *Disney Village* and grab a bite to eat at places like Planet Hollywood, Annette's Diner and the great-value Earl of Sandwich.

Alternatively, you could book lunch at the start of the day at one of the 4 full-

Riding Bullseye in Frontierland

service restaurants (Walt's, Auberge du Cendrillon, Blue Lagoon or Silver Spur Steakhouse) to guarantee a pleasant sit-down and some rest – especially with children.

(120) Frontierland

Okay, enough of the warnings – let's get to the fun! There is plenty in store, so let's take you on a full tour of the remaining 'lands' in the *Disneyland Park*. Starting immediately to your left from the Central Plaza brings you to Frontierland, a true rootin', tootin' cowboy town that oozes child appeal and has plenty of visual creativity and stimulation for grown-ups, too. It is a realm of pioneers and gold diggers,

Phantom Manor

the Wild West in vivid 3-D, with a big helping of some of the epic scenery that the real-life version possesses in places like Nevada and Arizona.

BRITTIP
Go to the top of Fort Comstock and you have a great spot to take memorable photos of Frontierland.

As in virtually all other areas of the park, Frontierland rewards the casual wanderer with some great little paths leading nowhere in particular but which reveal interesting details or amusing scenery, such as the Indian village encampment or the hot springs (complete with Old Faithful geyser).

Fort Comstock: Once again, the faithful re-creation of the era can be seen in every building and façade, none better than the main entrance here, which is an attraction in itself, with scenes from Legends of the Wild West. You can climb the wooden stairs to the ramparts, visit the US Marshall and Fort Jail, and peer into the stables and offices (see if you can spot Buffalo Bill). Kids will want to roam the ramparts and scan other areas of the park through the telescopes provided. It is a good place to let youngsters explore on their own, too. AA

Phantom Manor: Turn left after coming through Fort Comstock and head along the plaza past the Silver

Spur Steakhouse for one of the most clever and amusing rides in the Disney repertoire. This elaborate haunted mansion is a variation on the theme established in Anaheim and Orlando, with a ghoulish entryway leading to an underground ride of wonderfully creepy proportions. The introductory spiel is in French (while some aspects of the commentary are alternately in English and French). However, it needs little real explanation as the gloomy entrance parlour (watch for a remarkable trick here) takes you down to this spook-tastic world.

Thunder Mesa Riverboat

BRITTIP
Queues build up at Phantom Manor from mid-morning and, although they rarely top half an hour, this ride is a good one to do early or during a parade, when it's quieter. Or wait until the last hour before park closing when it rarely has a queue (people seem to overlook this corner of the park late in the day) and it is at its spooky best!

Under 5s may find the mock-horror elements a bit too convincing but otherwise the whole experience is more fun than frightening. The story of an elaborate socialite wedding that went tragically wrong, leaving the bride as one of the 999 ghosts, is a bit hard to follow, but the ride takes you right through the manor and into a realistic haunted town in best graveyard fashion.

BRITTIP
You can see a photo of a very young Walt Disney in Phantom Manor. As you leave the 'stretch' room, walk the hallway, cut around the corner and you will see it on a table on the right-hand side. A real Disney heirloom!

In the queue you can study the elaborate terraces and gardens outside the manor, while you exit into Boot Hill and some more pun-laced scenery that includes various graves – such as 'Here lies Shotgun Gus, holier now than all of us'. The more attentive will also notice the sounds of knocking from

Big Thunder Mountain

the largest of the mausoleums in the graveyard. This can be a great source of amusement when people notice it for the first time on dark evenings! AAAA (TTTTT for youngsters)

Thunder Mesa Riverboat Landing: Backtrack slightly along the plaza and you can hop on a boat offering a slow and picturesque ride around much of Frontierland on the Rivers of the Far West, including several sections that can only be seen from the water. The commentary is bilingual and it is quite a capacious ride, so there is rarely much of a queue. One of the two boats sailing that day, either the *Molly Brown* or *Mark Twain*, will provide an enjoyably authentic experience. This is a good ride to save for mid-afternoon when Phantom Manor and Big Thunder are busiest, but be aware the Landing closes earlier than other attractions. AAA

Rustler Roundup Shootin' Gallery: Fans of the old-style arcade shooting ranges can get a quick 'fix' here, where €2 (the only additional charge for an attraction in the theme park) will give you 10 shots at various audio-animatronic targets. TT.

◀️▶️ **BRITTIP** ─────
Need a little spot to relax and get away from the crowds without leaving the park? On the right hand side next to Rustler Roundup Shootin' Gallery is a little path that will guide you to a porch near the waterside overlooking Big Thunder Mountain. A place not many people discover or know about, but a great place to sit down and relax for a little while.

Big Thunder Mountain: This is one of Disney's trademark roller-coasters. While others may thrill (or terrify!) with their topsy-turvy antics, Big Thunder sticks firmly to the straight and narrow but is still as fun and inventive as most people desire, with this abandoned 'gold mine' showing it has plenty of life left in it in the shape of its runaway train. Again, you get a different version from other Disney parks; this one starts straight away with a dive into the dark under the lake before whizzing around

the mock sandstone monoliths and mine shafts in exhilarating fashion.

◀️▶️ **BRITTIP** ─────
If you head to Frontierland first, Big Thunder should be your opening ride, followed by Phantom Manor. Then return to the mine-train coaster and grab a FastPass for another go later!

With three different ascents (and plunges), the proliferation of clever scenery is never less than spectacular, so it usually needs at least two rides to take in all the detail (it looks great at night, too). This is one of the 5 FastPass (FP) rides, so this is well worth taking advantage of, as the queues can reach two hours at peak times. Afterwards, you can buy the souvenir photo of your ride (from €18–35; poster size €21; plastic coffee mugs €16). Restrictions: 1.02m/3ft 3in. TTTT (FP)

River Rogue Keelboats: This original park ride closed back in 2001 and re-opened in 2007 only to close once more because of operational difficulties. However, just in case it opens again, it features a gentle 20min tour of the Rivers of the Far West, following a similar path to the Riverboats but providing a more up-close experience of some of the sights and a different perspective, close to the water. Its real problem is that it is slow to load and queues build up quickly. AA

Pocahontas Indian Village: If the youngsters are too short (or apprehensive!) to ride Big Thunder, head for this straightforward play area with a mixture of slides, swings and climbs geared towards under 6s. Unfortunately, this area closes when it rains but, otherwise, it is a valuable place to allow the young 'uns to let off steam. NB: The play area may close during winter months and low season. TTT (for the right age group!).

Woody's Roundup Village: The former Critter Corral petting zoo, this is now a cowboy-style mini-village and smart character meet 'n' greet area. It started with *Toy Story* characters but, with Woody's new location next door at the Cowboy Barbecue Cookout, other Disney characters take his place periodically. Kids can enjoy more organised character interaction here, plus extra fun at Halloween and the all-new *Father Christmas Village* for the full festive season, with the chance to meet Santa and his helpers.

Chaparral Theatre: Opposite Woody's Roundup Village, this is one of the park's 4 live entertainment venues. The attractions are seasonal, with both a summer and winter programme. The **Tarzan Encounter** returned in 2011 after a 3-year break, to the delight of its fans. It tells the story of Tarzan as related in the Disney film but with new elements and extra music written and performed by Phil Collins in multiple languages. The performance itself features highly skilled acrobats who jump and fly through the air either with ropes or trampoline, plus a suitably well-built Tarzan. Children have the most fun, though, as they can join in by banging on pots and pans to add to the 'music'! The show is performed several times a day and it is advisable to be at the theatre 30mins early to grab a seat in the middle as some areas have an obstructed view because of the massive supports carrying the roof structure. AAAAA

Mickey's Winter Wonderland takes over in the Theatre from mid-Nov to early Mar, with an equally clever ice-skating show featuring Mickey and the gang (including a suitably hapless Donald Duck) that keeps youngsters enchanted for the full 25 minutes. It is a fairly straightforward song-and-dance pastiche, but once again the staging and lighting are impressive and its bilingual style ensures English speakers are not left out. AAAA

Frontierland Railroad Station: Often the best place to catch the theme park's steam train is next door, to take the slow chug all the way round. NB: During low season this station may close, making it a place where you can only hop off the train.

Shopping: Shopping is suitably cowboy orientated, with **Tobias Norton & Sons** – **Frontier Traders**, a leather emporium featuring hats, boots, wallets and belts; **Bonanza Outfitters**, offering the full range of Western apparel; and the **Eureka Mining Supplies**, which stocks a selection of typical cowboy-style foods and toys, including the inevitable hats and guns.

BRITTIP
If there isn't a queue, take the Railroad steam train for the best short cut to Fantasyland or Discoveryland. Whatever the queue, it is usually quicker to walk if you need the fastest way back to Main Street USA.

Dining: Your dining options feature 2 outstanding opportunities. The **Silver Spur Steakhouse** is a truly deluxe establishment, designed like a classic Western hotel, using rich, dark wood and plush upholstery. The subdued lighting provides an intimate dining style and there is a display kitchen at the back. Steaks are their stock-in-trade, but they also do excellent salmon, chicken, steaks and vegetarian pasta. Set, 3-course meals are €27–32/adult, while a 2-course Pony Express menu is served within 40mins at €20.50. A la carte dishes are €17.50–26.30 with wine €16–45/bottle. Children's menu is €14.10. Superb desserts (€6.60–8.50, €12.50 2-person) add to the high quality on offer here.

BRITTIP
A chocolate birthday cake can be ordered at most full-service restaurants for €27.50 but it is essential to do this in advance.

Lucky Nugget Saloon offers a fabulous Tex-Mex buffet lunch from 12–3pm, plus 6–10pm for dinner in high season. The restaurant is wonderfully styled like a two-storey Western saloon, with a stage and a long bar. The food is a serve-yourself buffet (€23.70 adult, €11.30 age 3–11s) featuring crudités, chicken wings, nachos, salsa, fajitas, spare ribs, chilli con carne, pasta, pizza and a large choice of desserts. Drinks are not included for adults, but one soft drink is included per child).

Last Chance Café

Cowboy Cookout Barbecue is a wonderful venue to enjoy some proper Western cookin' and meet Disney characters like Mickey, Tigger, Goofy and Pluto and many of the *Toy Story* gang. For a set price of €26, you can choose a starter, main course, dessert and a drink. The choices are limited, but you'll get plenty of time with the characters. Choices include chilli con carne, smoked chicken, pork ribs, and chicken salad. Children pay €13 for a set menu (check what's on the menu in advance as picky eaters might not be happy). At 5pm there is also a Tea Party with the characters, with a Pastry buffet set-up at €19 per person.

Fuente del Oro Restaurante goes down Mexico way for counter-service cantina style, with tacos, chilli and other Mexican specialities such as fajitas and nachos (one of the better counter-service options, but very busy noon–2pm). Choose from chilli con carne (€6.95), vegetarian taco salad (€6.50) or a chicken fajita (€8.50). There are 3 set meals (€9.99–12.99) and a children's menu, including a main dish, a side order, a dessert and a drink (€5.70).

Finally, the recently revamped **Last Chance Café** (in between the Silver Spur Steakhouse and Lucky Nugget Saloon) offers more cowboy fare with typical Western al fresco decor, serving turkey legs, salads and chips. They also offer a fun Texas Platter with meat and onion rings.

Interconnecting paths: A unique feature of this section of the park is the latticework of paths that interconnect between Frontierland and Adventureland. This surprisingly small-scale landscaping is a notable element of the European influence behind the overall design, and the paths are almost interwoven to provide an alternative way of getting around as well as highlighting different aspects of the lands (but keep your map handy in case you get lost!). For those following these tucked-away paths, Disney add some little extras to enjoy. See if you can spot a famous Disney snake and Disney bird once you enter the Adventureland section.

THE DISNEYLAND PARK

Mexican style at Fuente del Oro Restaurante

© DISNEY

Adventure Isle

BRITTIP

Try to get a view of the Castle from one of the small side paths between Frontierland and Adventureland, as there are a number of unusual perspectives offering good photo opportunities.

BRITTIP

Adventureland is the hardest 'land' to navigate, so hang on to your map to find your way from place to place.

Adventureland

Africa, the Caribbean and the jungles of Asia combine to provide a host of contrasting and thrilling experiences, all with lush landscaping. This is the 'land' with the fewest attractions, but the whole area has such a wealth of detail and fine architecture (take a close look at Skull Rock and the castle façade of the Pirates ride) that it is easy to spend a good deal of time just wandering and admiring. Even if you don't eat at most of the counter-service diners, it is worth looking into places like Colonel Hathi's Pizza Outpost and Restaurant Hakuna Matata to appreciate the interior design that gives them a real storybook feel. NB: Adventureland can close at least 1 hour before regular closing time in high season to prepare for the fireworks. This is generally marked on posters in both lands.

Indiana Jones and the Temple of Peril: If you come from Frontierland, turn left by Colonel Hathi's for this 5-star thrill ride. Not content with creating a ducking and diving coaster that seems to zip along much faster when you're aboard than when you're watching, the designers added a brain-scrambling 360-degree loop and have reconfigured

Indiana Jones

kwards or (at
The theming
euing area
rchaeological
style, before
l your rickety
know it,
und a tight,
twisting track with its sudden loop and
dramatic swoops, only to come to the
end of the track all too soon once your
body has got the hang of it!

BRITTIP
The scary aspect of the Indiana
Jones ride and its position at the
innermost end of Adventureland means
it is often overlooked by many park visitors,
hence it is a good ride to do during the
morning and even the afternoon at quieter
times of the year.

This is definitely not the ride if you
suffer from neck or back problems as
there is quite a bit of vibration but it
is also quite exhilarating and much
more fun than it looks. Indiana Jones
is a FastPass ride, which is handy for
coaster lovers as queues can be slow-
moving. The first couple of hours of
the day are rarely busy, and the queues
often don't build up here until mid-
afternoon. Restrictions: 1.40m/4ft 6in.
TTTT (FP)

Adventure Isle: Retracing your steps
slightly and turning left brings you into
this central portion of Adventureland.
The Imagineers have worked overtime
here to create something different
from existing themes in other parks.
They opted for an elaborate overgrown
adventure playground. This delightful
pot-pourri of attractions, mainly aimed
at children, is also eye-catching and
detailed enough to appeal to adults.

BRITTIP
Adventure Isle is just about the
only area of either park that is NOT
accessible for guests with disabilities
as it is simply not designed for the use of
wheelchairs.

La Cabane des Robinson: The
Swiss Family Treehouse is the first

attraction you come to on the Isle.
The re-creation of the treehouse of
the castaway Robinson family from
the 1960 Disney film is only a walk-
through attraction, but queues are
rarely a problem and there are great
views from the top. The tree looks
beautiful in the evening during
nightfall when it's completely lit up. AA

Spinning off the treehouse is a high-
level rope suspension bridge, **Le Pont
Suspendu**, which takes you on to the
five other sections of the Isle, **Skull
Rock** (a labyrinthine stone edifice that
towers over one end of the lagoon),
L'Ile au Tresor (a series of lookout
towers and spooky secret caves), **Le
Ventre de la Terre** (a series of galleries
under the tree), **Captain Hook's Galley**
(a rather tame pirate ship that actually
has little to explore) and **La Plage des
Pirates** (or Pirates' Beach, a clever play
area of slides and climbs expressly
for little shipmates). Kids will want to
dash off and explore Ben Gunn's Cave,
Ambush Alley and Dead Man's Bridge,
and it is a good area in which to let
them loose for a while. TTT AAA

Pirates of the Caribbean: Coming off
at the top end of Adventure Isle brings
you to one of Disney's trademark
unmissable rides. The original version
of this attraction was installed in
Disneyland California in 1967 and
remains an Imagineering gem to this
day, highlighted by their pioneering
work with audio-animatronics. These
are a series of life-like figures that
move, talk, gesticulate and, in this
instance, lay siege to a Caribbean
island! Your journey starts as you wind
down inside the Pirate Castle, through
secret streets and dingy dungeons,
until you reach your boat for a plunge
into the darkness of this pirate realm.
There are 2 minor plunges (and slight
splashes – front seat passengers may
get a little wet), the first of which
drops you into the middle of the island
siege, with the clever – and distinctly
amusing – action going on all around,
and a second that drops into the
pirate treasure caverns. Skeletons
and dungeons abound, and it may be
a little too intense for under 5s, but

there is little that is genuinely scary and the whole effect is so amazing you will probably want to have several turns to appreciate all the detail. While it is a popular ride, queues drop off towards the end of the day and it is often possible to ride with little wait (it is also a welcome place to cool down during the hotter months!). Did you see him? Jack Sparrow? If you didn't, he IS on the way. The US versions of the ride have both been retro-fitted with the Cap'n Jack character as well as a spooky Davy Jones 'waterfall' fog effect, and these are due to be added to the Paris ride in the near future, we believe, as part of the 20th Anniversary celebrations. It will help to give a contemporary twist to a classic attraction that inspired a film into an updated attraction inspired by the movie (if you follow us!). AAAAA (TTTT for under 8s)

BRITTIP

Pirates of the Caribbean has one of the most beautiful queue areas of all Disney attractions. Take your time as you walk through and enjoy the dark corridors and other surprises, too – it's all part of the attraction! Oh, and the best time to do it is about 30mins before closing so you can enjoy the scary queue … alone!

If you enter Adventureland via the main entrance off the Central Plaza, you will come straight into the **Agrabah Bazaar** area. Here you will find the **Passage Enchanté d'Aladdin**, a walk-through exhibit of the Aladdin story with some amusing tableaux and clever lighting tricks. AA

Other entertainment: Near the side entrance of the restaurant Au Chalet de la Marionette a small show will please the youngsters in the family. **Following The Leader With Peter Pan** is a fun street performance with the characters from Peter Pan. Children can interact while everybody is asked to sing along during this small but fun event. Shows start in the afternoon with several performances every day. **Rhythms of the Jungle** is a photo opportunity with a little 'Tam Tam' twist as children can

meet some famous characters from the Disney jungle (*Lion King, Jungle Book*) and then join in and play some music on the drums.

Shopping: The shopping options tend to be rather humdrum in this area. The array includes **Indiana Jones Adventure Outpost** (safari accessories and Indy souvenirs), **Les Trésors de Shéhérazade** (magic lamps, dolls, clothes), **La Girafe Curieuse** (jungle-themed curios and wild animal toys) and **Le Coffre du Capitaine** (as you exit the Pirates ride, with a suitable range of sea-themed treasures and toys) but they are worth a look more for their décor than the merchandise.

Dining: One of the real scenic highlights, though, is the magnificent indoor/outdoor shopping and dining scenario (straight out of 1,001 Nights) of the **Agrabah Café**, which offers a creative and appealing Mediterranean-oriental buffet, among the best on offer here. Selections include shwarma, chicken, lamb, couscous, salads and tempting desserts (€23.70 adults, €10.90 children; child's meal comes with drink and surprise). If you want to visit during busy lunch hours, it's highly advisable to make reservations as it is often hugely popular.

BRITTIP

Plan a special meal, even with the kids, in the Blue Lagoon and you won't be disappointed. Book at City Hall or with your hotel concierge. A perfect pit stop in winter when it is heated to tropical temperatures!

Adventureland is also home to one of our all-time favourite Disney restaurants, the **Blue Lagoon**, which is actually set inside the Pirates ride (so there are usually a few shouts of 'Bon Appetit!' from people setting off on the ride as you dine) and is the occasional haunt of Cap'n Jack himself (just outside for character meet 'n' greets and, periodically, inside as well). You enter just below and to the left of the ride entrance, and the setting alone is worth a look. You eat on a mock 'outdoor' terrace under dim lights,

Hakuna Matata

authentically furnished, listening to sounds that evoke the feeling of a warm evening on some distant Caribbean island.

The seafood-orientated menu is also a delight, with the likes of grilled swordfish with coriander, roasted prawns with basil, Jamaican pepper fillet of beef and chicken and seafood with Creole-style rice. The set Buccaneer's menu is €27 (€14.10 teens, €10.50 3–11s), while starters are €8.30–13.50 and main courses €15.95–29.95. The speciality set menu, Treasures of the Sea, features crab, scallops, tuna, ostrich steak and swordfish for a princely €32.60. Desserts are €6.60–8.50.

Café de la Brousse

BRITTIP

A 'secret' route goes from the park entrance all the way to the heart of Fantasyland, mainly under cover. Take Liberty Arcade up Main Street USA, turn sharp left into Frontierland, walk straight through Fort Comstock and follow the covered walkway into Adventureland. Skirt around Les Trésors de Schéhérazade (briefly in the open), then pick up the walkway alongside restaurant Au Chalet de la Marionnette and you end up at the Peter Pan ride. It is also a quick way OUT of Fantasyland when the park is busy.

Counter-service options here include **Colonel Hathi's Pizza Outpost**, serving up pizzas, salads and pastas (€6.50–8.95; set menus €9.99, €11.99 and €12.99) all in best *Jungle Book* style. A children's option is available at €5.70 and includes either pasta or a kids pizza, dessert and a drink. **Restaurant Hakuna Matata** offers a choice of 3 menus with one of the following; spice chicken, mixed meat platter or a kebab. Menus come with fries or vegetable rice and include their own dessert. You can also order à la carte (€9.99–12.99). **Café de la Brousse** and **Captain Hook's Galley** feature sandwiches, hot dogs, ice creams and drinks.

Fantasyland

Having arrived in the theme park's largest 'land' via Adventureland, here you will find the biggest selection of rides and the most concentrated fun for under 8s. This is the stuff of pure fantasy and the whimsical creativity on show is first class, from the huge Castle down to the tiny detail of the clock façade on 'it's a small world'. Unfortunately, it is also the most crowded area, with queues building up quickly from mid-morning and rarely abating until early evening (when it is open until 11pm). Parts of the back of Fantasyland also close from 10pm to prepare for the evening fireworks, so don't think you have the place to yourself all of a sudden!

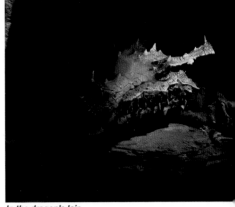

In the dragon's lair

BRITTIP

Don't be surprised to see people lighting up around the park, despite the no-smoking laws in France that limit smoking to specific outdoor areas. Cast Members don't seem keen to ask people to put cigarettes out.

If you have young children, Fantasyland should be your first port of call as it is likely to offer the most candidates for 'favourite ride' and it is not unknown for families to spend virtually all day here. If you come for 'rope drop' (highly recommended), you should head straight through the Castle and try to do Dumbo first, head over to Peter Pan next and visit the Carrousel straight after in quick succession. These are all painfully slow-loading rides where the queues build up almost immediately and remain slow all day.

Excluding Peter Pan but including the Mad Hatter's Tea Cups (another slow-loader), you might be inclined to say 'We waited for THAT?' at the end of the ride as they are not terribly exciting for grown-ups, being basically re-themed versions of standard fairground rides. However, children will almost certainly demand to ride Dumbo at least once and, if you manage to get it under your belt without waiting half an hour or more (and the queue can top in excess of a mind-numbing hour), you will have done well!

A princess in Fantasyland

Taking Fantasyland in a clockwise
direction starting at the Castle, you
have 12 main attractions from which to
choose, plus 7 restaurants and 7 shops
that include some of the most original
gift items in the park.

**Le Château de la Belle au Bois
Dormant (Sleeping Beauty Castle):**
This is a draw in its own right, having
two contrasting things to see. La
Galerie de la Belle au Bois Dormant is
easy to miss as you scamper through,
but is actually upstairs in the Castle
and tells the story in picture-boards
and words (in French) of Sleeping
Beauty. Check out the beautiful
Renaissance-style tapestries that line
the walls and the stunning (and highly
photogenic) stained-glass windows.
You can also walk along an external
balcony that provides a great view from
both sides. AA

Underneath **le château** and accessible
via 3 different portals (including a back
door of Merlin's shop, down a winding
stone staircase) is the magnificent **La
Tanière du Dragon**, or dragon's lair.
Here, the creature that turned many a
would-be saviour of Sleeping Beauty
to toast lurks in steamy, underground
splendour, wrapped in reptilian
fashion around the stalactites and

stalagmites, occasionally rearing his
audio-animatronic head to threaten
fire and brimstone on all those who
dare to disturb his slumbers. In the
semi-darkness, it really is a convincing
beast (watch its chest 'breathing'!) and
is usually far too menacing for under
5s. TTT (for under 8s)

Sword in the Stone: Stepping through
the Castle's rear gate brings you to
a courtyard and this great photo
opportunity. Occasionally, during high
season, small shows are produced on
this location and characters might
also appear.

Le Carrousel de Lancelot: Right in
front of you is this standard horsey
roundabout that youngsters love,
even if queuing can take an age and
mum and dad would rather be doing
something (anything!) else. AA (TTTT
for under 5s)

**Blanche-Neige et les Sept Nains (The
Adventures of Snow White):** Right next
door, this is a typical Disney kiddie ride
that is a fairly dark journey into the
cartoon world of the classic film. The
soundtrack is in French, which detracts
a little if you are unfamiliar with the
story (but then, how many people is
that likely to be?). All kids can relate
to this mildly scary trip into the realm
of the Wicked Witch, her evil plans
and the suitably happy ending. Under
5s may find parts of it menacing, but
most soon get over their fear of the
dark with parental encouragement.
AAA (TTT for under 8s)

Pinocchio's Fantastic Journey:
Following on is another dark ride, this
time in the company of Jiminy Cricket,
showing his attempts to keep the
wooden puppet-boy on the straight
and narrow. Again, it is a touch intense
for real young 'uns (especially with

the surprise menace of the whale) but most find it fun rather than frightening. The special effect at the end with the Blue Fairy is well worth seeing. AAA (TTT for under 8s)

Dumbo the Flying Elephant: Needing little explanation, this is a standard fairground whirligig with elephants as the flying 'vehicles'. The front-seat passengers get to make the elephant go up and down while circling gently round and round, and that's about it. There is little to look at while you are queuing, the queues move painfully slowly and the music is horribly repetitive, but kids seem to get a buzz out of piloting their elephant and it is a highly visible ride, thus hard for parents to ignore! Head here first thing or expect to queue for ages (the crowds do ease off a little during the parades, but there is no substitute for doing this early on). TT (TTTT for under 8s)

Peter Pan's Flight: Next door to Dumbo is Fantasyland's other serious queue-builder, which has the saving grace of being a FastPass ride (see page 105). Once you get to board your pirate ship, you rise up, up and away over the streets of London, turn right at the first star and straight on to morning, all the way to Neverland and a close encounter with Captain Hook and his inept pirates. It is another indoor dark ride (very dark as you go through the star-lit portion), but the overhead mechanism of your 'ship' and the elaborate scenery combine to create the right illusion, making it a big hit with all the family and a must-do ride for most kids. Be aware the waiting time can easily top an hour here and much of the queuing area is in the open, so your best bet is to try to take advantage of the FP. If the FPs have all gone (as often happens by 1pm), leave it as late as possible or wait until a parade has just started. AAAA (TTTTT for under 8s) (FP)

Meet Mickey Mouse: Step out of Peter Pan, turn left and you come to this brand new purpose-built venue to showcase Mickey himself. Formerly the Fantasy Festival Stage, it has been completely remodelled as a back-stage

area where Mickey can .. greet guests in high theat AAAA (FP)

Fantasyland Railroad Statio. entrance is to the left of the Fe. Stage. This will usually get you ɒ ᴋ to Main Street USA much quicker than walking, if there isn't a serious queue. However, if the queue is long avoid it, as only limited places on the train are freed by a limited amount of people hopping off at this stop.

Now, all the attractions so far are relatively faithful copies of Disney rides in other parks, but the next is a true *Disneyland Paris* original.

Alice's Curious Labyrinth: An interactive maze leading up to the Queen of Hearts' castle, this seems to have almost universal appeal for children up to about 12. There is a range of *Alice in Wonderland* tricks and motifs all along the way, including amusing signage, squirting fountains (kids *really* gravitate towards these, trying to catch the water as it 'jumps' from bush to bush), an encounter with the hookah-smoking Caterpillar and several scrapes with the Queen of Hearts and her guards (in various audio-animatronic guises). It is gentle stuff but keeps youngsters (and their parents) amused for a good 15–20mins and is an ideal place to visit when waits at Peter Pan and Dumbo hit an hour. AAA

Passing further along and under the railway bridge brings you to the little area right at the back of Fantasyland that gets overlooked by some (though it can be closed at quieter times of the year). But, if you have young children this is somewhere you won't want to miss, both for the instant kiddie appeal and the shorter queues. Both rides are copies from the *Disneyland Park* in California, but they possess a timeless charm for children.

Le Pays des Contes de Fées: This is a gentle boat ride into a fairytale world, with miniature depictions of stories like *Snow White, Peter and the Wolf, The Wizard of Oz, Beauty and the Beast* and *The Little Mermaid.* For the Aladdin

Peter Pan's Flight

section, your boat is 'swallowed up' by the giant lion's-mouth cave from the story, which can be a little daunting for the youngest passengers, but the whole thing proceeds at barely walking pace, so you have plenty of time to ease any apprehensions. AAA

> ### ✈ BRITTIP
>
> If you are at Le Pays des Contes de Fées out of peak periods, the boat ride is usually a walk-on attraction and has the great benefit for youngsters of being able to take them straight back on for another go. Again, be aware it may only be open during high season.

Casey Jr – le Petit Train du Cirque: Another guaranteed hit for the under 8 brigade. In reality, it is a fairly tame, junior-sized coaster, themed in eye-catching style after the circus train in Dumbo. Some of the cars are designed like animal cages, others are open and, of course, 2 can sit up front in the 'engine'. It glides along for some 5mins, encountering a couple of mild dips and gentle bends, but it gives just the right illusion of excitement to those of the requisite age (and any nervous parents!). AAA (TTTT for under 5s)

As you exit this 2-ride mini-land, you pass the disused Les Pirouettes Du Vieux Moulin, a big-wheel type ride that proved unworkable with even moderate queues and that has quietly been abandoned. It still looks good in non-working mode but sadly that is all you get from it.

Mad Hatter's Tea Cups: Another standard fairground ride, this has been given a bit of *Alice in Wonderland* top-spin to make it seem more than it actually is. Kids all seem to love the chance to ride in these manically whirling cups, which have a wheel to make them spin counter to the main rotation (uurgghhh! we say). We have to admit, going round in never-decreasing circles (or so it feels) was never our 'cup of tea' at all, but it remains a seriously popular ride, so it is best to do this one early in the day or later in the evening. TTT

Continuing our clockwise tour of Fantasyland brings you next to one of Disney's signature rides.

Mad Hatter's Tea Cups

THE DISNEYLAND PARK

'it's a small world'

'it's a small world': Designed under the direction of Walt himself for the New York World Fair in 1964, this ride has stood the test of time amazingly well for children under 8 and remains a big hit. The exterior façade is one of the most eye-catching in the park, with all manner of moving and static elements that add up to a wonderfully artistic collage. Inside, all it really consists of is a slow-moving boat ride through a colourful series of scenes featuring audio-animatronic dolls singing and dancing in various national-themed displays, from Britain to Brazil and Africa to the Arctic. It has an insidiously catchy theme tune (we challenge you NOT to be humming it when you exit!) and an imaginative winter wonderland final scene, but otherwise it just highlights the clever way in which Disney's Imagineers can take a routine ride and give it a whole new style and appeal.

Once again, it proves that if you give it the right scale and a proportionate amount of detail (with a little sprinkle of Disney 'pixie dust'), the ordinary can become quite extraordinary. Many adults are captivated by the spirit and vivacity of this attraction, and it is one that bears multiple visits. Queues rarely top 20mins and move quite steadily, so this is a good ride at most times, but especially in the afternoon

(and when it's hot). It can get very busy after the main Parade, though, as many head straight here after the last float passes by. AAAA

Other entertainment: Another lively piece of street entertainment is the *Once Upon a Time Sleeping Beauty* song and dance show in the Castle Courtyard area (by the Sword in the Stone set-piece), which features Aurora and her Prince several times a day (NB: may be seasonal only). The most important recent addition here is the **Princesses Pavilion** (right next to 'it's a small world') where young girls can go to meet their heroines and have

Merlin l'Enchanteur

their photos taken in true Princess style. There are two Princesses 'in residence' at any time and the queue is well organised (if slow moving) to give everyone a chance for some time with the Disney icons. Beware of the **Villains** though; they like to walk around Fantasyland, too, and are quite happy to pester unsuspecting guests while roaming the park! **The Wonderful World of Alice and the Mad Hatter** then provides a photo opportunity with the characters at the table of the famous Tea Party celebration just in front of the Labyrinth. You can also meet **Rapunzel** from the film *Tangled*. She has her own display near the Dumbo ride and does not appear in the Pavilion.

Shopping: For gift ideas, the interlinked group in and around the Castle offer worthwhile browsing. Pick from **Merlin l'Enchanteur** (a clever 'rock-carved' boutique featuring fine crystal, glassware – hand-made while you watch – and porcelain statuettes), **La Boutique du Château** (a Christmas-orientated offering), **La Confiserie des Trois Fées** (a great sweet shop in the company of good fairies Flora, Fauna and Merryweather from *Sleeping Beauty*), and the epic **Sir Mickey's** (featuring cuddly toys, jewellery, glass and ceramics, plus children's clothes, toys and games).

Dining: When it comes to mealtimes, Fantasyland has a gourmet offering in **Auberge de Cendrillon**, with an elegant ballroom-type setting. Open for lunch 11.30am–4pm and dinner 5.30–9.30pm, it features a set menu with several choices. The set meal is a hefty €60 (€25 for 3–11s), but the big attraction here is the character interaction. Suzy and Perla's Fantasies features the two mice from *Cinderella* and a host of Disney princes and princesses, dancing and interacting with guests (reservations strongly advised, on 01 60 30 40 50, from any Disney hotel concierge desk or from City Hall). There is also an outdoor courtyard, **La Terrasse** (where Cinderella's carriage stands – a gift from *Walt Disney World* to *Disneyland Paris*).

The other 3 outlets are all counter-service and fill up quickly for lunch at even mildly busy times: **Au Chalet de la Marionnette**, which has a rear entrance opening into Adventureland, serves 3 set menus with either a double cheeseburger, chicken nuggets or roasted half chicken, plus a range of salads and desserts; the stylish **Toad Hall Restaurant**, modelled in mock English country house style, à la *Wind in the Willows*, serving surprisingly good fish and chips, chicken burgers, salads and ice creams (set menus €9.95–11.95); and **Pizzeria Bella Notte**, an Italian diner modelled on *Lady and the Tramp*, offering basic pizza and pasta (€6.95–8.95).

BRITTIP

Of all the counter-service restaurants in busy Fantasyland, the Pizzeria Bella Notte is likely to have the shortest queues, as it is slightly off the beaten track.

More venues for a snack, ice cream or drink include **March Hare Refreshments**, **The Old Mill** and **Fantasia Gelati**.

Discoveryland

When the Imagineers set about designing the park's fifth and final 'land', their challenge was to come up with a new variant on a fairly well-worn theme. In both Anaheim and Orlando, this area had been developed as Tomorrowland, an unabashed attempt to predict and present the future in an amusing way. There is a mock retro styling about the previous examples, but that was felt to be an over-used idea when it came to *Disneyland Paris* and the call went out for something new. So, the Imagineers studied their European literature and came up with a new motif, that of a future world inspired by technology derived from historical luminaries such as Leonardo da Vinci and Jules Verne. This helped determine the overall look and feel of Discoveryland (a new title too, as Tomorrowland was felt to be too narrow a definition), hence the styling is a kind of 'antique' future, with much of the architecture borrowing heavily from Verne's 19th-century images of the future.

The two principal icons – Space Mountain: Mission 2 and the Café Hypérion – are magnificent re-creations of Vernean visions and help to create a visual stimulus that is both bold and exciting (can you tell we quite like this area!). The fanciful exterior of Space Mountain is one of the greatest examples of the ride designer's art because so much of it is totally unnecessary to the ride itself; it is purely and simply a statement of style that epitomises the creativity inherent in a Disney theme park. And the rides are pretty good, too!

BRITTIP

If you don't visit Space Mountain early in the day and can't get a FastPass, return in early evening to beat the worst of the queues.

Space Mountain: Mission 2: Completely re-themed and revamped in 2005, this breathtaking blast of a ride borrows from the Verne novel *From the Earth to the Moon* and gives it a contemporary twist. Whereas the original giant cannon Columbiad (of the Baltimore Gun Club) blasted riders to the Moon, now the over-sized gun barrel has been super-charged to send its vehicles much deeper into space, to discover the secrets of the universe! (Actually, the main ride is exactly the same, but the new theming is convincing.) You queue up through the heart of the ride itself before you reach your vehicle, which is 'loaded' into Columbiad. The dry ice flows, the music rolls, the lights pulsate and then … Pow! You are off at gravity-defying speed to explore outer space, dodging close encounters with meteorites and other cosmic phenomena, looping the loop, corkscrewing twice past thundering comets and evading an exploding supernova into 'a new dimension' as the unexpected climax to this 3-minute whizz. The high-tech light show alone is worth seeing and, if the description sounds disturbing,

don't let it put you off. This is one of the smoothest coasters you will ride and it is a big-time thrill. It is also a FastPass ride, which is vital for peak periods as the crowds flock here from early on. Souvenir photos are also available. Restrictions: 1.32m/4ft 3in. TTTTT (FP)

Les Mystères du Nautilus: As you exit Space Mountain, you encounter another *Disneyland Paris* original, a clever walk-through version of Captain Nemo's famous submarine. The realism as you go down 'underground' on a circular steel staircase is all-encompassing, bringing you into the Nautilus itself and a self-guided tour of this amazing Verne creation. Take your time to peer into all the nooks and crannies and admire the intricate detail, and sit for a moment at one of the big, circular portholes. Is that a giant squid moving in, too close…? You'll have to check it out for yourself! Children under 7 must be accompanied by an adult (11.30am–5.30pm only). AAA

Orbitron – Machines Volantes: Next door is this similarly eye-catching ride, which is really only a jazzed-up version of the Dumbo ride, spinning and climbing in regulation fashion as the front-seat pilot takes the controls. The clever circulation of the accompanying planets really makes this ride, however, giving it the look of something more intricate, and it is another one that is fun just to watch. However, while queues might *look* small for this attraction, it is actually a slow-going process and waits of 1 hour or more are not uncommon. TT (TTTTT for under 8s)

Star Tours: Behind Space Mountain is the impressive futuristic façade of Disney's collaboration with *Star Wars* director George Lucas. The queuing area alone is something of a masterpiece, as you are drawn into the make-believe world of squabbling 'droids C-3PO and R-2D2 as they prepare your Star Speeder for the light-speed trip to Endor. This is a faithful transplant of the classic first versions of the Star Tours attractions in *Disneyland California* and *Disney's*

Les Mystères du Nautilus

Hollywood Studios in Orlando, with the exception that the commentary provided by your robot pilot is in French. The ride itself, though, is a 24-carat thrill, as the realistic Speeders load and lift off for outer space, where various mishaps create a series of adventures. This was the bee's knees when it made its debut in Anaheim in 1987 and is still a magical experience for Disney newcomers (although those familiar with the ride from elsewhere may feel it is a little humdrum by now). Both US versions have since been up-dated with a new 3-D Star Tours experience, but there is no sign of a similar makeover for *Disneyland Paris* anytime soon. It is also a FastPass ride, though, which is handy as you can easily spend 45mins or more here at peak periods. However, if FastPass is no longer available for the day, try to ride in the last hour of the day when this part of the park tends to be quieter. There's no height restriction but those with bad backs/necks ought to pass it by, as should mothers-to-be. It's probably too intense for under 4s, too. TTTT (FP)

Space Mountain: Mission 2

The exit to Star Tours used to bring you into an amusing area of interactive games, L'Astroport Services Interstellaires, but sadly these have been scrapped in favour of some fairly standard (and rather dismal by comparison) video arcade fare, which you need to negotiate on your way out. Behind Star Tours is **Discoveryland Railroad Station**, but this is a good one to miss at busy times as it is second only to the Main Street station for drawing long, slow-moving queues.

BRITTIP

Head for Discoveryland first and you can ride either Space Mountain or Star Tours without much of a queue and pick up a FastPass for the other. The new Space Mountain: Mission 2 draws heavy crowds throughout the main part of the day.

Captain EO: or the return of a Disney classic. Captain EO opened in Paris on the first day of the park's official opening, 12 April 1992, but it closed after only a 6-year run to make way for 'Honey, I shrunk the Audience'. However, in June 2010, the 3-D Disney classic starring Michael Jackson as Captain EO returned to the park to battle one more time. The show starts in the pre-show waiting area where multiple TV screens show a short 'making-of' film. See how the special effects were created along with the impressive sets and how the dancers trained. The doors to the theatre then open and, once seated inside, you can pop on your 3-D glasses and get ready

THE DISNEYLAND PARK

for a classic musical Science Fiction adventure with Michael Jackson.

Now digitally remastered and sound enhanced, it is a 17min romp through space as Captain EO and his band of ragtag renegades set out to save the universe by bringing a special gift to the evil Supreme Leader: the key to unlocking the 'beauty within'. Jackson's signature dancing and the show's *We Are Here To Change The World* message keep the tone upbeat, but some of the darker thematic elements may frighten young children. It's a visually thrilling trip down memory lane for Disney fans, though, and good ultimately conquers evil – naturally! The movie was directed by the great Francis Ford Coppola and produced by George Lucas. Alongside Michael Jackson was Anjelica Huston, who played the Supreme Leader. AAAA (FP)

Autopia: Another attraction you need to visit early on unless you want a LONG wait. Rather old-fashioned, this mock Grand Prix track – a 'futuristic Formula One circuit' – is purely for kids and sits a little awkwardly among the more sci-fi laden offerings. It is often closed for maintenance (and at off-peak times) and is notoriously slow to load, so queues can easily top an hour and move slowly. And, unless you are under 9, you're unlikely to get much of a thrill from these tame cars that run on well-defined tracks, even if they provide the illusion of driving. Children under 1.32m/4ft 3in need to be accompanied by an adult but you

Videopolis

are not missing much if you bypass this one. T (TTT for under 9s)

✓ **Buzz Lightyear's Laser Blast:** This wonderful interactive family ride appeals to all ages and can be quite addictive. Riders are 'recruited' into Buzz Lightyear's Space Ranger galaxy defence force and kids in particular will not want to miss this chance to join the great *Toy Story* character in his battle against evil Emperor Zurg.

BRITTIP

Not only will you find one of the nicest Hidden Mickey's (twice) on the Planet Pollostroutt in Buzz Lightyear, it also offers a glimpse of the past. Once you start your journey, look to the right, before see the first target, and you'll see Nine-Eye, a character used in Le Visionarium, the attraction that used to be in the building before the Laser Blast.

You ride into action against Zurg's villainous robot army – and shoot

(137)

THE DISNEYLAND PARK

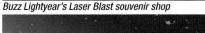
Buzz Lightyear's Laser Blast souvenir shop

them with laser cannons! You can spin your car from side to side and score points as you would in an arcade game, which ensures everyone tries it again to improve their score. Watch out for a gift shop and ride photo opportunity as you exit. It is extremely popular, though, and queues are long and slow-moving, so visit early in the day. FastPasses are often all gone by early afternoon. TTT (TTTTT for under 8s) (FP)

BRITTIP
The Buzz Lightyear robot targets have different values, with anything moving worth a higher score. Watch out for the large robot as you enter the first room. Turn your vehicle around and aim for the target on his hand – it's worth 10,000 points. Then aim for the middle of Zurg's chest and a direct hit will score 100,000pts. You'll need to hit Zurg several times, though, to reach that top score of 999,999 pts!

Videopolis/Cinéma Mickey: Sharing the impressive Café Hypérion building, Cinéma Mickey replaced the *Legend of the Lion King* stage show in 2009, with host Mickey Mouse formally introducing himself, in animation form, on the silver screen. Cartoons are shown on several big screens, from Disney classics, starring Mickey himself, to the Pixar shorts we know from the cinema today. Be careful when visiting with young children – they might want to see 'just one more' cartoon multiple times before they leave! NB: The impressive Lion King set is still visible on stage but is no longer used for any show. AA.

BRITTIP
Cinéma Mickey is the perfect spot for a mid-afternoon rest with a snack or a drink. Younger children especially appreciate the gentler experience of the classic cartoons as a break from the hectic pace of the parks.

Arcades Alpha and Beta: As a final word on the attractions, the inevitable video games also make an appearance here on either side of the lower entrance to Videopolis. Older children and young teens who need a break from the family shackles for a while can head to either of these (or the arcade inside the exit to Star Tours) and shoot up a T-Rex or play football or air hockey. Be warned, the games are not cheap – one token costs €2 and there is a one-token minimum per game. TT

Other entertainment: There is not much extra entertainment in Discoveryland, although **Star Wars** characters like Darth Vader, the Stormtroopers and even Chewbacca do make occasional appearances in high season. There is also a new statue of Wall-E and EVE between Space Mountain and the Cafe Hypérion building, near the Star Tours entrance. It's a perfect spot for an extra holiday picture with these two great characters in the background.

Shopping: There are 2 main gift shops here, the elaborate **Constellations**, (the shop you have to pass through after Buzz Lightyear's Laser Blast), with the usual range of souvenirs but a ceiling twinkling with a 'universe' of stars and **Star Traders**. This used to have a nice Star Wars section in the back but, unfortunately, it had to make space for other items. There are still some Star Wars items to be found, next to the Captain EO T-shirts and other goodies, but you'll find a greater range of Star Wars items in Disney Village.

Dining: When it comes to eating, the **Café Hypérion** is worth investigating even if you don't visit the counter-service diner, which serves very average cheeseburgers, chicken burgers and chicken nuggets. **Buzz Lightyear's Pizza Planet Restaurant** (easy to miss, but it's just to the right of Captain EO) is another buffet-style restaurant in the park. It includes a salad bar, pasta, pizzas, desserts and comes with unlimited cold drinks. Hot drinks are available at an extra cost. (€17.95 adult buffet, €8.95 for kids). There is a nice little play area in the restaurant that could keep the little ones quite happy for the duration of the meal (only for paying guests).

The **Rocket Café** at the back of Space Mountain offers some additional snacks and drinks that you can eat in relative peace and quiet at the back of the park near Space Mountain.

BRITTIP —
To prove Disney also thinks on a small scale as well as the large, check out the audio-animatronic pigeons (!) attached to the Hypérion airship at the entrance to Café Hypérion.

Parades, shows and tours

As if 5 'lands' weren't enough, you have several other sources of great entertainment along the way. Chief among these is the daily parade (or parades if you are here in high season or for a special event like Halloween or Christmas).

Disney's Magic On Parade: New for the park's 20th Anniversary (starting April 1, 2012), this takes over from the Once Upon A Dream Parade and will continue to be the daily highlight (except for Oct when it takes on a Halloween theme and the festive period from mid-Nov to early Jan when it becomes the Christmas Parade – see page 23). Highlighted by Sorcerer Mickey, this cavalcade of Disney film fantasy features a magical line-up of new floats, music, characters and dance, with some novel touches to provide fun interaction along the way.

BRITTIP —
Be aware people start staking out the best spots to watch the parades – along Main Street USA and around the Central Plaza – up to an hour in advance. There can also be a bit of push-and-shove as late-comers try to squeeze in.

The fairytale elements will enchant children and parents alike and ensure a dazzling celebration of favourites both past and present. If you have never caught a Disney parade, this is a must-see experience. Yes, the queues at many attractions get shorter while

the parade is run... to miss something...

BRITTIP —
For the main da... through Fantasyl... than elsewhere, while... Town Square in front of C... ...also a good place to wait as it is often overlooked and offers some shade when it's hot.

It starts in the Discovery Arcade corner of Town Square and continues up Main Street to the Central Plaza, where it turns right in front of the Castle Theatre Stage and moves into Fantasyland before exiting next to "it's a small world." The scale and elaboration of the huge floats has to be seen to be believed and it's a great chance for children to see a multitude of their favourite characters at close quarters. The music is memorable and the dancing amazingly energetic (especially in the heat of summer). The whole spectacle takes a good 25–30mins to pass by and you will take a LOT of photos – if you don't get sidetracked by watching children's faces around you. AAAAA

BRITTIP —
For Fantillusion, stake out a spot in front of the Castle, where you'll be able to see two out of the three stops, with the best view of the transforming dragon and the best photo opportunity with the Castle in the background.

Disney's Fantillusion Parade: This adds to the picture for the high summer and winter season evenings (usually after 10pm) and is equally stunning. It features an eye-popping cavalcade of Disney favourites in a high-tech setting of glittering lights and dazzling floats. The parade comes in 3 parts and unfolds with an almost balletic grace, first as Mickey himself brings the Gift of Light, then a darker section as the Disney villains threaten to take over (with some spectacular special effects as Jafar transforms into a serpent and Maleficent becomes the wicked dragon) and finally a joyful

Ready for the parade

conclusion as the glittering heroes and heroines, princes and princesses get together with Minnie to save the day.

It features a fabulous soundtrack by Bruce Healy and a seemingly endless fairytale pageant of shimmering, twinkling lights. The overall effect is so thrilling, even by Disney standards, that it is worth keeping the kids up to see it. The whole parade stops at various points for a few well-rehearsed routines from the costumed dancers, and it can take a good 30 minutes to pass by. But, whatever you do, don't miss this one! AAAAA+

THE DISNEYLAND PARK

BRITTIP

You can watch the Fantillusion Parade from the steps of the Railroad Station on Town Square, then, once it has passed, take one of the arcades up to Central Plaza to be ready for the fireworks while people are still watching the parade on Main Street!

Disney Princess souvenirs

Halloween Parade: This re-themed parade adds to the daily fun throughout Oct (check your park map for timings) and is another visual riot of creepy costumed capers, song and dance, with various characters joining the extravaganza. Here, the Disney villains have usurped the stage for a darker (but still fun) cavalcade of ghosts, goblins and witches, with some inventive, skeleton-inspired touches. AAAA

It is worth taking a mental step back from all the clever artistry of the floats to appreciate the non-stop energy and quality of the many dancers in the parades, who keep up their efforts for every second of every performance, day in, day out. It takes immense dedication, but they also have a lot of fun and get a real kick out of the reaction they get from their audience – especially the kids. So don't hesitate to smile and wave back, as they deserve all the encouragement and appreciation you can muster.

BRITTIP

The best place from which to watch the nightly fireworks is in front of the Castle or at the end of Main Street USA. The show is choreographed with, and symmetrically around, the château and the visual effect is stunning.

Mickey's Magical Celebration: This one-off nightly element was introduced on the Central Plaza Stage for the Magical Moments Festival in 2011, with Mickey joining forces with the Genie from Aladdin and the Fairy Godmother from Cinderella to become the Sorcerer's Apprentice from *Fantasia*. To celebrate his magical skills, Mickey also called on Merlin, the princesses and their princes to dance on the big stage, with some special pyrotechnic effects. However, the Central Plaza Stage is likely to be removed as part of the new night-time spectacular, Disney Dreams! (see below).

Disney Dreams!: Every day there is now a whole new nightly special effects finale, in honour of the 20th

Anniversary. Unique to *Disneyland Paris*, it features a variety of superbly colourful fireworks (colour is a big key for this show), lasers, water fountains and spray effects, all brilliantly arranged with additional lighting on and around Sleeping Beauty Castle and choreographed to a wonderfully evocative musical soundtrack. It begins with Peter Pan's shadow playing tricks and carrying guests off on a 15min fantasy of classic Disney dreams and magic, featuring literally thousands of lights and enormous fountains (all newly built in and around the Castle). The pyrotechnics burst above the park with almost balletic grace (and there is more emphasis on light than sound with the park's fireworks, in deference to the neighbours), while the lasers add even more layers of colour and the Dreams conclude with a burst of visual effects that transform the look of the Castle. It is a genuinely jaw-dropping experience, using a whole array of unique effects, all new to *Disneyland Paris*, so there should be no trying to sneak off before the end! Be warned, however, the scale of the fireworks can still scare young children.

There's more!

Want to learn more about the history of the *Disneyland Park*? Sign up for a Guided Tour at City Hall early

The Jungle Book characters on parade

in the day (subject to availability; maximum 25 people) and you can take a walking tour in the company of a highly knowledgeable Cast Member who will show you what makes the theme park tick. At €15 adults (with 2 paying adults; a single adult will pay €20) and free for under 12s, the tours lasts 2hrs and will give you extra, in-depth insight into the creation of this magnificent entertainment venue.

If you have always wanted a private tour, Disney's **VIP Tour** offers groups of up to 10 the chance to book a 2-park tour, with, priority seating at shows and parades and assistance with dining reservations at the restaurant of your choice. At €550 (regardless of party size) this isn't a budget option,

Fantillusion

The Disneyland Park: 20 years in the making

Disneyland Paris is celebrating its 20th year in 2012, a young park, but with enough history to fill a book (or two!). Here are some of the highlights from the resort's history.

Mid 1980s: The Disney Company is looking at the European market to build a Disney park.

1984: Robert Fitzpatrick was appointed to become the Euro Disney president.

1985: December 18, a first letter of agreement was signed by Michael Eisner, then the Disney CEO.

1987: Marne la Vallee, near Paris, was picked to become the new home for Euro Disney. Paris was up against Spain's Costa del Sol, which had better weather, but it was the massive Paris population and demographic location that won the day.

1988: Construction began in August.

1990: In December the preview centre 'Espace Euro Disney' opened to the general public. Here guests could see what resort would look like.

1991: Disney Casting Centre opened in September, looking for 14,500 employees to operate the park and the hotels.

12 April 1992: Euro Disney opened as planned with mixed result as 'only' 50,000 people turned up for opening day. The main reason could have been the RER strike that day and a warning by the media to stay away from a first day over-crowded park.

30 July 1993: Indiana Jones and the Temple of Peril opened for its first official ride.

1994: Euro Disney changed to Euro Disneyland Paris but, before the end of the year, changed to just Disneyland Paris. Both Le Pays de Contes de Fées (Storybook Land Canal Boats) and Casey Jr – Le Petit Train du Cirque (Casey Jr. Circus Train) opened.

1 June 1995: The indoor roller coaster 'Space Mountain De La Terre à la Lune' opened to the public.

9 September 1996: A disastrous day as a fire destroyed a big part of the Sequoia Lodge hotel.

1999: Disney Village expanded with the Rainforest Café and the popular McDonald's.

28 March 1999: Honey, I Shrunk the Audience replaced Michael Jackson's Captain EO.

26 December 1999: A big storm damaged a lot of the Davy Crockett Ranch, the new Crescend'O tent in the Disney Village and even forced Disney to close the park for a day.

16 March 2002: The official opening of the *Walt Disney Studios*. No longer a one-park set-up, another name change took place as the resort was now known as Disneyland Resort Paris and the original park became the *Disneyland Park* (English) or Parc Disneyland (French).

5 July 2003: The Fantillusion parade came to Paris.

2004: The fantastic The Lion King show celebrated its first performance in Discoveryland.

9 April 2005: Space Mountain: Mission 2 opened to the public with new music and special effects (but on the same track layout).

8 April 2006: Buzz Lightyear's Laser Blast opened.

9 June 2007: Crush's Coaster opened in the *Walt Disney Studios* as well as the children's attraction, Cars Quatre Roues Rallye (Cars Race Rally).

22 December 2007: Opening day for the fantastic thrill ride The Twilight Zone Tower of Terror.

22 March 2008: Stitch Live! debuted in the Studios.

2009: Disneyland Resort Paris dropped 'resort' and became just Disneyland Paris.

12 June 2010: Captain EO returned to Discoveryland.

17 August 2010: Three new attractions opened at the Studios – Toy Soldiers Parachute Drop, RC Racer and Slinky Dog Zig-Zag Spin.

12 April 2012: Happy 20th Birthday Celebration of *Disneyland Paris*.

2013/14: Ratatouille attraction in the *Walt Disney Studios*.

Ready for the next 20 years...

Andy De Maertelaere

The Disneyland Park with children

Here is a rough guide to the rides that appeal to different age groups. Obviously, ch[...] in their likes and dislikes but, as a general rule, you can be fairly sure the following w[...] to the ages concerned (also taking into account the height restrictions):

Under 5s

Disneyland Railroad, Main Street Vehicles, Thunder Mesa Riverboats, Pocahontas Indian Villa[...]age des Pirates (Pirates' Beach) play area, La Cabane des Robinson, Blanche-Neige et les Sept Na[...]s (Snow White), Pinocchio's Fantastic Journey, Le Carrousel de Lancelot, Peter Pan's Flight, Dumbo, 'it's a small world', Le Pays des Contes de Fées, Casey Jr, Alice's Curious Labyrinth, Buzz Lightyear's Laser Blast, Orbitron (not recommended for babies), Autopia, Les Mystères du Nautilus, Cinéma Mickey, Disney Magic On Parade, Princesses Pavilion.

6–8s

All the above, plus Phantom Manor (with parental discretion), Fort Comstock, Rustler Roundup Shootin' Gallery, Big Thunder Mountain, Adventure Isle, The Tarzan Encounter, Pirates of the Caribbean, Le Passage Enchanté d'Aladdin, La Tanière du Dragon, Mad Hatter's Tea Cups, Star Tours, Captain EO.

9–12s

Phantom Manor, Fort Comstock, Rustler Roundup Shootin' Gallery, Big Thunder Mountain, The Tarzan Encounter, Pirates of the Caribbean, Adventure Isle, Indiana Jones and the Temple of Peril, Peter Pan's Flight, Mad Hatter's Tea Cups, Alice's Curious Labyrinth, Arcades Alpha and Beta, Buzz Lightyear's Laser Blast, Orbitron, Space Mountain: Mission 2, Les Mystères du Nautilus, Captain EO, Star Tours.

Over 12s

Phantom Manor, Big Thunder Mountain, Rustler Roundup Shootin' Gallery, The Tarzan Encounter, Pirates of the Caribbean, Adventure Isle, Indiana Jones and the Temple of Peril, Mad Hatter's Tea Cups, Arcades Alpha and Beta, Buzz Lightyear's Laser Blast, Orbitron, Space Mountain: Mission 2, Captain EO, Star Tours.

but the chance to spend 4hrs getting tips, enjoying priority access to some rides, and asking questions about the parks and attractions could prove a magical experience indeed!

BRITTIP
Andy de Maertelaere points out the *Disneyland Park* tour goes inside the Star Tours building for a rare view of the simulator with the lights on – a real treat for Disney die-hards.

And that, folks, is the *Disneyland Park* in all its detailed splendour. Hopefully, after a day here (even when crowds are at their heaviest), you will agree with us in judging this to be a work of art in the business of having fun. Take time to acquaint yourself in advance with all that's here and you should be well prepared to get the most out of these immensely diverse attractions. As we advise for visiting any Disney park, try to take some time along the way to slow down and appreciate all the intricate detail that's involved.

BRITTIP
Unless you are particularly speedy in leaving the theme park at closing time, you might be better off taking the 15–20min walk back to the big hotels such as *Disney's Hotel Santa Fe, Cheyenne Hotel* and *Newport Bay Club*, as the crowds at the shuttle bus stop can mean yet another lengthy wait.

There is just so much packed into this theme park in particular, it would be a shame if you went home without seeing the history of Dapper Dan's barber shop, the nostalgia of the 2 arcades and the whimsy of restaurants like Pizzeria Bella Notte and the Blue Lagoon. It is a wonderfully complete and immersive environment that really does transport you a million miles from everyday life, so make sure you get the most out of it. But we can't stop here. There is a whole new park to explore yet. It's on to the *Walt Disney Studios…*!

7 The Walt Disney Studios

or Lights, Camera, Action!

While the original park is the grande dame of *Disneyland Paris,* the *Walt Disney Studios* is more the brash teenager – fun, lively, a bit raucous but also not yet fully polished or refined.

It is certainly a smaller development and a completely different entity to its older sibling, something that complements the first park but doesn't attempt to copy its formula of non-stop rides and 'pixie dust' magic. There are far fewer attractions, but what there are tend to be much bigger in scope and offer a contrasting experience. There's more emphasis on shows, plus the iconic Twilight Zone™ Tower of Terror, while the movie theming is extensive. The Studios keep on growing with new attractions, like the Toy Story Playland area that opened in August 2010, and the forthcoming unique Ratatouille attraction that will add significantly to the park's appeal. It used to be the case that you could do this park in half a day, but that is certainly no longer the case.

There is also a major difference in the geography and topography between them, as well as the newer park being almost half the size (although with scope to continue to grow). It consists of just 4 main areas (with Toy Story Playland being part of Toon Studios as one of them) and, aside from the imposing Tower, there are no great distinguishing features once you have passed through the entrance complex known as the Front Lot. It is an easy park to negotiate, though, and getting from one area to another for the various shows is a lot less problematic than it can be at the older park. You can walk from one end to the other in little more than 5mins and it positively invites you to step outside for lunch in *Disney Village* as it's all so simple.

Another notable difference is in the sound of the 2 parks. In the *Disneyland Park,* the accompanying music provides a background to all the fun and rides. In the *Walt Disney Studios,* the music is right up front, setting the scene and providing a soundtrack almost everywhere you go, most notably in the Backlot area. This dramatic musical accompaniment underscores the film-orientated nature of the Studios and adds an important extra layer to the overall theming.

Slinky Dog ZigZag Spin

Get with the theme

There are 17 out-and-out main attractions as well as the daily parade, on which to concentrate. Of course, being Disney, there are always some delightful extras along the way and here you have several other live elements, and a lot of character meet 'n' greets, adding to the fun factor.

The depth and elaboration of the theming, both architecturally and in the landscaping, is not on the same scale as the *Disneyland Park* either. Some say the Studios environment is actually lacking imagination. But, as one Cast Member explained, 'Well, our theme is a movie studio. What do you expect a movie studio to look like, apart from a collection of big, warehouse-like buildings?' Of course, there is more to it than that, but it is a pertinent point.

The whole idea is to surround you with the magic of the movies and, to that end, the collection of large studio soundstages that house most of the attractions can look functional by comparison with the neighbouring park. However, Disney's Imagineers are adding extra embellishments all the time and the internal effects are rarely short of spectacular (witness the lobby inside the Twilight Zone™ Tower of Terror!).

The one possible concern for parents with younger children is there isn't as much for them to do here as next door. There are 6 main kiddie rides (including those in the new area) and 3 shows that are primarily for them, while several attractions are not ideal for young eyes and ears (too loud, fast or scary). The daily parade, however, is a genuine source of family fun, and

The Walt Disney Studios at a glance

Location	Off Exit 14 of the A4 autoroute, proceed to the clearly signed car park; or turn right out of the Marne-la-Vallée RER and TGV station; or through the *Disney Village* if staying at a resort hotel
Size	27ha/67 acres in 4 areas
Hours	10am–7pm winter and spring off-peak weekdays; 9 or 10am–7pm all summer (Extra Magic Hours from 7 or 8am for Disney Hotel guests on select days)
Admission	Under 3 free; 3–11 €51 (1-Day/1-park Ticket), €62, €109, €130, €151 (1-, 2-, 3- and 4-Day Park Hopper), adults (12+) €57 (1-Day/1-park Ticket), €69, €122, €151, €179 (1-, 2- 3- and 4-Day Park Hopper); Annual Passports (per person): Fantasy €139, Dream €199, Classic €99. NB: All prices subject to annual increase: see disneylandparis.co.uk
Parking	€15
Pushchairs	€7.50 (Pushchair shop to left of Studio Photo, on right-hand side of entrance courtyard)
Wheelchairs	€7.50 (Pushchair shop)
Top Attractions	Twilight Zone™ Tower of Terror, Rock 'n' Roller Coaster starring Aerosmith, Moteurs… Action! Stunt Show Spectacular, Crush's Coaster, Studio Tram Tour, Cinémagique, RC Racer, Toy Soldiers Parachute Drop
Don't Miss	Disney Stars 'n' Cars Parade, Studio 1, Toy Story Playland
Hidden Costs	Meals — Burger, chips and coke €10.95; Buffet dining €24 for adults and €11.50 for kids (Restaurant des Stars); beer €3.99–5.90; wine €7; Kids' meal €5.70
	T-shirts — €15–35
	Souvenirs — €2.50–100+
	Sundries — Face-painting €8–12

the high level of character interaction helps to round out the experience. You should certainly find it easier to meet Mickey and Co here as there are several regular set-piece meeting points, plus a select programme of entertainment on the Production Courtyard stage and inside Studio 1, while there are frequent character appearances throughout the park.

BRITTIP

As with the *Disneyland Park*, you can take advantage of the Disney Shopping Service for purchases you make here. Instead of having to carry them around, they can be sent to *Disney Village* for you to pick up at the Disney Store from 6pm, or back to your hotel.

Staying dry

The other clever element of the Studios is that nearly all of the attractions are under cover, which is vital in winter and quite welcome in summer, too. With the exception of the Flying Carpets Over Agrabah, Cars Quatre Roues Rallye, and the new Toy Story Playland area, the attractions provide a much longer and more involving experience, too. Several of the shows last half an hour or more, which means you can spend longer doing fewer things than in the *Disneyland Park* (with less time spent queuing) but there should still be enough to keep you occupied for a full day (with the option to move between parks with the multi-day Park Hopper tickets – see page 101).

Another difference between the parks is the dining. While the *Disneyland Park* has a comprehensive mix of restaurants, cafés and snack bars, the *Walt Disney Studios* is limited to just 3 counter-service options and 1 buffet-style restaurant, plus a series of snack wagons (there will be a dramatic new restaurant when the Ratatouille attraction opens, though). With *Disney Village* just a 5min walk from the front gates, it is easy to argue you have plenty of choice (plus a chance to escape the hubbub), but we look

forward to the future development of this aspect of the park. At least one full-service restaurant is needed to provide a bit of breadth to the studio style (anyone who has eaten in the Sci Fi Dine-In Theater or the 50s Prime Time Diner at *Disney's Hollywood Studios* in Orlando will know what we mean). However, there are also fewer shopping opportunities in this park and you don't feel quite so much a target for the big sell.

Right on queue

One lingering concern about the park is its ability to handle the queues, especially around its big-draw attractions of The Twilight Zone™ Tower of Terror and Crush's Coaster. With fewer attractions but some hugely popular rides and shows, the park struggles at times to manage the crowds, as well as the capacity of some of the rides themselves. There are only 4 FastPass attractions and, while they are not always needed at quieter times of the year, this can also add to the congestion at peak times as FastPass distribution is not always predictable.

At park opening, the initial crowd heads for one of The Twilight Zone™ Tower of Terror, Crush's Coaster or Toy Story Playland. While the attractions are not immediately open, guests can head to them up to 30mins before the official opening time and queues are allowed to form in an orderly fashion, eliminating the old rope-drop rush.

Other rides that continue to draw big queues – like the Studio Tram Tour and Flying Carpets Over Agrabah – are now less pressured and the shows continue to have the ability to soak up large numbers at one time. Queues at these attractions only start to form when the rides themselves open.

Queuing for the big Stunt Show Spectacular has improved in recent years and the big arena also helps to manage the crowd flow. There is no need to arrive especially early, unless you want to sit in the centre of the arena (which does fill up first) as there are no bad seats.

Hollywood Boulevarde

Towards the end of the day you should be able to enjoy rides like Rock 'n' Roller Coaster and the Flying Carpets with very limited waits. However, since Toy Story Playland opened, the park does stay pretty busy until closing time, which wasn't always the case.

Enter, stage centre!

Okay, without any further preamble, let us introduce you to the *Walt Disney Studios…*

If you approach from the main car park, the Studios will be straight ahead of you as you come through the moving walkways. From *Disney Village*, bear left past the Gaumont Cinemas and the new World of Disney Store, or from the bus or train station, continue straight on, passing *Disney Village* on your left. The park is subdivided into 4 main areas, although there is little visual distinction between them, and your adventure starts as soon as you walk through the imposing gates.

The grand layout in front of you makes it clear what's in store – film adventure and lots of fun in the inimitable Mickey style. The 33m/108ft water tower edifice (based on the same structure at Burbank, California), topped by a large pair of mouse ears (we kid you not), is called… wait for it… the Earful Tower (!), and sets out the visual style in no uncertain terms, as well as providing a handy marker for the front of the park.

Talking tactics

Unlike the *Disneyland Park*, this is not somewhere you need to be right on opening time (unless you have youngsters who are keen to try out the new Toy Story Playland rides, much like Fantasyland in the older park). With so much of the entertainment centred on the big show times, such as the Stunt Show and Cinémagique, you can arrive in more leisurely style, head for the shows first and be reasonably sure you can get into most of them with only minimal queuing. With that said, if the lure of the Tower, Crush's Coaster or the 3 new Toy Story rides is especially strong, plan to be here by opening time – or be ready to stand in long queues!

BRITTIP
Although the shows have large capacities, it is still advisable to arrive 10mins early to benefit from being the first to be seated.

If you are after the thrills, your best plan is to start by going to either The Twilight Zone™ Tower of Terror or Crush's Coaster immediately upon park opening. If you have young children with you, visit Toy Story Playland or Cars Quatre Roues Rallye first, as the various kiddie rides are slow loading and draw long queues for much of the day. If you prefer a gentler start, make the Studio Tram Tour your first stop. Waiting times can top half an hour later on. If you then take in Armageddon and Rock 'n' Roller Coaster, you will have 3 (or 4) of the biggest crowd-pullers under your belt early on. Alternatively, if you have younger children, they will certainly want to ride the Flying Carpets Over Agrabah after visiting Cars, as this is another ride where slow-moving queues can build up.

Front Lot

Once through the turnstiles, you come into a lovely Spanish-style courtyard that marks the entrance to the first main area, the Front Lot

WALT DISNEY STUDIOS

Front Lot
1. *Walt Disney Studios* Store
2. Studio Photo
3. Disney Studio 1
4. Les Légendes d'Hollywood
5. Restaurant en Coulisse

Toon Studio
6. Art of Disney Animation
7. Animagique
8. Flying Carpets Over Agrabah
9. The Disney Animation Gallery
10. Crush's Coaster
11. Cars Quatre Roues Rallye (Cars Race Rally)

12. Ratatouille (opening 2013/14)

Toy Story Playland
13. Slinky Dog ZigZag Spin
14. RC Racer
15. Toy Soldiers Parachute Drop

Production Courtyard
16. Cinémagique
17. The Studio Tram Tour
18. Catastrophe Canyon
19. Stitch Live!
20. Playhouse Disney Live
21. Twilight Zone™ Tower of Terror
22. Restaurant des Stars
23. La Terrasse
24. Place des Stars

The Backlot
25. Armageddon: Special Effects
26. Rock 'n' Roller Coaster starring Aerosmith
27. Moteurs...Action! Stunt Show Spectacular
28. Le Café des Cascadeurs
29. Blockbuster Café
30. Rock Around The Shop

Place de Frères Lumières: This is the 'office' part of the theme park and houses the more functional elements such as pushchair and wheelchair hire, lost property, lost children centre, baby-care centre, first aid station, cash dispenser and currency exchange. You will also find the **Studio Services** here, for any queries about the park (like when and where to find the characters). Visitors with disabilities can also pick up a *Guide for Guests with Special Needs* if they haven't done so already and the Assisted Access Card, if required, which allows guests with a disability incompatible with waiting in the regular queue to wait in an alternate area (see page 28).

This area is an extremely elegant piece of design, with the central **Sorcerer Mickey fountain**, flanked by palm trees, providing a great photo opportunity. The left-hand side of the courtyard is taken up by the *Walt Disney Studios* **Store**, the theme park's biggest shop, while on the right is **Studio Photo**, for all your photographic requirements (although it is better to bring your own).

From 10–noon and 2.15–4pm, you can meet several **Disney characters** here (usually Goofy, Pluto, Minnie, Donald, Daisy and Chip 'n' Dale), and it is worth pausing to enjoy the classic 1930s-style architecture as the theme park transports you into the world of movies, Hollywood style.

BRITTIP
The Front Lot courtyard, **Place des Frères Lumières**, makes a good place to visit in early afternoon if the park is busy. Grab a drink or snack inside Disney Studio 1 and head out to enjoy the relaxing surroundings.

Disney Studio 1: You really get the full effect as you walk through these doors (remember to pick up a park map as you enter). It is almost an attraction in its own right, even if it is in many ways just a covered version of Main Street USA in the *Disneyland Park*. It is long, 35m/115ft wide and making it the second-

largest 'soundstage' in Europe (okay, it isn't actually a working facility, but the impression is pretty good). The overall effect is as if you have walked into the middle of a Hollywood film shoot, with all the paraphernalia of movie-making.

BRITTIP
You can get films processed in 2 hours at the Studio Photo in the Front Lot courtyard. It's not cheap, but you can check your prints while you still have a chance to retake them! Photo CDs are also available.

The film 'sets' are all unfinished and provide almost a kaleidoscopic montage of scenery in each direction, with a series of façades and hoardings, which change the perspective in a multitude of ways with the aid of some brilliant lighting effects. Down the left side is **Les Légendes d'Hollywood** store, while on the right flank is **Restaurant en Coulisse**.

BRITTIP
Restaurant en Coulisse gets pretty busy from noon–2pm but is ideal 3–4pm for a late lunch or early tea.

The shop is cleverly disguised behind no less than 6 different façades, giving the impression of a whole movie 'street' modelled on various Hollywood stores – both real and imagined – from the 1920s to 60s.

BRITTIP
One of our favourite 'hidden gems' in the Studios park is playing with the lighting effects inside Studio 1. Look for the 2 big lighting consoles, one in front of Club Swankadero (marked 'Illuminazione Produzione'), which changes the lighting on the Hollywood & Vine façade, and the other inside the Liki Tiki, which lights the jungle roof and starts a thunderstorm!

Designs that stand out include Last Chance Gas (a mock Route 66 petrol station), The Alexandria Theater (a classic Los Angeles 'movie palace') and The Gossip Column (a news and magazine stand) and, of course,

Waiting for opening

If you arrive half an hour before the official opening time, you will still be admitted through the main turnstiles of the *Walt Disney Studios*. This brings you into the Place de Frères Lumières courtyard in the Front Lot and you can then pass into Disney Studio 1. Once you pass through Studio 1, you can select the attraction that appeals to you most.

For example, if you want to ride Crush's Coaster first, you will be directed to queue in an outside area. About 15mins before opening, the covered queue area is opened to let people advance. Once it hits opening time, you will be able to enter the building itself. At Toy Story Playland, guests are stopped at the entrance of the area until park opening. Once the park officially opens, so will Toy Story Playland. Cast Members will guide the first guests into the land where they then can choose from one of the three attractions.

If you are looking for the thrills first, the highlight of The Twilight Zone™ Tower of Terror is straight ahead of you (it's hard to miss!). Turn left for the Backlot area and Rock 'n' Roller Coaster while, for Crush's Coaster and Toy Story Playland, go sharp right into Toon Studio. If you have young children, you should concentrate on this area and head first for Cars Quatre Roues Rallye, which quickly builds up some of the slowest-moving queues, and the Toy Story rides.

you can buy a range of film-related souvenirs as well as the usual Disney souvenirs. Also here is **Shutterbugs**, a fun photo studio that can put YOU in the Disney picture with various well-known characters (€16.50–25).

On the other side, the restaurant is a combination of another 6 imaginary 'sets', with the counter-service diner concealed behind such legendary establishments as **Schwab's Pharmacy** (a classic 1940s' American chemist's), the **Brown Derby** (the famous Hollywood restaurant in the shape of a bowler hat), **Club Swankadero** (an imaginary nightclub), the **Gunga Den** (a well-known bar) and the **Liki Tiki** (a wonderful thatched South Seas-themed bar).

BRITTIP
The Studio 1 area has a handy **Restaurant Reservations** kiosk, where you can book meals for later in the day at the full-service restaurants in *Disney Village* and the *Disneyland Park*. However, the kiosk isn't always open and, in that case, you need to visit **Studio Services** in the Front Lot for your reservations.

Here, the fare is French continental for breakfast and standard burger-style the rest of the day, with pizza, lasagne and salads as your alternatives. If

you haven't had breakfast, stop here for a set meal of orange juice, a hot drink, and a croissant (€5.50; 8–11am). For lunch or dinner, choose from 5 set menus (€9.95–11.95) including a burger with chips and a soft drink or double chicken burger or bacon cheeseburger with chips, cake and drink. Upgrade your soft drink to a beer for an additional €1.

There are actually 670 seats for dining here, so it absorbs a lot of people, and the upstairs terracing – 'Carmen's Veranda' (ouch!) – also provides a great view over the whole of Studio 1, as well as the best seats in the house for watching the hustle-bustle below.

BRITTIP
Check the Information Board as you exit Studio 1 to find out the waiting times at the attractions and which queues to avoid.

Toon Studio

Turn right as you exit the doors of Disney Studio 1 and you are immediately in the area of the park that caters mostly for younger children (it was Animation Courtyard until Crush's Coaster and the Cars Race Rally opened in 2007). As well as more chances to meet, photograph and get autographs from the characters, you

© DISNEY

The Magic of Disney Animation

have 2 genuine kiddie rides here, the most enchanting of the park's shows and the wildly popular thrill of Crush's Coaster, plus the all-round fun of the new Toy Story Playland.

The Magic of Disney Animation: The first big set-piece attraction, located under the giant Sorcerer's Apprentice hat, this is a 4-part adventure into the history, creation and magic of animated film. The first section concentrates on the history and is the least interesting for younger children. It is basically a pre-show area, with a series of exhibits around the room, showing how animation developed from its most basic into the art form that Walt Disney helped to pioneer. The highlight, amid several hands-on gadgets (like a Zoetrope and a Magic Lantern), is one of only 2 surviving multi-plane cameras, a breakthrough in animation developed by Walt in the 1930s.

BRITTIP
Check out the carpet in the post-show area of the Art of Disney Animation. Can you pick out a certain set of Mouse ears in the pattern…?!

As the doors close behind you, a large video screen comes to life and Walt pays tribute to the European pioneers

of animation, along with former Walt Disney Co chairman Roy Disney (Walt's nephew). Annoyingly for us, it is all dubbed in French (you would have thought one of the showings would be kept in English) with English subtitles, but it sets the stage for the 225-seat Disney Classics Theatre next. The doors underneath the screen open and you pass into the mini-cinema for 8 minutes of highlights from the Disney classics (including some recent Pixar hits) that are sure to keep everyone more than happy.

Stage 3 is another theatre-like auditorium, set up like an animator's office, where a part live and part film show brings Mushu from Mulan to life and explains how this dragon-character came into being (with an amusing voice-over from Eddie Murphy). The interaction between the live 'artist' and Mushu is wonderfully scripted and, although the on-stage part is in French, there are headphones to provide a full translation (watch out for the finale as the Murphy-dragon imagines himself as The Mushu of Nôtre Dame!).

You exit the theatre into a final room of 6 'animation stations', which give you the chance to try your hand at drawing, colouring or providing a voice or sound effects for various characters. It is great fun for children of 6 upwards, and the Animation Academy with a real artist is presented in both French and English. In all, it is a fascinating and thoroughly enjoyable look at the artistry of feature animation and the queues move steadily here, so you are rarely waiting long. AAAA

BRITTIP
Try to arrive a few minutes early for the Animagique show as the 1,100-seat theatre comes to life with a series of clever sound effects that ring and echo in delightful style around the auditorium before it begins.

Animagique: Opposite the Sorcerer's Apprentice hat, this is a unique live show featuring the innovative Czech art of 'Black Light' stagecraft and Japanese 'Bunraku' puppet manipulation. If that sounds a bit dry, prepare yourself for 25mins of pure Disney fun in the company of Mickey, Donald Duck and the cast of *Dumbo, Pinocchio, The Jungle Book* and *The Lion King.*

The story (partly in French and Donald Duck-ese!) sees Donald stuck for inspiration at the drawing board. Ignoring Mickey's warnings, he opens the Disney vault and unwittingly lets loose a host of animated characters who run riot on stage, with a big song-and-dance finale that will have you humming the catchy theme tune as you leave. Some excellent effects surprise you along the way (which we won't reveal) but be prepared for some extra fun, especially if you are in the first dozen or so rows. The high-tech show (involving digitally synchronised lighting, audio and machinery effects, in addition to the puppetry) is presented 6 to 7 times a day and show times are posted both outside and on the park maps. AAAA

BRITTIP
If you have children, try to sit in the central section of the theatre, no more than 10–12 rows back and you will enjoy one of the best special effects of Animagique.

Cars Quatre Roues Rallye (Cars Road Rally): Located opposite Animagique, this attraction borrows from the 2006 Disney-Pixar film *Cars*. It visits Radiator Springs, where Lightning McQueen is starring in a movie being filmed down in the canyon,

and you're invited to co-star. But be warned: you'll be doing your own stunts and spin-outs as they are all part of the action! In all honesty, this is just another variation on the basic spinning tea cups ride and it is a fairly short experience (barely 2mins), but it has great kiddie appeal, so you should head here early if your children will want to do it. The ride has that swing-'em-around motion (3 revolving platforms that then add an extra spin with each car) that pre-schoolers seem to love. The crowds do build up quickly here and it is a slow-loading ride, hence the queue is pretty slow moving. TT (TTTT under 7s)

Flying Carpets Over Agrabah: This children's ride, which is another variation on the Dumbo/Orbitron attractions of the *Disneyland Park*, can be found at the innermost end of Toon Studio. It has been transported with a slightly different theme from Orlando's *Magic Kingdom*. Here you line up (in a loosely themed area like a film 'green room', where actors prepare for their next scene) to take part in 'casting' for a role in a movie, with the Genie (from the 1992 Disney film *Aladdin*) as the director (in French and English). Once aboard your 4-person 'flying carpet', there are controls in the front seats to make it go up and down and in the rear seats to add a bit of tilt 'n' turn. In all honesty it is a fairly tame ride, but children under 10 always seem to get a thrill from it. However, the queues can build here through the middle of the day, so it is best to visit early on or wait until the last hour of the day. TT (TTTT for under 10s) (FP)

Flying Carpets Over Agrabah

Crush's Coaster: This is a breathtaking, high-speed journey along the 'East Australia Current' (or EAC) from the film *Finding Nemo*. The surfer-dude turtle, Crush, allows you to ride on his back as he plunges and swirls through a mock undersea world, full of inventive lighting and special effects, with a brief plunge outdoors before diving back inside again. You board your 'turtle shell' alongside a Sydney harbour fishing village (each shell holds 4 riders sitting in back-to-back pairs), where guests facing forward at the start soon find themselves spinning backwards (and the back seats become the front), dipping and swirling through the great bubbly blue. The ride includes a slower-paced dark section where you meet Nemo and Squirt in their undersea habitat (courtesy of some high-tech visual effects) before you are bumped into the main part of the ride, a wild and twisting spin both up and down the EAC before Crush guides you back to safer waters. It's righteous, dude!

The attraction will probably appeal to most of the family, although it may be too dynamic for under 6s (top speed is only 37mph/57kph but it feels faster with all the tight twists and turns). It is also something of a slow-loader, hence queues build up quickly and often remain at an hour-plus for much of the day. Try to do this early on, especially as it is NOT a FastPass ride. Restrictions: 107cm/3ft 5in. TTTT

BRITTIP

When you enter the minefield area on Crush's Coaster, have a good look at the big decoration painting and see if you can spot the Hidden Mickey made out of 3 mines (Hint – it is only visible for those riders facing forwards at that point).

Toy Story Playland

This 'land within a land' opened in August 2010 and took the Studios to the next level in entertainment terms. While most of the Studios merely reflect a backstage film theme, Toy Story Playland brought the theming firmly into the park. It starts with the giant talking Buzz Lightyear who greets guests at the entrance. Once you enter, you see all kinds of toy-style decorations – over-sized toys, building blocks and even benches looking like Scalextric. There are a couple of neat photo opportunities here – a talking Rex the dinosaur, a Toy Box and the Parachute background. Position yourself just right and it will look as if you are really parachuting! The key part of this area is the 3 attractions, and, while Toy Story Playland appeals to children, some rides might be a little scary for the youngest visitors.

Toy Soldiers Parachute Drop: Joining a mission with the Army Men from Andy's bedroom, young guests will get the chance to be lifted up the 25m/82ft tower and then 'parachute' down again. This tower ride (on 6 lines for 2 riders each) offers quite an exhilarating drop and bounce for children 6–12, as well as providing a good view of the park at the same time. Queues here build up VERY fast, though, and will rarely be under an hour, but the single-rider line does help to speed things up if your child doesn't mind riding by themselves. Restrictions: 0.81m/2ft 8in, TTT (TTTTT, under 12s)

Slinky Dog Zigzag Spin: Taking another leaf from standard fairground rides and giving them a heavy Disney overlay is this circular spinning ride. While Woody's classic slinky toy friend chases his tail (around a huge fire hydrant!), riders will revolve around and up and down on a fairly lively round track. Like the Mad Hatter's Tea Party in the *Disneyland Park*, don't expect anything startling, but children are sure to enjoy this pooch-with-attitude. However, while it might not have the long queues of the Parachute Drop, it is another slow-loader and wait times soon get up to an hour. TT (TTTT under 12s)

RC Racer: This is the one element that may scare a few young 'uns – and thrill their teenage siblings! Riders board a version of the Remote Control Racing Car (again from Andy's bedroom) and zoom backwards and forwards on a big U-shaped track, which eventually takes them up the full 35m/114ft height for 2mins of high-speed hither and thither. The technical terminology for this kind of ride is a 'half-pipe' but it is a whole lot of fun. The ride time might appear short but for some stomachs it's quite long enough! Again, there is a single rider line that can save valuable time with queuing. Although riding the attraction might be the most important aspect, do take time to look at the fantastic queue area, with the over-sized Scalextric track right under your feet. Restrictions: 1.21m/4ft. TTT (TTTTT+ under 12s)

Ratatouille Attraction: This new dark ride attraction is planned for a 2013/14 opening. It will take guests into the world of Remy, the haute cuisine-inspired rat from the Oscar-winning 2007 film *Ratatouille*, with everyone being shrunk to rodent size. Passing through the kitchens, back-streets and, yes, even the sewers of the film's Paris setting, visitors get to travel with Remy on his adventurous journey to become a chef (with the help of his hapless human companion, Alfredo Linguini). As good as the story is likely to be (and we expect it to be an amazing adventure), the real scene-stealer will be the new technology Disney are wheeling out for this ride, a novel trackless system coupled with state-of-the-art digital film projectors using domed screens to create a totally immersive, 3-D environment. Riders will feel like they are in the movie and the latest special effects should add an extra layer of ride fun. The one drawback is the unknown timescale for the ride's opening with so much technical equipment to install. AAAAA+ (expected)

Toon Studio Plaza: Just behind Crush's Coaster and in front of the Toy Story Playland area is this small but fun photo opportunity location. A colourful display is used as a background for meet 'n' greet with some of Disney's newest characters. It's also the place where you are most likely to see Mickey Mouse appear when he is in the Studios.

Other entertainment: As you exit Animagique, watch out for the **New Stars**, characters from the latest Disney films, as they often appear in the Courtyard in front of the Art of Animation (and in the specially designed scenery of Toon Studio Plaza). **Buzz Lightyear** (or Buzz L'Eclair, as is he known in France) is often to be found here, too. For another great photo opportunity, visit the **Monsters Inc** display between Studio 1 and Animagique – and see how loud you can be on the Scream Monitors. Mike and Sulley, from the *Monsters, Inc* film, also appear here for photo opportunities periodically. **The Green Army Men's Meet, Greet & Play** takes place in Toy Story Playland, where the Soldiers will come out and drill children keen to become their newest recruits (high season only).

> ⟨flag⟩ **BRITTIP**
>
> As you walk out of Studio 1, be sure to check the Information Board right in front of you for all the show and wait times for the various attractions – a great help when planning your *Walt Disney Studios* day.

Shopping: There are only a couple of shopping options, the best being **The Disney Animation Gallery** at the exit of the Art of Disney Animation (inside the giant Sorcerer's Apprentice hat). It offers a rather upmarket range of souvenirs and serious collectables – figurines, statues, books and genuine Disney film cels – for those with a fascination for the true art of Disney. Toy Story Playland has its own little shop, **The Barrel of Monkeys**, filled with Toy Story-related goodies and then there is a small kiosk in the Courtyard area with a small selection of general Disney items.

Dining: For a snack in this area, the **Studio Catering Co.** has 2 outlets, themed like truck trailers, offering hot dogs, burgers, fish and chips, club sandwiches, popcorn, ice cream, doughnuts, muffins and cookies, as well as drinks.

Twilight Zone™ Tower of Terror

Production Courtyard

Retracing your steps brings you into the Production Courtyard area. This middle section offers 5 main attractions, including Playhouse Disney – Live on Stage.

The Twilight Zone™ Tower of Terror: Enter a new dimension of sight, sound and high-speed, hair-raising fear! The Hollywood Tower Hotel's glamorous heyday lies dormant beneath layers of dust and abandonment, hinting at the tragedy that befell its last visitors – and now awaits you! Pass through the lobby into a dimly lit library, where Rod Serling (the original TV programme host) warns of the Tower's terrible past and then invites you to step aboard a maintenance service elevator heading directly to...The Twilight Zone. Sounds from the boiler room prompt you forward through grim and grimy surroundings until you finally reach the elevator and, once inside, your fate is sealed.

The remainder of the ride is a thrill-seeker's dream, with astonishing special effects and moments of sensory deprivation that will leave you shaking – and eager for a second ride! And do ride again. With a drop-and-rise sequence that leaves you breathless, you may well miss some of the clever details en route, so you will need several visits to take it all in. Unmissable both visually and as an attraction, the Tower represents Disney Imagineering at its finest. Most importantly, it is also a FastPass ride, but with the ride's popularity it is not unusual for FastPasses to run out by early afternoon. Restrictions: 102cm/3ft 4in. TTTTT (FP)

BRITTIP
The queue is so spectacular even non-riders should do it just to enjoy the theming. They are then free to duck out of the ride without boarding.

Cinémagique: One of the park's undoubted highlights and a real high achievement of imagination, this half-hour film show, exclusive to *Disneyland Paris*, starts out superficially as a tribute to the history of both European and American cinema, but soon takes an unexpected dramatic turn. It ends up as a hilarious series of scenes featuring comedian Martin Short as a hapless time traveller moving through a range of cinematic genres linked by a wonderful love-interest storyline.

BRITTIP
Waiting in the holding pens for Cinémagique is fairly dull, but the large capacity of the theatre ensures everyone usually gets in, while you can often wait until the last minute and still find a seat. There are up to 6 shows a day in high season, and it is quite likely you'll want to see this more than once.

The show includes numerous funny scene shifts (the cowboy shoot-out scenario is inspired) and a couple of eye-popping special effects, which we won't reveal but that add hugely to the fun (hint: an umbrella might be a good idea!). French actress Julie Delpy is the co-star and the show takes place inside

A Towering achievement

The original art deco-style Tower of Terror opened in Orlando in 1994, themed as an episode of the popular television show, *The Twilight Zone* (1959–64). The show's host, Rod Serling, recounts that fateful night when a bolt of lightning struck the Hollywood Tower Hotel – a glamorous Hollywood Hills retreat catering to the brightest stars of the late 1930s – propelling 5 unsuspecting guests into the Fifth Dimension, never to be heard from again. But their ghostly figures haunt the hallways, and the door they passed through into the unknown has opened again. This time, *you* will step through it…!

California's Tower opened in 2004, based on the same storyline, although the façade is *pueblo*-deco and the setting is downtown Hollywood. The ride is essentially the same, but Orlando's ride vehicles utilise a continuous circular loop technology, with vehicles moving horizontally into a separate drop shaft, and guests loading and unloading in separate locations, while the versions in California, Tokyo and now Paris all feature independent drop shafts, with ride vehicles that move horizontally back into the shaft before making their hair-raising journey.

The *Disneyland Paris* Tower, opened in early 2008, continues the Twilight Zone theme, again in a late 1930s *pueblo*-deco style setting. Orlando's Fifth Dimension element (ghostly apparitions appearing before the vehicle enters the drop shaft) is replaced by a mysterious-looking glass effect, in which riders see their own reflections before their image morphs into ghostly figures.

The version in the *Disneyland TokyoSea Park* changes the storyline completely. This gothic-style edifice is known as Hotel Hightower and the setting is New York in the late 1890s. The hotel's owner, Harrison Hightower III, collector of rare artefacts, has unwittingly transported Shiriki Utundy, protector spirit of the tribal Mtundu village, into the hotel, where the idol takes revenge, plunging Harrison to his death inside an elevator. But his body has never been found. Years later, in an effort to save the abandoned hotel, guided tours are being offered, but the curse – and the mystery – persist.

The Tower of Terror is arguably Disney's most recognisable ride worldwide. The artistry that went into creating a totally convincing environment, from Rod Serling's seamless delivery (Serling himself died in 1975, at the age of 50, and his presentation was achieved by the laborious process of splicing together segments from the TV show, then adding a voice-over where needed) to the placement of props from famous episodes, the Tower's eerie silence, broken only by screams coming from the elevator shaft, will convince you to…Fear Every Drop! The one drawback here in *Disneyland Paris*? The attraction has a French voice-over with English subtitles.

a beautiful 1,100-seat theatre with an art deco theme harking back to classic 1930s' Hollywood movie palaces.

BRITTIP

In Cinémagique, the Western sequence involving different snippets from *The Magnificent Seven, Once Upon a Time in the West, The Wild Bunch, Tombstone* and *The Good, The Bad and The Ugly* is an absolute *tour de force* and worth going in to see on its own.

It probably won't hold the attention of younger children (say, under 4s) for the full 30mins, but there is enough amusing on-screen action to keep older children entertained. Adults will enjoy the clever interweaving of scenes, with Short popping up in all

manner of unlikely but well-known film scenarios. AAAAA

Studio Tram Tour: This large-scale, 15min ride has been adapted from *Disney's Hollywood Studios* in Orlando and enhanced with several

Studio Tram Tour

DISNEY ©

new elements, making it a must-see attraction. Cleverly arranged with an English-French soundtrack, it is a tour of heavyweight proportions.

The tram takes you on a behind-the-scenes look at a movie studio, learning some tricks of the film trade, such as location sets, props and special effects. Each tram has a video screen with a full commentary (the English version supplied by a wonderfully laconic Jeremy Irons) that points out the key areas along the way. You pass a whole array of film props and scenery (notably the imposing Waterfall City façade from the *Dinotopia* mini-series) before entering the tour highlight, Catastrophe Canyon.

◀🇬🇧▶ BRIT TIP

Young children may be scared by the loud and dramatic special effects in the Studio Tram Tour. An explanation and reassurance that it's safe and just a film trick is a good idea. The left-hand side of the tram may also get a little (?!) wet.

Catastrophe Canyon: Here, you are supposed to get a dry-run version of an elaborate special effects set-up but the director mistakes the tram for his film extras and starts the action with you in the middle! Before you know it, the tram has been hit by earthquake, fire and flood, and the culmination, when 265,000l/58,300g of water are dumped on the flaming set, is breathtaking. Having survived the canyon, you continue on past some more film props before passing the **Star Cars** garage exhibit of well-known movie vehicles (like Cruella de Vil's car from *101 Dalmatians*, the Humvee from T*he Rock* and the sports car from *Runaway Bride*). Finally, you enter the smoking ruins of London, circa 2022 (or at least a remarkable film-set facsimile). Here, for anyone familiar with the summer 2002 blockbuster film *Reign of Fire*, you get a close encounter with one of its stars. Well, not actually one of the dragons, but a fairly hot close-up of its fiery breath, which blasts out twice on the right side of the tram.

The shock effect, the noise of the fire and the feel of the heat will definitely scare young children (and some adults!), so think carefully before taking your youngster on this tour. However, the encounter is over pretty quickly and the rest of the set is something to marvel at. Avoid this just after a Stunt Show has finished in the Backlot area, as many of that 3,000-strong crowd head straight here (and there's not much to see while waiting). AAA/TTTT (FP)

Stitch Live: This is your chance to interact with the mischievous blue alien when Disney Studios send a satellite beam directly into outer space for a live audio and visual connection between Stitch and the studio audience. Children can ask questions and Stitch responds directly to each child – and may even ask a few questions of his own! Each encounter is personalised, unpredictable, hilarious and filled with the sort of gentle irreverence that makes Stitch a family favourite. The 20min theatre-style show, located inside the former Walt Disney Television Studios, runs up to 3 times per hour, with shows alternating in French and English (check the times schedule posted outside the attraction). Although the attraction is geared for youngsters, the technology is so convincing (if you have seen Turtle Talk With Crush at the *Epcot* park in *Walt Disney World*, you will have some idea of what to expect), even older children and adults will be enchanted. AAAA

Playhouse Disney – Live on Stage: New in 2009 (and also occupying part of the old Disney Channel TV Studios building) was this show performance – a mix of live actors, costumed characters and puppetry – based on various characters from Disney's TV Playhouse programmes but centred on the Mickey Mouse Clubhouse. The likes of Handy Manny, Winnie the Pooh and The Little Einsteins also appear, providing plenty of lively fun, sing-alongs and audience participation for the pre-school brigade, and the show is performed up to 10 times daily, alternately in English, French and Spanish (check the board outside for details of which language the next show will be in). Everyone sits on the floor but the theatre takes up to 480 at a time, so there is rarely a long wait to get in, and it is a guaranteed hit with younger children. AAAA (under 6s)

Other entertainment: On the small Place des Stars stage, guests can enjoy a small musical show with the characters that drove in during the **Stars 'n' Cars** parade. The stage is also used as a platform for other performances throughout the year (especially during high season). The Christmas season used to see a Santa-themed Post Office here but that is now located in Santa's Village in Frontierland for the festive season.

Shopping: The lone option here is a gift shop at the exit of the Tower of Terror, with a range of Tower-specific merchandise. There is also another small kiosk with general Disney items.

Dining: When it comes to grabbing a bite to eat, the Production Courtyard has the best of the theme park's dining in the shape of the **Restaurant des Stars**, a 300-seat café-type diner in full art deco style, which offers a set-price buffet meal. The speciality is a meat carvery but the range of food is extremely broad (similar to the Plaza Gardens Restaurant in the *Disneyland Park*), from baked fish to penne pasta Bolognese, roast chicken, vegetable lasagne and a wide variety of salads (€23.70 adults, €11.30 3–11s, including one soft drink). The walls display a fine array of authentic Hollywood photos and film memorabilia. **Remy**, from *Ratatouille*, also makes periodic daily appearances both inside and outside the restaurant. It's a charming encounter, worth seeking out when you are in the area.

If you like your coffee, visit the **Cafe** window next to the restaurant for a hot cup of espresso, cappuccino, latte machiatto or even an iced cappuccino for the hotter days. But be warned: don't come here when the Stunt Show has just finished and 3,000 people are in the vicinity!

The Backlot

The Backlot area is past the Restaurant des Stars and features some more action-packed offerings, with 3 contrasting thrill elements.

Armageddon: Special Effects: This unique, elaborate show that puts YOU at the heart of the action (although it's not one for young children) is the first of the thrills. You enter a pre-show area, full of models, exhibits and diagrams from the blockbuster film starring Bruce Willis (there are 2 studios, 7A and 7B, and the array of models does vary), where a Cast Member greets you and acts as the show's director.

With the help of your director and a video that explains the eye-popping scenario of the film, your role as extras in a special effects scene is explained in amusing detail (in English and French). The screen is then turned over to a tribute to Frenchman Georges Méliès, who is credited with inventing film special effects. It shows how the movie world has taken his ideas and developed them with astonishing creativity in the last 100 years. The video continues with the explosive arrival of Michael Clarke Duncan, another of the *Armageddon* stars, who explains how the film's technical wizardry was carried out (in dubbed French, with English subtitles). You are then invited to see for real how it is done, under directorial guidance, in an amazing mock-up of the movie's Russian space station – just as it comes under threat from a meteor shower!

The ensuing chaos, as the station almost literally blows up all around you, is brilliantly scripted and the array of effects incredibly realistic, with smoke, sparks, bursting pipes, buckling doors and a huge central fireball that adds real heat to proceedings.

In our opinion, the sights and sounds (it is pretty loud) are much too intense for under 7s, but there are no real warnings of this outside. However, the space station itself is a work of art and the hectic action is suitably breathtaking. They could do with adding a bit of interest to the plain waiting area outside, though. TTTT

BRITTIP
It is a good idea for an adult to experience an attraction first to check on its suitability, if you are worried that certain elements might be too scary for your children.

(160) **Rock 'n' Roller Coaster starring Aerosmith:** This next attraction is a real blast of a ride, rocketing from 0–100kph/62mph in just 2.8 seconds! It is a revised version of the Orlando ride, making it a different experience.

Here, you enter the rock 'n' roll world of American supergroup Aerosmith, as they discuss the creation of this unique rockin' ride, described as a 'revolutionary musical experience' produced by Tour De Force Records. As the record company's VIP guests, Aerosmith invite you to enter the research and development area to try it out at first hand and you pass into the launch area, complete with

Rock 'n' Roller Coaster

© DISNEY

sound engineers and computer models of the ride systems, which feature 'Soundtracker' cars. These are fitted with 5 state-of-the-art speakers per seat so you literally 'ride the music'.

BRITTIP
Listen out for Aerosmith lead singer, Steve Tyler, completing a clever 'sound check' as you board the Rock 'n' Roller Coaster – it adds considerably to the fun.

Once you are harnessed into your seat, the countdown begins and you blast off into a topsy-turvy 'rock video' that features 2 loops and a corkscrew as well as some eye-popping lighting effects. There are 5 music tracks to accompany the ride, hence 5 variations on the ride experience.

BRITTIP
Some say the best spot on Rock 'n' Roller Coaster is the first row, others say it's the back. To find out for yourself, ask a Cast Member if you can wait for either of these rows – it's worth it.

Aerosmith have even re-recorded a couple of their tracks, so see if you can notice the new lyrics (hint: the adapted songs are 'Love In An Elevator' and 'What Kind of Love Are You On?'). Waiting time can hit an hour at peak periods but there is rarely much of a queue for the first few hours or in late afternoon. The queue area also displays some rare rock memorabilia like signed instruments and European tour posters – great for music fans. Although the attraction has FastPass, the machines often stay closed in low season as the queue is a fairly fast-moving one. It is not recommended for anyone with back or neck problems or for pregnant women. Restriction: 1.2m/3ft 9in. TTTTT (FP)

BRITTIP
The queue for Rock 'n' Roller Coaster drops off during a performance of the Stunt Show next door but it should be avoided just after the show finishes as many people make a beeline for it.

Moteurs…Action! Stunt Show Spectacular: Next door to the Rock 'n' Roller Coaster, this is one of Disney's most remarkable shows. Full of genuine high-risk stunts and hugely skilful car and motorbike action, it will have you shaking your head in amazement for a while afterwards.

BRITTIP
People start queuing for the Stunt Show a good half-hour before a performance at peak times (3 to 4 a day) and the middle shows of the day are often packed. It is better to head for the first one or stay until the last to minimise your wait.

Seating starts a good 20mins prior to show-time, and there is some amusing pre-show chat (in English and French) and freestyle show-boating by one of the bike riders to keep people amused before the serious stuff starts. An audience member is also recruited to help in one of the scenes and a roving cameraman picks out people from the crowd to highlight on the big video screen in the centre of the square. The huge set is based on a typical Mediterranean village and is magnificently crafted to have an aged appearance. Once the preliminaries are completed, you are treated to a 45min extravaganza of daredevil stunts, with a Car Ballet sequence, a Motorbike Chase and a Grand Finale that features some surprise pyrotechnics to complete a truly awesome presentation (keep your eyes on the windows below the video screen at the end). Each scene – featuring a secret agent 'goody' and various black-car 'baddies' – is set up and fully explained by a movie director (and the need for bilingual commentary is handled skilfully). The results of each shoot are then played back on the video screen to show in detail how each effect was created and how it is all spliced together to create the desired end product.

All the cars were specially created for the show by Vauxhall and there are some extra tricks in between the main scenes. The whole thing

Moteurs ... Action! Stunt Show Spectacular

was designed by Frenchman Rémy Julienne, the doyen of cinematic car stunt sequences, who worked on the James Bond films *Goldeneye* and *Licence to Kill* and other epics such as *The Rock, Ronin, Gone in 60 Seconds* and *Enemy of the State*. It all adds up to a breathtaking show, and kids are sure to want to come back – another good reason to see it early on. There is nothing like it in any other theme park in the world (except for the copycat version in *Disney's Hollywood Studios* in Orlando), and the fact so much of it involves genuine, live co-ordination makes it truly thrilling. Kids will also enjoy the special guest appearance of Lightning McQueen from the film *Cars* as he encounters a villainous rocket-equipped car. His cartoon friend Tow-Mater also appears on the big screen to help out.

BRITTIP
Be aware there is some loud mock gunfire during the Stunt Show, which can upset young children, while the motorbike scene includes a rider catching fire, which can be quite frightening for them.

However, the exit is quite a scrum as 3,000 people have to leave through 2 fairly narrow thoroughfares and it can take 10–15mins to get clear of the auditorium. So, although a Cast Member will direct you to a seating area, if you can sit towards the front either on the right or left of the grandstand, you will be out quicker. TTTTT

Shopping: The only shop around here is **Rock Around The Shop**, at the exit to

Halloween at the Walt Disney Studios

While children can enjoy the gentle, largely scare-free fun at the *Disneyland Park*, things are a little more intense for October in the *Studios*. Make that a LOT more intense. The **Terrorific Night** started off as a trial event in 2009 and, by 2011, had quickly become a big Halloween weekend success, with 2 sold-out nights and zombies and monsters everywhere! Unlike the character fun of Mickey's Not So Scary Halloween Party, Terrorific is a full-scale scare-fest, with special shows, roaming creatures and genuine horror-movie style. The Studios get their own elaborate Halloween makeover, with some of the rides – notably the Studio Tram Tour, which has its own show en route – specially decorated to add distinctly ghoulish overtones. Here, the Villains *really* take over and have full licence to terrorise the guests. In truth, it is a lot of fun and is performed with a lot of panache but it is certainly NOT an evening for children (or under 14s at least). While it's all make believe, the element of gruesome realism is quite high, hence it is a handy alternative to the *Disneyland Park* for older teens and adults. It's quite likely this could expand to even more nights in future, so be sure to check out **www.disneylandparis.co.uk** for details well in advance. Tickets are usually around €26, so why not step up and enjoy Disney's alternative Halloween atmosfear?!

Rock 'n' Roller Coaster, offering a range of Aerosmith and rock-related goods, plus the chance to buy your ride photo.

Dining: When you need something to eat, **Le Café des Cascadeurs** is an imaginative little diner (themed as an art deco studio café for the stuntmen and women) around the corner from Armageddon, serving a fairly simple selection of salads, sandwiches, burgers, hot dogs and crisps, but the train carriage setting is good fun.

The newly re-themed **Blockbuster Cafe** (formerly The Backlot Express) is a counter-service café with the interior split in 2 parts, one for High School Musical (with a full array of banners, posters and film props) and the other in *Pirates of the Caribbean* movie style (with props and decorations straight from Davy Jones' Locker, or somewhere nearby!). The costumes shown in the Pirates area are merely duplicates, not originals used in the movie, and, in truth, the new theming is less extensive and interesting than the prop-intensive Backlot Express version. The food is fairly ordinary – Mickey pizza (€4.95), toasted sandwiches, baguettes and salads (€6.00–€6.50) and a set sandwich, crisps, dessert and drink meal (€11.95), but it holds up to 500, plus there is outdoor seating in summer.

Other animation: Disney characters now roam the Backlot, too, so make sure you have a times guide (along with your park map). They are more numerous in high season and also tend to appear after mid-day.

BRITTIP

In Le Café des Cascadeurs, help yourself to a selection on the classic 1950s-style jukebox.

Here comes the parade

In best Disney park fashion, no visit is complete without the daily procession. **Disney's Stars 'n' Cars** parade left *Disney's Hollywood Studios* park in Orlando in 2009 and found a new home here. This is themed like a 1930s Hollywood film première, with a series of genuine vintage cars and clever replicas being used to mount a cavalcade of Disney showbiz favourites. It provides the likes of *Aladdin, Mary Poppins, Mulan*, the *Muppets* and *Monsters, Inc.* with a chance to show off in larger-than-life fashion. Watch out for the *Star Wars*™ 'Land Speeder' with a radio-controlled R-2D2. If you haven't seen your favourite characters yet, this is a good chance to get a wave and a photo of several in a relatively short time. Wait in the Production Courtyard and you should get a great view as the parade stops for a character display at Place des Stars where the characters will step out of their cars and star in a special

Walt Disney Studios with children

Here is a rough guide to the attractions in this park that are most likely to appeal to the different age groups (taking into account any height restrictions):

Under 5s
The Art of Disney Animation, Playhouse Disney Live, Animagique, Toy Story Playland play area, Slinky The Dog Zigzag Spin, Flying Carpets Over Agrabah, Toon Studio Plaza, Cars Quatre Roues Rallye, Stitch Live, Moteurs…Action! Stunt Show Spectacular (with parental discretion), Disney Stars 'n' Cars Parade, Toon Train

6–8s
All the above (except Playhouse Disney Live), plus Toy Soldiers Parachute Drop, Studio Tram Tour (with parental discretion), Crush's Coaster, Disney Studio 1, Cinémagique, Armageddon (with parental discretion)

9–12s
All the above (except Cars Race Rally), plus RC Racer, Rock 'n' Roller Coaster starring Aerosmith and The Twilight Zone™ Tower of Terror

Over 12s
Crush's Coaster, Disney Studio 1, Art of Disney Animation, Studio Tram Tour, Cinémagique, Armageddon, Rock 'n' Roller Coaster starring Aerosmith, The Twilight Zone™ Tower of Terror, Moteurs…Action!

musical production before retracing their steps and making their way out of the park. Times can vary, so do check the daily programme. AAAA

BRITTIP
If you want to see the show during the Stars 'n' Cars parade, you will have to get a spot at least 30mins before the parade starts. However, if you only want to see the parade, it's safe to wait until 5mins before it starts. Stand by the starting gate in the Toon Studios area and you should be in a relative crowd-free zone.

Other entertainment: The park has additional fun provided periodically by alternating performing acts, who pop up to give impromptu shows that have a central theme but include some improvisation. Special acts perform at Halloween and Christmas (including an *a capella* carol group), so once again it pays to check the daily programme for details when you enter the park. Look out also in the Backlot for occasional appearances by *Push, The Talking Trashcan*, a remarkable interactive 'performing rubbish bin' that moves, rattles and even talks to passing visitors.

For those keen to learn more about the park, there is a 1½hr **Guided Tour** (€15 adults with a €5 supplement for just one adult; children 11 and under free), which gives an in-depth view of the park's history and architecture. Book at Studio Services when you first arrive (subject to availability).

As with the *Disneyland Park*, the *Walt Disney Studios* looks even better in early evening, when all the clever (and hidden) lighting effects come into play. There is definitely room for improvement, but the high quality of the attractions here (Twilight Zone™ Tower of Terror, Cinémagique and Moteurs…Action! are real works of art) still provides a rich and rewarding experience. You will also leave with an improved knowledge of the movie business and a heightened respect for those who work in it. The essence of a theme park is that it envelops you with its sense of design and purpose and we feel the *Walt Disney Studios* does this, ensuring you believe you have truly had a movie-world adventure.

Right, that should be enough theme parks for now. But the fun doesn't stop here. Oh no! There is still plenty to do and see when we visit the *Disney Village*, Val d'Europe and more. It's time to go beyond the parks…

Beyond the Theme Parks

or Shops, Activities, Dinner!

Having led you, quite literally, up the theme park path, it is now time we took you beyond those confines and explored some more of what makes this resort – and this whole area of the Ile de France region – so enticing.

To backtrack slightly and put things in context, the Ile de France is the central region of France, the 'island' around which lie the other great regions of Normandy, Picardie, Champagne-Ardennes and Burgundy. The Ile itself is made up of 8 *départements*, namely **Yvelines**, **Essonne**, **Seine-et-Marne** and **Val d'Oise** (that form a large outer ring) and then **Hauts-de-Seine** (immediately to the west of the city), **Seine-St-Denis** (to the north-east), **Val-de-Marne** (to the south-east) and **Paris** itself. The *département* of Val-de-Marne should not be confused with Marne-la-Vallée, where *Disneyland Paris* is situated, which is actually in the *département* of Seine-et-Marne.

Before 1989, when construction began, there was little here apart from sugar beet fields, but the development since has been swift and dramatic. There is, in fact, no real town or village of Marne-la-Vallée, it is a made-up name given to the RER/TGV station here, which acts as the terminus for the RER's Line A. The nearest sizeable village is Chessy, hence the RER station

Disney Village entrance

is properly known as Marne-la-Vallée Chessy. However, to all intents and purposes, Marne-la-Vallée IS the site of *Disneyland Paris*, hence this is how the majority refer to it.

Marne-la-Vallée is also (confusingly) a sub-district of the Seine-et-Marne *département* closer to Paris (between the towns of Noisy-le-Grand and Lognes). When driving, therefore, you should always aim for 'Les Parcs Disneyland'.

More to see and do

When it comes to the associated attractions beyond the theme parks, there are 5 distinct topics to cover. First and most obvious is all the fun, fine shopping and dining of **Disney Village**. Second, Disney has also developed its own sporting connections – at **Disneyland Golf**, plus the novel challenge of **Davy Crockett's Adventure** nearby. Next, the neighbouring development of **Val d'Europe** offers another scintillating array of great shops and restaurants, including the Auchan hypermarket and the outlet shopping village of La Vallée. Finally, the highly family-friendly **Sea Life** aquarium centre is situated inside the Val d'Europe shopping centre and is another good reason to go beyond the parks.

The golfing opportunity is obviously for devotees of the sport but the others should all be on your must-see list if you are here for 4 days or more (or if you are on a repeat visit). The **Panoramagique** balloon flights over *Disney Village* are quite breathtaking and especially worthy of note.

As this is primarily a new-town area (the great Disney trail-blazing has given rise to a flurry of modern suburban development), there are not many other out-and-out tourist attractions here, but it does make a great base from which to explore Paris and some of the more genuinely historic points of interest in the region (notably the towns of Provins and Meaux, see Chapter 9).

Disney Village

Starting at the top, it is almost impossible to miss this hugely colourful entertainment centre situated between Disney's hotels and the theme parks. This impressive complex was designed by American architect Frank Gehry, who was also responsible for the Guggenheim museum in Bilbao, Spain, and it originally featured a host of complex, almost abstract ideas designed to link the Village to the railway station. However, some of these were removed in 2005–06 (notably a series of large towers), giving the Village a more open, cleaner look.

If you come straight in by car or train, you might not notice *Disney Village* on your left as you scamper headlong straight for the *Disneyland Park*, but otherwise it is fairly obvious. From one end (nearest the theme parks), it is dominated by a massive gateway topped by a huge red banner with 'Disney Village' emblazoned across it. From the hotels end, you enter via the Lake Disney entrance, with a spread of restaurants – Café Mickey, Rainforest Café, Earl of Sandwich and McDonald's – before you.

In a way, it is easy to see the Village as one big merchandising opportunity. There are a dozen different ways to spend money here – from the shops to video games – and even some of the restaurants have their own gift store. But, ultimately, this has the hallmark of the Imagineers once again (even if the Rainforest Café, Planet Hollywood, Earl of Sandwich, McDonald's and Starbucks all have their own internationally recognisable stamp). It has a wonderful outdoor café style, especially in the evening, and the brilliant lighting is well worth stopping to see. The main concourse provides periodic live entertainment (weather permitting) and there are other stalls, vendors and games from time to time, which all help to create a carnival atmosphere (as well as set-piece seasonal events, such as St Patrick's Day and St David's Day in March, Halloween in October and the

Disney Village What's New

The basic form of *Disney Village* has changed little since the early days of the resort. King Ludwig's was added in 2003, a new **Starbucks** café in 2009 (replacing the old Buffalo Trading Co shop) and the **Earl of Sandwich** in 2011. The NEX Game Arcade and bowling alley opened in 2007 only to close again after a serious flood, finally re-opening in summer 2009 following a heavy refurbishment.

The BIG new development, though, in every sense, is the arrival of the **World of Disney** store. Orlando-goers will already know this massive emporium of all things Disney – from souvenirs to house-wares – from the Downtown Disney area in *Walt Disney World*, and now it is opening here in *Disneyland Paris*.

On the corner of the IMAX Cinema facing the *Walt Disney Studios*, the World of Disney will also be the catalyst for a lot of other changes when it opens later in 2012 (another part of the 20th Anniversary celebrations). Its basic function as THE shop for all themed merchandise will make the current crop of stores in the main thoroughfare (The Disney Store, Disney Gallery, Hollywood Pictures and Disney Fashion) largely redundant, hence there will be some refurbishment here, too. The Disney Store will close to make way for a new restaurant while the other three will be amalgamated to offer more specialist shopping, notably in Disney collectibles such as Vinylmation and original artwork (like the Art of Disney in Orlando).

At the same time, the opening of World of Disney is the beginning of a whole new (long-awaited) phase of development for a second 'street' of shops and entertainment. As yet, there are no confirmed plans for what else will be here, but with the success in the US of specialist shops like Little MissMatched, Design-A-Tee, Basin and Tren-D, we can expect to see more of this name-brand style being added to the Village, too, along with more dining choice.

Christmas festivities). When you add in the entertainment possibilities of Buffalo Bill's dinner show, the cinema complex and the live music of Billy Bob's, you have a serious array of choice as to how to spend your time.

What's there

Roughly speaking, you can divide the offerings of *Disney Village* into the **Restaurants and bars**, the **Shops** and the **Entertainment**. But, to get maximum enjoyment, you need to be aware of a couple of things. Firstly, the restaurants normally start to fill up from 6–7pm. In high summer, when the theme parks are open until late, the peak period for the restaurants and shops is more likely to be 9pm. Unless you've made a booking (and only 4 of the restaurants actually accept reservations), you are likely to find queues of half an hour or more for places such as The Steakhouse, Planet Hollywood and even Annette's Diner.

◀◀▶ **BRITTIP**

The restaurants at the theme parks end of Disney Village fill up the quickest, with Planet Hollywood and Annette's Diner being the most popular venues.

The other factor is the weather. On a fine evening, it will be easier to get a table; but, if it is wet, everywhere fills up extremely quickly, so you need to anticipate the rain to avoid being left out in it! It is also worth pointing out the Village is relatively quiet during the day, so it is the ideal spot for a more relaxed lunch away from the parks and some leisurely afternoon shopping. You have free pick of all the restaurants (apart from Billy Bob's, where the buffet is evenings only) and it is particularly convenient if you are in the *Walt Disney Studios*, where there is no table-service dining. If you just need a quick snack, there are a handful of fast-food carts dotted throughout where you can buy hot dogs, pancakes or other small items.

Restaurants and bars

Planet Hollywood: Taking *Disney Village* from the theme parks end, as soon as you come through the gateway you face the immediately recognisable two-storey edifice of this popular international chain. Planet Hollywood is a huge draw from early evening until late, and reservations can be made in early evening only, which takes care

Planet Hollywood

of most of the queues. But, if there is a queue, there is a great bar area and some snazzy bar staff to make the wait more fun. An unhurried lunch is also available at any time. If the queue can be seen outside, you'll be looking at a good 30min wait for a table.

BRITTIP

When the *Disneyland Park* is open until 11pm, head to Planet Hollywood for dinner at about 6pm and you should have your pick of their best tables.

The huge variety of movie models, costumes, portraits and other memorabilia in this 500-seat restaurant are subdivided into differently themed areas, each with its own video screen that shows well-known film clips, music videos and (worth looking out

Annette's Diner

for) special trailers for forthcoming movies. The memorabilia, which will certainly get film buffs wandering around to study it, varies from James Cagney to Wesley Snipes, Arnold Schwarzenegger and Sylvester Stallone. The upstairs section includes a sci-fi dining area and an adventure area, as well as the lively bar, while downstairs there is a *Raiders of the Lost Ark* section and the Zebra Room (for obvious, stripy reasons). In the inevitable gift store, also downstairs, you will probably find the brand souvenirs a bit cheaper than London.

Different nationalities seem to dine at different times of the day. The Brits tend to eat earlier, hence there will be a UK predominance in the restaurants from 5–7pm, while the Spanish are almost invariably the last ones out! The menu has also been adapted for the more European mix of customer, so several dishes have been tweaked (and their lasagne is a house speciality).

BRITTIP

Can't decide what to choose at Planet Hollywood? Look for the VIP Platter for starters (€18.50), which comprises 4 of their best offerings, while the delectable desserts include a White Chocolate Bread Pudding and some heavenly speciality coffees.

DISNEY VILLAGE

1 Planet Hollywood
2 Annette's Diner
3 King Ludwig's Castle
4 Sports Bar
5 New York Deli
6 Billy Bob's Country & Western Saloon
7 The Steakhouse
8 Rainforest Café
9 Earl of Sandwich
10 Café Mickey
11 McDonald's
12 The Disney Store
13 Starbucks
14 The Disney Gallery
15 Disney Fashion
16 Hollywood Pictures
17 World of Toys
18 Gaumont Cinema
19 Buffalo Bill's Wild West Show
20 Marina Del Ray/Panoramagique
21 IMAX Cinema
22 NEX Arcade
23 World of Disney

The full range offers starters (€6.90–11.75), salads (€14.50–14.90), sandwiches and burgers (€15.50–16.50), steak, chicken, ribs, salmon, boeuf bourguignon and fajitas (€15.90–24.50), pasta dishes (€14.90–16.90) and pizza (€14–14.50), while desserts run from €5.70–9.90). Vegetarian options are available and extremely good and for the youngest in the party, there is the Kid's Menu (up to 11, €11.50).

Of all the Planet Hollywood restaurants we have visited, the food here is usually the best, which we ascribe to that extra bit of French flair. They also freshen the menu from time to time and have some tempting cocktails, including an exclusive Summer Specials menu. TVs in the bar show all the major sports events, and the latest football results are usually available (in English).

If you haven't been to a Planet Hollywood before, you will probably be wowed by their lively entertainment mix (even their soundtrack is carefully balanced so you can talk at the table without having to shout), so you should make a beeline for this one. If you are already familiar with their style, head here anyway and try their LA Lasagne (a layered pasta that is rolled, cut in half, deep fried and then smothered in their tomato sauce), which will make your taste buds quiver with delight and your waistline shudder!

We will admit to being slightly biased in our liking for the brash cinema-style motif of Planet Hollywood, but we reckon it is one of the most fun dining experiences in the resort. Hours 11.30am–11.30pm, but it stays open until the last person leaves!

Annette's Diner: Opposite PH stands this classic 1950s' rock 'n' roll-style restaurant. Straight out of *Grease* and *Happy Days*, the bright, vivid decor provides a suitably fun, family atmosphere, with waiters and waitresses who dance on the bar top at various moments. The large icons are all typical Americana from this period, and the menu is equally in keeping with the theme, with a line-up of

burgers, hot dogs, chilli, fajitas, salads and sandwiches. The restaurant has 2 (rather noisy!) levels, the mezzanine floor offering the best views of the restaurant. There used to be a classic Cadillac and Corvette by the entrance but only the Cadillac remains, now placed next to the Village Exit.

Open from 10am for their American-style breakfast (until 1pm, €11.40), there is also a featured set Kids' Meal for lunch/dinner (for under 12s) at €11.40, while the burgers are €13.50–18.75 (for the humongous Annette's MAXI Incredible Burger at €22.80 – finish it all and qualify for a free milkshake!). The desserts are possibly their best feature, with a range of ice creams, sundaes and shakes to appeal strongly to those with a sweet tooth. Drinks can come with a little twist; just order a Cherry Cola or Cherry Sprite and you'll get a regular Coke or Sprite with cherry syrup in it, while their Old-Fashioned Lemonade is the best in the resort. When the queues get long (as they often do), there is a handy take-away window at the side, a faster and even cheaper option to enjoy a good burger. Annette's Diner is open 10am–midnight.

◄█► **BRITTIP**
To book any of the restaurants in *Disney Village*, up to 2 months in advance, call (from the UK) 00 33 1 60 30 40 50 or make a reservation through the concierge at your hotel.

King Ludwig's Castle: Continuing along the main *Disney Village* thoroughfare brings you next to this hugely elaborate establishment, which opened in June 2003, with a 2009 expansion adding a bar area. Inspired by the Neuschwanstein Castle in Bavaria (built by 'mad' King Ludwig II), King Ludwig's has been designed primarily for German visitors but will, we think, appeal to anyone who enjoys good beer, Bavarian food and castles in general. With more than 300 seats on 2 floors, the interior of the restaurant is redolent with castle theming, including wooden panelling, flags and ornate carvings.

BEYOND THE THEME PARKS

The menu is designed to appeal to international tastes, with starters (€6.20–8.90) like Caesar salad and a good potato and leek soup and an impressive array of main courses (€17.95–25.50) such as Black Night's Schnitzel, Stroganoff Godomar and Royal Sauerkraut (smoked pork loin, bacon, sausage and potato on a dome of sauerkraut). Desserts (€6.20–7.80) include various strudels and a delicious chocolate cake. There are also more straightforward salads and pastas, plus burgers and even a tandoori chicken dish, as well as a simple kids' menu (€10.90), but the feature dishes are all well worth trying. On select days King Ludwig's Castle offers the kids menu at a discounted price (€8.90), as advertised on a big board outside the restaurant.

This can all be washed down with a good choice of beer and schnapps, plus a Happy Hour from 5.30–7pm with various beer specials. There is also a set menu at €19.95 (a starter and main course, or main course and dessert). A magnificent design inside and out, the castle has a fantasy-orientated and whimsical touch rather than the usual more formal approach. Their gift shop sells branded merchandise – glass, porcelain and the inevitable plastic swords – under the mark of Prince Luitpold of Bavaria (a direct descendant of King Ludwig II and the owner of the Kaltenberg brewery). It is open from 11.30am–11pm (Sun–Fri) and 11.30am–midnight (Fri and Sat).

Sports Bar: Diagonally opposite the Castle, this regular haunt for many Brits is the nearest the Village gets to a proper pub. With an outdoor terrace, indoor seating and a cinema-style video screen at one end (plus a dozen TV screens sprinkled through the bar), this is the place to come for a British-style beer, a quick snack and, more importantly, the footy on telly at weekends and midweek! They show a great variety of European action and keep all the latest scores and tables on big blackboards behind the bar.

Popular with Disney Cast Members, the Sports Bar can be a lively place most evenings, but especially at weekends when the locals come out to play. The draught beers are usually Kronenbourg 1664, Fosters, Beamish (stout) and Carlsberg, while there is a good choice of bottled beers, including Heineken, Guinness, Budweiser, and Strongbow. Open 2pm–1am Mon–Fri, midday–2am Sat and midday–1am Sun (with food until 11pm), it serves hot dogs, pizza, nachos and chicken nuggets; chips and crisps are also available (with a set meal of a hot dog and fries, or chicken nuggets, plus a brownie and a soft drink for €11.99, or a beer instead of a soft drink for €12.99). It is usually packed for the big European football games and can be a bit rowdy, so it is not an ideal atmosphere for children, although they are always welcome.

New York Deli: Next door to the Sports Bar (and sharing the outdoor terrace), this rather nondescript offering has undergone various small changes and tweaks in recent years, moving away from the 'sandwiches' style since the opening of the Earl of Sandwich (which does them much better) to a more obvious deli counter. It features take-away or dine-in options for pasta, pizza, salads, hot-dogs, paninis and baguettes, with cookies, brownies, doughnuts and muffins for dessert. A hot dog (with fries) is €7.50 and baguettes (also with fries) range from €7.90–9.50. Pasta starts at €6.80 and a slice of pizza at €5.90. Open 9am–midnight (Mon–Thurs), 9am–11pm (Fri and Sat) or 9am–midnight (Sun).

Billy Bob's Country & Western Saloon: Just down from King Ludwig's Castle, you come to this wonderful mock cowboy saloon, with a large bar and a stage for live music every evening. House group, The Billy Bob's Band, perform on stage from Sunday to Thursday from 10.30pm. You can also come to learn some rock 'n' roll dancing on Wed from 8pm and traditional line dancing on Thurs from 8pm. Fri and Sat the stage is reserved for guest bands with the likes of Elvis tribute performers, soul, rock and even Salsa fun. The 3-storey Grand Oprystyle building (copied from an original in Austin, Texas) is superbly designed, with tiered balconies all providing a good view of the stage. Just sit back with a drink and enjoy the house band, who are genuine exponents of the Country & Western genre. Even if it's not your usual cup of musical tea, their live style is worth checking out.

BRITTIP

If the other restaurants are heaving in the evening, try Billy Bob's Buffet upstairs in La Grange Restaurant. Not many people notice it and it is usually possible to get a table without much of a wait.

Bar snacks include chicken nuggets, spare ribs and nachos, or try out the excellent Tex-Mex buffet upstairs at **La Grange Restaurant**, which is at the top of the bar at the back (take the stairs to your left and keep going up). La Grange is only open 6–11pm, but offers a great value meal (€25.80/adult and €12.80/child) featuring salads, roast pork and beef, fajitas, chilli con carne, rice, pasta and vegetables, chicken wings, spare ribs, cheese tray and a huge choice of desserts. La Grange restaurant can be booked in advance through your hotel concierge while Billy Bob's is open 6pm–1am (Sun–Fri) 6pm–2am (Sat), with snacks (€3.50–13.50) served from 6–10.30pm. To book before you go, call 00 33 1 60 30 40 50 from the UK.

Starbucks: Okay, we moaned long and loud about there being no decent coffee bar in *Disney Village*, and the powers-that-be must have listened because this finally opened in summer 2009. And, while it is not in the best European traditions (of Lavazza and Illy), it definitely increases the quality of the dreadful counter offerings in the parks. Be prepared for a surprisingly low-key and whimsical atmosphere in keeping with its Disney location. There is also an obvious commitment to 'going green', from countertops made of recycled mobile phones to entry mats created from recycled French aeroplane tyres. Be ready for the usual Starbucks premium pricing, though: €4.10 for a grande latte or €4.20 for a grande cappuccino, and €5.70 for a mocha frappuccino. Open from 8am–midnight (Sun–Thurs) and 8am–1am (Fri and Sat).

The Steakhouse: Right next door, this offers the real fine-dining opportunity in *Disney Village*. In fact, only the California Grill in the *Disneyland Hotel* and Hunter's Grill in *Disney's Sequoia Lodge* can rival this for quality. It is a spectacular venue, with a Chicago-style warehouse interior in 3 sections – the main warehouse, the smart bar and the conservatory-like annexe. It is all decorated in 1930s' Americana, with lots of dark woods, rich upholstery, wood panelling and elaborate candelabra lighting

BEYOND THE THEME PARKS

King Ludwig's Castle and Planet Hollywood

effects. The bar area is straight out of the TV programme *Cheers*, but it is also extremely elegant for such a large restaurant and provides a great backdrop for a special-occasion meal (although it is also popular with families early in the evening and you will find a lot of children here).

The mouth-watering menu is pretty broad-based, although the obvious speciality is steak (filet, entrecôte, rump steak, sirloin, Brazilian strip, rib-eye and steak tartare) along with spare ribs, a couple of excellent fish dishes, a chicken curry and a vegetarian lasagne. The à la carte prices are not too outrageous (steaks are €26.90–34.90, while starters are €8.75–17.95) and there is a set menu, Chicago, for €30 that offers a choice of 3 starters, 4 main courses and 3 desserts. For those wanting only 2 courses, they can opt for the Jazz Menu at €24.50. Arrive before 7pm for their Early Bird Specials.

For children, the Scrooge McDuck Menu (€13.30) is also a cut above usual kiddie fare (although they can still get the ubiquitous chicken nuggets). Reservations are highly recommended at most times and the restaurant is open daily noon–midnight. This is also the place to come for a superb **Sunday Brunch** with Disney characters, noon–3pm. It's a tad pricey at €35/adult and €10/child (no Half Board on Sun) but it does make a memorable meal and is rarely crowded, so the kids have plenty of time with the characters. Call 00 33 1 60 30 40 50 (from the UK) to book.

Rainforest Café: This unmistakable international chain restaurant, providing a larger-than-life jungle adventure and whose decor owes a lot to the artistry of the Imagineers, is next up on the Village restaurant tour. Here you will find tropical aquaria, waterfalls, streams and a host of (animatronic) animals to accompany your meal, all in a realistic rainforest setting punctuated by thunderstorms and rainfall. You don't just go to eat here you go 'on expedition' and it is as much the decor and atmosphere as the food that creates the experience.

Rainforest Café

In truth, the food is fairly regular diner fare given a bit of a twist and a few fancy names (Rasta Pasta is penne pasta with chicken, broccoli, peppers and spinach tossed in a cream sauce, while Mojo Bones is barbecue ribs with coleslaw and chips), but the portions are huge and usually good value. Salads, pasta, burgers and grills (try the Oriental Safari Starter for 2, Wanton Shrimp and Brochettes of Chicken or go even bigger with the Awesome Appetizer Adventure starter) range from €17.90–25.90 and the Cha Cha menu will let you pick one of 4 main courses and one of the three desserts for €19.95. Starters on their own range €4.30–7.90, with the appetizers to share starting at €12.90. Cocktails and desserts are both specialities of the house, and the Chocolate Diablo Cake alone is worth coming in for, along with the delicious Bamba's Pancake.

BRITTIP

Visiting the Rainforest Café? Then you should certainly leave room to indulge in the Volcano. This dessert is one big mountain full of ice cream, cake and chocolate sauce. Don't try to eat one alone, says Andy – it's impossible!

Children in particular love the rainforest style and pick up on the many environmental messages, while the kids' menu (€12.90) is one of the best. The café doesn't accept reservations, so you just have to turn up and wait, but there is a gift shop to inspect before you eat and plenty of audio-animatronics to keep the kids happy (the big alligator outside seems to provide an almost endless source of amusement). The Rainforest Café is open 11.30am–midnight every day, with the gift shop open from 9.30am.

⚓ BRITTIP
Arguably the best value food in *Disney Village* comes from the **Earl of Sandwich**, as this surprisingly innovative café chain offers some delicious and well-priced alternatives.

Earl of Sandwich: Next to Rainforest Café and across from Cafe Mickey is the newest eatery that opened in mid-2011 and turned into an instant success with both guests and Cast Members (see them turn up here during their lunch break!). While it may *sound* like a British idea (and it WAS started by the Earl of Montague himself – a direct descendant of the original Earl of Sandwich, credited with inventing the original bread snack in the 18th century), the first café actually opened in Orlando's *Downtown Disney* area in 2004 and it wasn't until April 2011 that one opened in London (the first outside the US, where it has proved a huge success). The *Disney Village* version opened in June 2011 as Europe's second outlet. Sandwiches (obviously) are their stock in trade, all made fresh to order at the counter, and there is a highly appetising array – 16 at the last count – including the Original 1762 (freshly roasted beef, sharp Cheddar cheese and creamy horseradish sauce), All American (roast turkey, buttermilk ranch dressing, cranberries, Cheddar cheese, lettuce and Roma tomatoes) and Le Frenchy (ham, Brie cheese and the Earl's mustard sauce). There is also a fun Cannonballs (with meatballs), Tuna Melt, and Veggie. Sandwiches are set at one price of €5.50 and are a

nice alternative to the other fast food options. There are salads and wraps for the same price. Desserts start at €2.50 and will not set you back more than €3.95. There is even a breakfast option for €3.95. The restaurant has a nice but small indoor section on the ground floor and extra seats on the second. There are multiple outdoor terraces, at the side of the restaurant and on the second floor at the back.

⚓ BRITTIP
Get yourself a take-away from Earl of Sandwich to enjoy on a bench on the way to your hotel, or in the comfort of your hotel room. It's an ideal option for families with young and tired children who still need to eat before bed-time and want to avoid a crowded restaurant.

Café Mickey: This is another fun and lively venue that stages character meals throughout the day. Once again, the decor is bright without being garish and amusing without being obvious. The upstairs dining area has a magnificent view over Lake Disney from the terrace. TV screens showing classic Disney cartoons help to keep children happy if the food doesn't (and the food is usually above average here), but it is more likely to be the excellent character visits that make their day. A big breakfast buffet runs 7.30am–10.30am, where Disney hotel guest pay a €16.20 supplement per adult and €11.40/child (regular price is €23.80 and €16.20). Lunch is available noon–5pm and dinner 5–11pm (Sun–Fri) or 5pm–midnight (Sat). The dinner menu is an extended version of the lunch fare (hotel supplement €17/adult, €12/child; full price €25 and €17).

You can perhaps see the European influence at work here most, with a wide-ranging choice and a highly thoughtful and appetising selection (from pizza and pasta standards to seafood, vegetarian dishes and salads), way above usual diner fare. Try the Fantasia Mushrooms starter (garlic mushrooms beautifully roasted with pesto and parmesan), then progress to Pinocchio Pasta (creamy wok-cooked penne pasta with chicken and broccoli) or Little Mermaid's Favourite (fish risotto of cod, salmon, scallops and shrimp), or give their wood-fired oven pizzas a try. Then follow up with a wonderfully tempting array of desserts (of which Woody's Campside Chocolate, a rich fondant cake, is quite dreamy!). The 3-course set meal is €31/adults. Children (under 12) get their own menu (€15.20) and a special Mickey surprise. The characters circulate fairly constantly to keep everyone happy and the smart decor ensures adult sensibilities are not forgotten. Booking highly advisable in the evening to avoid a big queue (although lunchtime may be quieter). In France, call 01 60 30 40 50.

BRITTIP
Missed out on reservation for **Café Mickey**? Not to worry. Visit the restaurant about 5.40pm and you should benefit from their quietest period of the day, beating the crowds that usually wait for the 6pm characters appearance. By the time your food is at your table, you'll be the first to enjoy the characters.

McDonald's: Completing the impressive spread of restaurants is the inevitable (and huge) McDonald's, albeit quite a smart, almost high-tech version of the ubiquitous American burger chain. Open 8am–midnight (8am–1am Fri and Sat), it is a major draw in the evenings as it is obviously one of the relatively cheaper options (with a Big Mac costing €3.60 and a Happy Meal at €4), but it also has a high capacity with an outdoor terrace, providing a pleasant place to sit in the right weather. The original architecture is based on Italian theatre and the split-level arrangement also offers a games area for the kids.

BRITTIP
Don't think you will save a lot of time going to McDonalds. Queues can be massive and, for some reason, this fast food restaurant is one of the slowest we have witnessed.

Kiosks: Finally, if you're after an evening or late-night snack, there are a couple of kiosks where you can grab a hot dog, popcorn, crêpes, ice creams, frites, chicken nuggets, pizza or even some salads.

Shopping

Okay, if that sums up your eating opportunities in the Village, the retail therapy offerings aren't quite so wide ranging (at least until the World of Disney store is fully open), as you will find much of the merchandise recurring in different shops. However, there is still an imaginative array of interior styling and it is worth wandering through the likes of The Disney Gallery and the Rainforest Café shop just to have a look at the splendid and imaginative decor.

BRITTIP
If *Disney Village* is too crowded for your tastes or you can't get a table for dinner, try going to *Disney's Hotel New York* (see page 70) for their Parkside Diner, or the upmarket Hunter's Grill at *Sequoia Lodge* (see pages 71, 73–4). Both have great bars, too.

The Disney Store: At the time of writing, this is still first on your left when you enter *Disney Village* from the theme parks end. It's the biggest in the resort, and a huge character emporium that offers a good variety of souvenir goods and clever ways of displaying them. It sells the widest selection of character and souvenir wares, from books and cuddly toys, to DVDs, watches and jewellery, plus an extensive clothing selection and, nearer the festive season, an array of Christmas decorations, too. Kids will love browsing (if they can be prevented from trying to buy everything in sight!), while above them are a host of wonderful things to watch – large-scale moving models, mobiles and Mickey Mouse flying a spaceship. NB: We believe this will close later in 2012 to make way for a new dining option in due course.

World of Disney: This will be the new 'gold standard' of Disney shopping when it opens in summer 2012. Taking its cue from the two American versions of the store, it will feature a whopping 1,400m²/15,000ft² of sales floor, with a truly mind-boggling array of wares. Never mind watching the children, the grown-ups could easily get lost in this retail wonderland! Having seen the construction stages, it is clear this will be the new European flagship for all kinds of Disney merchandise; toys, cuddlies, clothing, home goods, jewellery, pins, princess accessories and much, much more will be collected under the capacious roof. The design is also wonderfully eye-catching, with a 19th-century French conservatory architectural style, highlighted by a massive globe and 2-storey foyer, complete with an array of clever lighting and other special effects. Look for more Disney whimsy and invention inside, too, to ensure shopping here is as good as it looks. Tinker Bell fans should also enjoy her 'top of the World' pose!

Planet Hollywood: This gift store, downstairs from the restaurant, offers themed souvenirs and other movie memorabilia. You can also check out the movie and TV star hand prints on the wall outside.

Café Mickey

King Ludwig's Castle: Next door, this fun restaurant also has a specialist shop, with various Bavarian souvenirs as well as a selection of toys and the all-important swords and shields for kids to re-stage the Battle of Waterloo!

Disney Gallery: This is opposite the Starbucks, offering a more upmarket selection of gift items for cinema and art fans. Disney collectors will want to make a beeline here to check out the range of limited series lithographs and original animated film cels. There are some great books (here's where you might still get a copy of Didier Ghez's superb book *Disneyland – From Sketch to Reality*) and photographs, and it also has the latest collections of china figurines and snow globes, plus novelties like a Mickey telephone (every home should have one!). Fans of the new collectible craze of Vinylmation should also head here – a lot of shelf space is given over to these cute figurines.

Disney Fashion, Hollywood Pictures and World of Toys: Immediately next door, you enter these 3 interconnected shops (handy in the rain) and, while you will probably have seen some of the merchandise already, there is more novel stuff, too. Disney Fashion is a rather ordinary clothing store (everything from hats to shoes), Hollywood Pictures offers an array of

Buffalo Bill' Wild West Show

film-themed clothing, photo albums and gifts (and the inevitable cuddly toys), and World of Toys is almost a reprise of The Disney Store, with yet more kids' playthings (beware the pirate paraphernalia and swords!), costumes and a big sweet counter. *Star Wars* fans are also well catered for here.

BRITTIP

We expect these 3 shops to get a heavy makeover after the opening of World of Disney as much of their wares is likely to end up in the bigger, newer store.

Rainforest Café: Finally, inside the main entrance to this café lurks an animal-themed gift shop just waiting to ensnare the unwary with another line-up of soft toys, games, clothing and environmentally aware souvenirs. Their audio-animatronics make it fun for children and should keep the kids amused while the grown-ups browse the merchandise.

Others: Essential services are provided by a **currency exchange** next to The Disney Store, two regular **cash dispensers**, an **Information & Ticket** kiosk and **Baby Change** facilities (between The Disney Store and the Sports Bar), while there is also a big **tourist information office** just outside the *Disney Village* gates in front of the

main railway station. The **post office** can now be found inside the Marne la Vallée station. You can't miss it as it is right next to the main entrance.

Village entertainment

If all that isn't enough to keep you occupied, Disney has a third array of opportunities to entertain and amuse. Foremost of these is Buffalo Bill's show, but there is also live music and other periodic street entertainment throughout the Village, including a small outdoor circus ring with clowns and jugglers. When you consider the big seasonal events, like Christmas, St David's Day, St Patrick's Day, Halloween and Fireworks Night, which are all either based or have a significant presence here, this can be an exceptionally lively scene at times.

Gaumont and IMAX Cinemas: One of the most eye-catching features of the theme parks end of the Village, is the modern 15-screen Gaumont Cineplex. However, unless you speak French this is probably not going to appeal to you as they no longer screen any films in English, sadly. The IMAX offers both the signature giant-screen films and 3-D movies, as well as DMR productions – digitally re-mastered versions of normal films.

Buffalo Bill's Wild West Show

Next door to the Gaumont – and arguably the most prominent feature of the Village – is Buffalo Bill's Wild West Show…With Mickey and Friends, a 90 minute sit-down dinner spectacular that relives the myths and legends of America's cowboy country. The huge indoor arena, some eye-catching stunts and the full Western style ensure this is a hit with all the family (but especially children in the 4–12 age range).

BRITTIP
Buffalo Bill's is not advisable for anyone who suffers from asthma or other respiratory complaints as the animals kick up a fair bit of dust in the indoor arena.

Food: The food is unremarkable, but there is always plenty of it: Camp Cornbread, Cattleman's Chilli, Texas Skillet with Meat, Corn on the Cob and Old-Style Potato Wedges. Dessert is a warm apple pie with vanilla ice cream. The choice of drinks are either water, beer, or Coca-Cola and coffee or tea at the end – and there is a separate children's platter (roast chicken, sausage, potatoes and ice cream, plus Coca-Cola or mineral water), which always seems to go down well. There is a constant supply of either beer or Coke (with the meal only – you pay for drinks in the pre-show Colonel Cody's Saloon) as part of the entrance price.

BRITTIP
In summer, watch out for Wild Bill's Show Parade in the *Disney Village* at 6pm as a prelude to the first show of the day (weather permitting).

Get involved: Everyone gets a cowboy hat, and you sit in one of 4 colour-coded sections corresponding to the different cowboys in the show, who go through a series of games and competitions to decide the 'numero uno' for the evening. You need to be in best audience participation and hat-waving mood as you cheer and clap for your cowboy and hiss and boo the others, and it all adds up to good fun, raucous stuff. After a revamp in 2009, Mickey, Minnie, Goofy, Chip 'n' Dale all now play a special role in the show, adding guaranteed child appeal at regular intervals, while Annie Oakley, the 'Queen of the Winchester', also puts in an appearance, literally shooting the lights out. There are some magnificent horse-riding tricks and skills, too, and much of the narration is in English as the 60 performers are nearly all American. A Native American element also features and, at one point, the curtain at one end of the auditorium rises to reveal a majestic rocky outcrop, which complements the superb lighting and sound effects. There are wagon trains and cattle drives, cavalry charges and rodeo games, along with a big finale with the inevitable stagecoach – and it is all performed with great gusto and zest by the large cast.

BRITTIP
A vegetarian or pork-free menu is available upon request at Buffalo Bill's. You can also order wine or champagne (at additional cost).

The degree of authenticity is remarkable, with the Native Americans from a variety of tribes (including Blackfoot, Sioux and Cherokee), the buffalo from Canada and longhorn cattle from Texas, while the horses are all original Pintos and Appaloosas (for the Native Americans) or quarterhorses (for the cowboys). It is staged twice a night – at 6.30 and 9.30pm. Guests can arrive up to 45mins before and enjoy the saloon bar atmosphere and live music, and there are two categories of seating, €71 and €59 for adults and €57 and €45 for children for their mix of entertainment, spectacle and fun. You can book in advance by calling (from the UK) 00 33 1 60 45 71 00, but it is usually possible to book when you arrive, either at your hotel or at the ticket office in *Disney Village*.

The *Disney Village* used to have one nightclub, Hurricanes. Unfortunately for those with the energy to party after park closing, the club shut down in 2010. You can still see the building and its exterior decoration behind Rainforest Cafe, but there are no current plans to redevelop it.

Fun, games – and Panoramagique

Disney Village is sprinkled with various types of fun games (all of which require a few extra euros), such as mechanical bull-riding and Ring the Bell (the typical fairground attraction). The more energetic might also like to try their hand (and feet) on the bungee trampolines at either end of the Village, which adds another – extra cost – element to the entertainment line-up.

BRITTIP
The Village's main toilets are located between the Sports Bar and The Disney Store. However, their cleanliness often leaves something to be desired, so using those across the plaza at The Steakhouse is usually better.

La Marina: From here on Lake Disney, you can hire pedaloes (€10 for 20mins), Hydrobikes (€5 for 20mins) or electric boats (€30 for 20mins). All can be hired from 3–9pm at weekends and public holidays. Or take a gentle pedal round the whole of Lake Disney on a **quadricycle**. These multi-seat bikes are available Mon–Fri 5–10pm, Sat 4.30–10.30pm, and Sun 11am–1pm and 3pm–10pm (€10 per 20mins 2–4 seat, €15 per 20mins for 6–seat). On a summer evening, it is a great way to while away some time.

Street performers: At peak times and for seasonal events, the Village comes alive with a series of performers such as jugglers, stilt-walkers and diabolo throwers, which all helps to enhance the carnival nature and intent of this long entertainment thoroughfare. There is also a summer season **Village Circus**, with a clown, juggler and acrobat performing along the main street. It is a lively, and occasionally even raucous, affair (not a big hit with seniors usually), although the atmosphere is decidedly different in the cold and/or wet.

NEX Games Arcade: Underneath the IMAX cinema is the renovated high-energy video and games arcade, which features a host of high-tech amusements, many offering the latest gaming technology. Downstairs you will find a unique car and motorbike racing set-up, along with flight simulators, shoot-'em-ups, basketball and dancing. Upstairs is a clever mini bowling alley (a scaled-down version of 10-pin, with lightweight bowling balls and no need for special shoes), plus online games, table football and pool tables. There is also a dedicated area just for younger children, mostly operated by tokens (€2 each, or 3 for €5, 7 for €10 and 15 for €20). Open 3pm–1am Mon–Fri, to 3am on Sat, and 11pm on Sun.

Panoramagique: This is a magnificent tethered balloon that takes flight over Lake Disney up to 6 times an hour, soaring to 100m/328ft (dependent on the wind) over the Village, with a superb view in all directions. The flights last around 6mins and can carry up to 30 passengers at a time. It is one of the largest of its kind in the world, taking off and landing from its own purpose-built platform on the water, and is styled in best Jules Verne Victorian fashion. It can fly in most weathers (although you wouldn't want to go up when visibility isn't good) but winds of more than 35kph/22mph will see the balloon grounded for a while. It costs €12/adult and €6/child (3–11) and, on a clear day, it is possible to see all the way to Paris and the Eiffel Tower.

BRITTIP
Save €1 per person by booking your tickets for Panoramagique in advance online at **www.panoramagique.com**.

However, the real fascination is getting a true perspective on *Disneyland Paris* itself, seeing how all the elements fit together, including the hotels of Val

Panoramagique

de France, getting a bird's eye view of the parks and looking at all the areas of possible future development. It is amazing just how much you can take in, while the smooth take-off, ascent and landing – plus the huge size of the cage-like metal basket – mean you feel totally safe. We would certainly rate it a must-do attraction for the resort. However, be aware that those who have a fear of heights or suffer from vertigo may not agree.

> **BRITTIP**
> Susan – not the happiest of people with heights – found she could ride Panoramagique quite comfortably as long as she looked out to the sides and not down the middle at the balloon's cable system!

Getting about

If you are staying at a Disney hotel or one nearby, you are very conveniently placed for *Disney Village*, and the multi-storey Vinci car park, which brings you out by the IMAX cinema. Once on site, everything is within a short walking distance and it is so easy just to wander around, sample a

variety of different establishments and then wend your way home again in this safe, well-organised and thoroughly entertaining environment.

> **BRITTIP**
> You can save €7 per day on parking for the parks by using the Vinci car park instead of the big open air main car park. The former is only a maximum of €8/day while main parking is a whopping €15. And the Vinci's multi-storey nature keeps it protected from the weather, too!

Of course, for those without a car or a Disney hotel booking, the usefulness of the RER station is paramount. Here, you can enjoy the convenience of a public transport system that runs on schedule 99 times out of 100 and keeps working until a little after midnight each day, ensuring you can get back to the many hotels linked to the Line A (and within walking distance of the stations along the way). It is an efficient, user-friendly and good value service. Miss out on a night in Disney Village at your peril!

> **BRITTIP**
> The Vinci car park, which costs €2/hour (up to a maximum of €8 for a whole day), is also free to Disney hotel guests and the Disney partner hotels. Just take your ticket and show your hotel ID at the office on the ground floor when you leave.

Disneyland Golf

Golf aficionados will be keen to indulge in their favourite sport at the **Disneyland Golf Course** in the neighbouring village of Magny-le-Hongre, barely a 10min drive from the resort itself. Although quite a modern set-up, it has all the characteristics of something more mature and its three 9-hole courses should provide a good test for all standards, as well as offering what amounts to 3 different 18-hole rounds. All the courses start and finish in front of the clubhouse so they can easily be combined.

Open year-round, 7 days a week, the facilities are second to none in the Paris area (there is another good course at nearby Bussy-St-Georges, but the variety and challenge at Disneyland Golf are still superior).

A driving range and practice green (complete with a well-known Mouse head silhouette!) are situated to either side of the clubhouse, which has an extremely pleasant bar and restaurant, and an outdoor terrace where you can enjoy the best of the summer weather.

From the striking circular restaurant building, the view over the green of what is, effectively, the 18th hole, the driving range and the practice green is superb and highly conducive to a satisfying lunch. There is also a well-equipped pro shop that hires electric and manual carts, full sets of clubs and golf shoes, as well as offering the usual range of equipment and clothing to buy. A TV lounge, changing rooms and showers complete the clubhouse set-up and there is a large car park.

Green fees start at €30 for a winter weekday 18-hole round and go up to €65 for a summer round on a weekend or bank holiday. For a 9-hole round, prices are €25–45, with reduced

Disneyland Golf

rates for under 18s. Club hire is €5 per club or €25 for a full set, while hand-carts are €8 and electric ones €30 for an 18-hole round. A bucket of 30 balls for the driving range costs €5, 5 buckets is €15 and 11 buckets €35. Tuition is available from one of the 2 fully qualified instructors from €30 for a half-hour lesson to €85 for an accompanied round. For more details about playing there, visit the website **www.disneylandparis.co.uk** and click on 'and even more', 'sports', then 'golf'.

Getting around in Paris

Davy Crockett's Adventure

Thrill-seekers with a love for the outdoors will surely enjoy this unique forest adventure next to *Disney's Davy Crockett Ranch*. The **Davy Crockett Adventure** comprises 5 trails with more than 80 activities in 5 levels of difficulty, from green – the easiest, accessible to children at least 1.10m/3ft 7in tall – to black, for real daredevils. The activities are linked by platforms and ropes that blend in with the environment. Each course features suspended stations (Tyrolean traverses, monkey bridges and swings) linked by platforms and cables, and adventurers move from tree to tree using special harnesses, tethers, karabiners and pulleys. The course includes creeper-swinging, suspended bridges, wobbly tree trunks and monkey bridges, as well as a dizzying 200m/656ft suspended footbridge and their trademark 16m/52ft Tarzan leap.

Davy Crockett's Adventure covers 5ha/12 acres of the Grains national forest full of 100-year-old oak trees. The entrance is just to the right of *Disney's Davy Crockett Ranch* (see page 78), just after the reception (off Exit 13 of the A4). Access, parking and reception are all located at the Ranch (and you will have to drive here as no transport is laid on). There is a 30min initiation on the equipment and safety rules, but then participants are on their own to tackle the course progressively, under the close watch of the course supervisors. It should provide around 3hrs of physical challenges in the great outdoors and costs €25 for those over 1.40m/4ft 7in tall and €15 for those shorter (or €3 just to watch). It is open from 9am in high season (first departure at 10am, last departure at 4pm) and from 1pm in low season (last departure at 3pm). However, you MUST book in advance online at **www.aventure-aventure.com**.

Val d'Europe

Leaving the immediate environs of *Disneyland Paris* behind, the nearby **Val d'Europe** shopping, leisure and business complex is well worth taking at least half a day to explore. Opened in October 2000, it has its own RER and bus stations and has given rise to a sprawling but smart new-town development. Covering some 24.5ha/60 acres, the central portion is basically a glorified (but very attractive) mall, with 2 additional elements (the Sea Life Centre and a big health and fitness centre called Moving), plus the associated development of **La Vallée Village** (outlet shopping) in an outdoor pedestrianised area at one end.

BRITTIP
If you find it too expensive to feed your brood at *Disney Village*, head for Val d'Europe where prices are lower and you can stock up on snacks etc, at the Auchan hypermarket.

As well as the mall and associated development, the main street through the town (outside the RER station) also boasts a number of pleasant restaurants, cafés and hotels, notably the pub/brasserie of **L'Agape Café**, the **Asian Wok** and the **Pizza Di Roma**.

BRITTIP
Need petrol? The Shell service station in the Val d'Europe car park is rated the cheapest in the Ile de France, so it is the ideal place to fill up for the journey home. However, you CANNOT use the ground-level petrol pumps (they accept only French credit cards), so you must use the services in the underground car park.

For anyone who enjoys retail therapy, this should definitely be high on their list of priorities. The 2-level mall has a huge number of high-quality shops (around 130 stores, restaurants and cafés), many of which are internationally recognisable (Adidas, Benetton, Claire's, Esprit, Etam, Gap, H&M, Levi's, Mango, Naf Naf, Quiksilver, Sephora, Swarovski, Swatch and Zara) or uniquely French and wonderfully chic. Choose from the likes of L'Occitane en Provence (candles, perfumes and cosmetics, made with plants and flowers from southern France), Yves Rocher (make-up and beauty products with the accent on health), Carnet de Vol and Brice (men's fashion and sportswear), Carré Blanc (household items such as towels and carpets, all with that essential French style), Maisons du Monde (some fabulous interior decor items from around the world), Petit Bateau (the must-have women's T-shirts), Armand Thierry (men's and women's fashions), Le Tanneur (leather handbags, luggage and wallets) and – women take note – Orcanta lingerie.

BRITTIP
July usually means *Sales!* in French shops, so don't forget to check out the mall and La Vallée for some bargains if you're here in the summer. The key word to look for is *Soldes!*

There are 6 shoe shops (check out Beryl, San Marina and Eden Shoes for the latest fashions), 10 jewellery outlets (including Louis Pion and Agatha), 8 for children's clothing shops (including Sergent Major which offers a range from 1 month to 14 years, and the fun Zoekids), and 5 sports stores (notably Go Sport and Planet Jogging), plus one of our favourites, the Belgian chocolates and ice cream of Jeff de Bruges. There is even a high-quality Paris souvenir shop, Articles de Paris, where you can get that essential mini Eiffel Tower; and another Disney store, Rendez-vous Disney, which is worth checking out for periodic sales.

Services

The clean, airy, uncluttered confines of the mall, some wonderful architecture (inspired by the great Parisian styles of the late 19th century) and the user-friendly way of doing things all add up to a true 21st-century shopping experience, enhanced by an array of tempting cafés and rest areas (around 250 armchairs are dotted throughout the mall). If you avoid the weekend,

you will also find it free of crowds and easy to negotiate – no queues here!

There are 5 'welcome points' (including 2 in the huge car park) to assist with finding what you need, along with baby-care centres for nursing mothers where hostesses can even provide jars of baby food. Four free play areas are available for children, with a variety of slides and climbs (excellent for 3–8s). Other services include valet parking, shoe repairs, photo printing, hairdressers (3) and opticians (3).

Tired of walking? Take **Le Petit Train** that goes from one end of the mall to the other and back again at regular intervals (for a small fee). It also stops at each of the main 4 entrances to the mall.

BRITTIP
There are 2 pharmacies in Val d'Europe, located between the RER station and the mall entrance, notably Forum Sante.

Hypermarket

Also here, and on both levels, is the **Auchan hypermarket**. If you have brought the car, this is where you can fill up with essentials such as wine, beer, spirits and a host of other items. The lower level features all the food (a huge choice in serious quantities, with a magnificent wine selection at very reasonable prices!) while the upper (ground floor) level stocks a massive range of domestic goods, clothes, books, CDs, toys, Disney merchandise and even furniture. The levels are linked by a sloping moving walkway, which means you can take your trolley around the whole store with ease.

BRITTIP
If you regularly take the car to Calais to stock up at the many hypermarkets, Val d'Europe offers a much more civilised and user-friendly way to do your shopping.

The Auchan chain is well known all over France and offers considerable savings on comparable goods in

Val d'Europe

the UK, so it is worth having a good look round. The whole store covers some 21,000m²/5+ acres and is open 8.30am–10pm, independent of the rest of the mall. Look up more on **www.auchan.fr**.

Les Terrasses

The Val d'Europe RER station is only 5mins from Marne-la-Vallée, and the mall is only a couple of minutes' walk from the station (turn right as you exit and it is straight ahead). Walk right through the mall and you come to the main café area, **Les Terrasses**, a monumental conservatory-style annexe, with luxurious vegetation filling the iron and glass construction. Here, your choice of dining options is both wide and mouth-watering – from a small café and a fine tea-house and crêperie (just called Paul) to a proper Italian pizzeria, a fine seafood restaurant (the boat-themed **La Criée**), an elegant Chinese (**Le Dragon d'Europe**) with set menus at €19.50, €13.50 and €12, plus a kids' menu at €7.50), a wonderfully fresh and inviting café **La Croissanterie**, the eclectic **Hippopotamus** (beef, lamb, steaks and kebabs) and the inevitable **McDonald's** (although even that has a much smarter appearance than usual).

Other highlights include **Le Paradis du Fruit** restaurant for natural drinks, salads and desserts, the new **Kyoto** Japanese restaurant and the Lebanese cuisine of **Noura**, with sandwiches, salads and meze. You will also find live entertainment, with shows for the children and music in the evenings for an older audience.

The shopping part of the mall is open 10am–9pm Mon–Sat (closed Sun) but Les Terrasses is open 9am–midnight every day. Visit **www.valdeurope.fr** (then click on English version and 'Vos magasins') for more information.

> **BRITTIP**
> For an excellent cup of tea and the chance to sample some exquisite crêpes, give yourself a break at Paul and just sit and admire the wonderful architecture of Les Terrasses.

Sea Life Centre

On the lower level of Les Terrasses (down the escalators) is the Moving health and leisure centre and the excellent **Sea Life Centre**. If you have children aged 2–12, this interactive aquarium (belonging to UK-based Merlin Entertainments Group, which runs 11 similar Sea Life Centres in

Koreana

Britain and another 19 in Europe and beyond) will keep them amused for a good couple of hours, and provides a welcome diversion from all the hectic theme-parking.

Many hotels offer a free daily shuttle to Val d'Europe, so you can usually come straight here or you can just get a bus to the Marne-la-Vallée RER station and take the 5min train ride. Seasonal special offers for Sea Life – such as 'free child entry with every full-paying adult' – are worth looking out for.

BRITTIP
The centre is fully accessible to the disabled.

Opened in April 2001, this 'aquatic park' offers a marine journey through 55 contrasting displays, exhibits and shows that trace an underwater journey from the source of the Seine river out into the Atlantic and on to the Caribbean. From tiny shrimps to menacing sharks and moray eels, from small tanks to the gigantic main aquarium holding 600,000l/132,000g of water, there is plenty to amuse, entertain and educate young minds.

The journey starts with a gentle introduction to the sea through a mesmerising exhibit, Jellyfish, Keepers of the Dark, then into the world of predators and a trip along the Amazon. Children can pick up a scratch card at the entrance, which invites them to visit the 10 question panels throughout the centre and choose the right answer on their card. Get more than 8 correct and they win a prize! All the explanations are bilingual and staff can give talks and answer questions in English.

BRITTIP
The Sea Life Centre is a good alternative when the weather turns cold and wet. It is also worth a visit when the temperature outside goes sky high, as it is air-conditioned and blissfully cool on hot days.

Each fish tank and aquarium is presented in a different way. The highlights are the walk-through underwater tunnel (a 360-degree experience with sharks, rays and other fish swimming all around you), the Pirates – The Legend of Blackbeard

Susan at La Vallée

challenge, the Stingray Pool (where children can actually touch these fascinating creatures if they are patient and gentle), a film presentation on the Atlantic Ocean (and how deep-sea exploration developed), the jellyfish exhibit and the Coral Reef tank.

The interactive theming, with different walkways, passageways and alcoves, invites you to explore every nook and cranny – and learn quite a bit along the way. Talks and demonstrations featuring sharks, stingrays and the touch-pool are given at regular intervals, while various feeding times add still further to the experience. At the end, there is a handy little seating area, with vending machines, where parents can grab a drink and sit while they unleash their offspring in the play area, which has a ball pool, climbing structure, nets and slides, and kiddie rides – a very thoughtful addition. Sea Life is open daily (but not Christmas Day and 1 January) 10am–5.30pm and costs €16/adult and €12/child 3–11 (under 3s free; children under 14 must be with an adult). For more details, call 00 33 1 60 42 33 66 (from the UK) or visit their website, where you can purchase tickets online at a discounted price that can save you €4 for an adult and €3 for a child; **www.sealifeeurope.com**

BRITTIP

You can come and go as you please once you have bought your Sea Life Centre admission. That means you can go shopping and come back later in the day if there is a particular show or demonstration you want to see.

La Vallée Village

Completely separate to Val d'Europe but right next door is this wonderfully chic world of self-contained outlet shopping and cafés. The discount basis of all the stores will appeal to all dedicated shoppers as all prices are guaranteed to be reduced by at least 33% on high street stores and you can often save much more. The 90 shops vary from homeware, luggage, shoes and accessories to high fashion, but most

are clothing stores, with the accent on designer names and famous labels. Luxury goods feature strongly, too, but, at prices like these, they are more akin to regular high street offerings. The shopping options include **Paul Smith**, **Dolce and Gabbana**, **Jimmy Choo**, **Guess**, **Polo Ralph Lauren**, **M Missoni** (part of the Valentino fashion group), top French crockery and ceramic company **Villeroy & Boch**, the French fashions of **Sandro** and the Italian women's style of **Pinko**.

There is a **Starbucks** coffee shop and 2 French restaurants when you need a drink or a bite to eat – the delicious kiosk offerings of **Amorino** (for hot chocolate and ice cream!) and the upmarket fast-food alternative of **Natalie's Cafe**.

The Village design, with its winding streets, encourages you to stroll the length of the complex and all the shops are unfailingly inviting, with courteous staff seeming light years away from the usual high street surliness and disdain you encounter. There is a useful **Welcome Centre** to get you started, a well-designed children's play area and clean, well-maintained toilets and baby-changing facilities. Start by visiting the Welcome Centre for the latest news and store promotions, and you can also use their pushchairs and umbrellas, if necessary.

Decoration and homeware: Here you have the choice of Bodum, Anne de Solène (household linens) and Lalique (one of the leading French brands), while the Samsonite store, the French Lancel and Lamarthe and the Italian Furla offer a wide range of luggage, handbags and accessories, along with Reminiscence, a renowned French costume jeweller.

Children's wear: There's fashionable Bonpoint and K.I.D.S. Teenagers can choose from well-known names such as Calvin Klein, Guess and Cerruti Jeans. If you are hunting for designer shoes, check out Robert Clergerie, and Heschung (French), Salvatore Ferragamo (Italian) or Manfield-Bowen (international).

High fashion: Women's fashion is represented by Anne Fontaine, Façonnable, Kenzo, Gerard Darel, Celine, MaxMara, Givenchy, Furla, Zadig & Voltaire, Nitya and Ventilo, plus the Lingerie Shop, Chantal Thomass, Wolford and Chantelle for lingerie; while the men can choose from the likes of Café Coton, Porsche design, Charles Tyrwhitt, Feraud Homme, Kenzo and Burberry.

International brands positively abound and you will find tempting outlet stores for all of the following: Longchamp, Diesel, Trussardi and Tommy Hilfiger, plus other well-known fashion names such as Puma, Timberland, Dunhill and Pepe Jeans. And there is plenty more besides.

BRITTIP
Book a session with La Vallée Village's **Personal Shopper** for an expert look at your perfect wardrobe. Two-hour sessions include style tips and individualised guidance in selecting your optimum styles.

For serious shoppers it is a veritable Aladdin's cave of desirable items, all with some major mark-downs, which makes you wonder why we ever bother paying the usual high street rip-off prices (you can tell we enjoy shopping here!). There is so much packed in, you can't fail to come away with a major bargain or more.

BRITTIP
Unlike Val d'Europe, which closes on Sun, La Vallée is open 7 days a week.

La Vallée is open 362 days a year (closed on Christmas Day, New Year's Day and 1 May) 10am–7pm all week long. A useful daily shuttle bus service also operates from the Disney and Val de France hotels. Check with your hotel concierge for details and visit **www.lavalleevillage.com** for all the latest news, as they still add new shops to their line-up periodically.

And there's more

Wander outside the immediate confines of the Val d'Europe mall and La Vallée and you will encounter some charming (and usually traffic-free) streets and pedestrian areas where there are several other notable shops and restaurants.

La Place de Toscane: At the north end of Les Terrasses is a delightful circular plaza of restaurants and apartments, with a central monument and fountain. Here you will find the likes of **Le Menhir** crêperie and **Canas y Tapas** Spanish-style café, both with lovely outdoor terraces for al fresco dining (or just watching the world go by). You can also try **Epices & Chocolat** for some tempting chocolate treats, drinks, spices and ice cream. Our favourite, though, is **Koreana** barbecue grill, a Korean cuisine where you grill your food at the table and they serve up some mouth-watering combinations of meats, vegetables, sauces and spices.

Place D'Ariane: This is other notable thoroughfare, with more cafés, brasseries, shops and the Hotel Elysée, has an award-winning **Pop Art** restaurant and the Japanese **Sakura**. More outlets are opening all the time, though, as this busy town develops (in partnership with Disney), hence it rewards a casual meander anywhere in the vicinity of the mall. Try it – you never know what little treasure you will discover!

And that sums up all the various alternative fun and entertainment on offer away from the theme parks. A meal in Les Terrasses is highly recommended at any time, while the general opportunity to travel easily thanks to the great convenience of the RER line (and the good road system) comes as a major bonus for those who like to explore. But let's not stop here. There is much more to be seen in the city itself – and beyond – so we'll conclude with a closer look at the main attractions of the city of Paris and the Ile de France.

9 The Attractions of Paris

or Getting an Eiffel of the City

Okay, we will admit to a bias here but Paris is a wonderful city and we reckon you'd be crazy to spend several days nearby and not consider paying a visit. Even with children to keep amused, there is a huge amount of family-friendly fare on offer, while the Eiffel Tower itself remains one of the greatest sources of child fascination and wonderment in the world.

Given that it is so easy to get into the city from Marne-la-Vallée on the RER (and even easier from some of the off-site hotels in the vicinity of Line A), visiting some of the great monuments, parks and museums of Paris is a natural add-on to all the theme park frolics. Public transport in the city is plentiful and reliable, and is far and away the best, cheapest and most hassle-free way to see the sights (driving – with the eternal bugbear of parking – is not recommended, even if you are comfortable with using your own car in France).

 BRITTIP

For all-day public transport in Paris, consider the **Mobilis** card (from any Metro or RER ticket office), which is slightly cheaper than the similar go-anywhere **Paris Visite** ticket. You will need one for Zones 1–5 from DLP.

It takes just 35–40mins to go from Marne-la-Vallée into the city centre,

Sacré Coeur

which means you can have almost a full day in one of the Disney parks and then head off for an evening in Montmartre, the Latin Quarter or for a stroll along the Champs-Elysées.

Getting around

Thanks to the comprehensive and integrated public transport system, involving the trains (RER, or Réseau Express Régional), underground (the Métro) and buses, getting to the sights is a doddle. Sign-posting is usually clear, the modern buses each have a route map and a board indicating each stop, and reliability is outstanding. The Métro system will get you to every tourist site in the city with only the minimum of walking and it runs until around 1am every day, while the last RER service back to Marne-la-Vallée is around midnight (check **www.atp.fr** for public transport details – in English as well as French).

Paris Visite: This card is almost an essential adjunct to sightseeing and can be purchased at any Métro ticket office, RER and SNCF railway station, bus terminal counter, airports and Paris tourist offices. The card provides unlimited travel on the whole Paris public transport system, including the SNCF (suburban) trains and the Montmartre funicular. The system is divided into 6 regional zones, with *Disneyland Paris* in zone 5.

BRITTIP

The real bonus of the Paris Visite card is that it comes with an array of discounts and special offers from 18 tourism partners, including the Cité des Sciences (the excellent Museum of Science), Bateaux Parisiens river cruises, the Musée de l'Armee and Paradis Latin cabaret and dinner-show.

Do it all with Disney

With all these possibilities on the doorstep, it stands to reason Disney would see a way to give guests even more value and purpose to staying

on-site. So they have teamed up with **Cityrama** bus tours, offering a daily sightseeing excursion into and around the city on one of their big, modern double-decker coaches. Because we believe it is the ideal way to visit the key experiences in Paris with minimal effort and maximum use of time, we highlight Cityrama in this chapter.

Tours run daily at 9.45am from *Disney's Hotel New York* and are usually very popular, so it is advisable to book early – with your tour operator in advance or at the hotel concierge desk when you check in. The tour returns at about 6pm, so you still have some park time left at the end of the day. The Cityrama buses are extremely comfortable and well equipped, with air-conditioning, toilets, drinks service and audio commentary on multi-lingual headphones.

The basic route takes you first into the heart of the city and provides a well-narrated overview of the geography, architecture, art, history and culture. The history is graphically illustrated with sites such as **La Bastille** (one of the city's oldest districts, now transformed into a more upmarket and happening area, with nightclubs, restaurants, piano bars and cafés) and **Le Marais** district, a mini-city in its own right, full of little streets, markets and several substantial mansions, now occupied by chic art galleries, cafés, health food shops and piano bars, plus the beautiful Sacré Coeur.

At the heart of Paris is the **Ile de la Cité**, the original settlement site, dating back to the 3rd century BC. The tour continues through the **Quartier Latin** (Latin Quarter), the famous Left Bank district that has been the centre of the city's university life for more than 700 years, and offers a cheaper selection of cafés and shops for more student-like budgets. You then pass the magnificent **Palais du Luxembourg**, with its 20ha/50-acre gardens, and travel along **Rue Bonaparte**, Paris's version of Bond Street, for exclusive shopping.

Les Bateaux Mouches

Paris is famous for its river tours along the Seine, providing both a great view of many well-known monuments as well as a relaxing and highly enjoyable form of transport. The collective name for the half a dozen or so companies that run these tourist boats is Les Bateaux Mouches. They ply their trade along the central section, from the Eiffel Tower to the Ile de la Cité and back, with plenty of history during the day and a generous helping of romance in the evening, when you can choose just an alternative view of Paris by night or a more elaborate dinner cruise. Tours must be booked in advance. Call 00 33 1 76 64 14 45 (from the UK) or visit **www.bateauxparisiens.com**.

The Louvre

Across the **Pont Neuf**, one of the 12 main bridges that link the 2 halves of the city, you drive past the **Louvre**, the massive repository of just about every example of artwork known to mankind. Its principal claims to fame are the exhibits of the Venus de Milo, Mona Lisa and Van Gogh's Sunflowers, but you could easily spend a day or more investigating the wealth of art on display. It is divided into 7 departments – Oriental Antiquities (including Islamic Art); Egyptian Antiquities; Greek, Etruscan and Roman Antiquities; and, for the modern period, Paintings, Sculptures, Art items, Prints and Drawings (**www. louvre.fr**).

Continuing your coach tour, you head back along the Left Bank and through the St Germain area, passing the **Musée d'Orsay**, another of the great repositories of French artwork. A conversion of the Orsay Railway station inaugurated in 1900, it houses an art gallery of the finest order, featuring works from 1848–1914 (**http://musee-orsay.fr**).

Champs-Elysées

A drive around the vast octagonal expanse of the **Place de la Concorde** reveals more of Baron Haussmann's outstanding design, especially as you continue along the **Champs-Elysées**

and into the **Place Charles de Gaulle** (aka Etoile), at the centre of which stands Napoleon's magnificent **Arc de Triomphe**.

Along Avenue Kleber you can marvel at more monumental architecture, especially as you enter **Place du Trocadéro et du 11 Novembre**, where a statue of the First World War military leader Marshall Foch stands in front of a grand vista representing 3 centuries of architecture. The view across the Seine to the Eiffel Tower is breathtaking and on a par with any of the great landmarks of the world such as the Sydney Opera House, the Acropolis and Statue of Liberty.

BRITTIP
If you are going into central Paris on public transport, the main Métro stops to look for are Concorde, Charles de Gaulle–Etoile, Trocadéro, Palais Royal–Musée du Louvre and Cité.

The **Hôtel des Invalides** is another significant 17th-century landmark and its Musée de l'Armée showcases 2,000 years of military history, from antiquity to the end of the Second World War, in an opulent setting. The Dôme within contains the tomb of Napoleon Bonaparte.

BRITTIP
Many Paris museums are free on the first Sunday of the month (though queues will be longer). The museums owned by the Ville de Paris (except the Catacombs) are free every Sunday. See **http://parisinfo.com/museum_monuments** for details.

River trips

After all this coach-bound sightseeing, it is time to step on to a different mode of transport (all part of the Cityrama tour) and view the city from the Seine on the **Bateaux Parisiens**. Here, either under a glass roof or out on deck soaking up the sun, the English commentary (on a hand-held audio device) continues to cover just about every angle of the city, ensuring you

The magnificent Nôtre Dame cathedral on Ile de la Cité

get a well-rounded experience and an in-depth view of the history and accomplishments of Paris and its people (or just a fabulous view if you choose to put your feet up and watch the vistas as you sail by).

Nôtre Dame

Your boat drops you off back in the Ile de la Cité for lunch, and an

From the top of the Notre Dame

opportunity to visit the stunning cathedral of **Nôtre Dame**. This masterpiece of Gothic architecture was built from 1163–1345, and is free to enter to view the awe-inspiring serenity of its vast interior. There are some serious queues here at most times of the day (you'll be used to that at Disney!) but they move steadily. There is a small fee to visit the belfry and you may have to wait 30 minutes or so for your turn. You have a good 90-minute break here, so you can divide your time between the cathedral and lunch.

BRITTIP
There are 2 handy, quiet restaurants on the Quai de Montebello, on the south bank of the river flanking Nôtre Dame. Stroll to the rear of the cathedral, turn right across the bridge and the crowds quickly disappear.

Up the Eiffel Tower

You get back on the boat at the Ile de la Cité pier and continue your hour's cruise, finally returning to the marina at the Port de la Bourdonnais in front

Eiffel Tower

of the **Eiffel Tower**. Your city tour then finishes in style with an organised visit to the tower itself. Your tour guide will lead you up the steps and across the Quai Branly to one of the lifts and a trip to the first floor (the second and third floors are extra, but you usually have time if you wish to go the extra distance yourself). This 324m/1,063ft, 10,100-ton steel edifice is a breathtaking sight close up, and the trip up by lift or stairs is a rewarding one, both for the view and the story of the tower told along the way. The perspective on the city is quite startling (especially from the glass-sided lifts between the first and second floors!) and totally unequalled. There is even a high-quality restaurant on the second floor – the Jules Verne – that you can book separately. If the price tag (in excess of €100) puts you off, try the first floor 58 Tour Eiffel, a chic Parisian brasserie (book from the UK on 00 33 1 72 76 18 46 for 58 Tour Eiffel and 00 33 1 45 55 61 44 for Jules Verne).

BRITTIP
At peak times in summer (midday to around 5pm), the Eiffel Tower often stops selling tickets for the top floor, and the second floor becomes extremely crowded, too.

The Eiffel Tower has 3 lifts (at the north, east and west legs) and 3 staircases (south, east and west), and ticket office queues reach beyond an hour in high summer. However, if you are travelling independently, arrive early and you will enjoy this amazing attraction at its very best, while the evening sees it in truly sparkling mode, with a magical lighting presentation. From dusk to 2am (1am in winter), the Tower's 20,000 special light bulbs (requiring 40km/25mls of electrical cord and 120kw of power) come to life in a glittering display each hour on the hour for 10mins. Once you have been up this modern marvel, you can walk the gardens of Le Champ de Mars for the full ground-level perspective.

BRITTIP
The Eiffel Tower draws some sizeable crowds during the day, attracting the inevitable vendors (selling bottled water and trinkets) who are a constant nuisance. Take extra care with your belongings.

At the north leg you can check out the memorial to Gustave Eiffel, while ticket-holders have access to the clever

lift machinery that he designed under the east and west pillars. A bureau de change can be found in the concourse under the Tower, plus a Paris Tourist Office (not to be confused with the ticket office), souvenir shops (as well as those on the Tower itself), and a cafeteria-style snack bar. For more info, www.tour-eiffel.fr.

All in all, the Cityrama day tour provides a pretty comprehensive beginner's guide to the city and the perfect way to get an overall appreciation of all the main sites in just a few hours. Tickets can be purchased at any of the Disney hotels or those in the Val de France area and it costs £63/adults and £33/children 3–11. NB: This is also a free activity option on the *Kids Under 12s Go Free* season from Jan to the end of Mar; one child with each adult booking.

Paris by night
If that is the story by day, Cityrama's **Illuminations** tour, also organised by Disney, is the city by night. Paris fully deserves its alternative title of 'The City of Light' and the tour portrays this to the full. The English commentary, via individual earphones, is specially adapted to the ambience of Paris by night, bringing its history to life with amusing stories, accompanied by background music and French songs that celebrate the city. The Cityrama coach departs every Mon–Sat at 8 or 9pm from the front of *Disney's Hotel New York* and returns to the hotel at around midnight (depending on traffic). It costs £43/adults and £14/3–11s and is again a free activity option in the Under 12s Go Free season.

A Versailles visit
In 2011, Disney introduced a new exclusive coach excursion to the Royal Palace of **Versailles**, taking in the full splendour of King Louis XIV's 17th-century château. Run by the Visual Tourisme group, it departs daily from *Disney's Newport Bay Club* hotel at 9.30am for a full exploration of this truly amazing site (returning around 4.30pm). It is a self-guided tour

once you are there, with information provided and an audio-guide available, discovering the main Palace, the Hall of Mirrors, the immense Gardens, the Grand Trianon, Marie Antoinette's secret estate and the State Apartments. Lunch is not provided but there is plenty of opportunity to grab something on the way or step outside to one of the many wonderful crêperies nearby. It costs £48/adults and $32/children 3–11 (with the free option during the *Kids Under 12 Go Free* season).

Paris information

Of course, there are dozens of other museums, churches, monuments, gardens, memorials and parks, not to mention the shops, restaurants and nightclubs and other modern city paraphernalia that make Paris such a deliciously heady place. Here are your contacts for essential information.

- **French Tourist Board:** 300 High Holborn, London WC1V 7JH, 020 7399 3545. Information: 090 68 244 123 (60p/min); email **info. uk@franceguide.com**, or **http:// uk.franceguide.com**.
- **Ile de France Tourist Office: www. new-paris-ile-de-france.co.uk**.
- **Paris Tourist Office:** 08 92 68 30 00 (in France), **http://en.paris info.com**.

BRITTIP
The Paris Museum Pass costs €35 for a 2-day pass, €50 for a 4-day and €65 for a 6-day. It gives no queuing, no-limit access to 70 museums and monuments in Paris. It is on sale at the tourist office, FNAC shops and online at **http://parismuseumpass.com**.

The jewels of eastern Paris

Seine-et-Marne: If you would prefer to escape from the hubbub for a while, this region can offer some more down-to-earth but equally enchanting sources of fascination. With a car, there are some wonderful possibilities a little more than an hour's drive from Disneyland Paris, where you can get a feel for rural France, untouched by the hectic rush and modernity of the city.

BRITTIP
The Seine-et-Marne region has an excellent tourist office in Fontainebleau (00 33 1 60 39 60 39 from the UK, **http://tourisme77.net**). They also have a very handy and friendly tourist office next to the Marne-la-Vallée RER station open 9am–8.45pm every day.

Vaux-le-Vicomte: Barely half an hour from the Disney resort is this magnificent 17th-century masterpiece, a historic château and gardens some 24km/15mls to the south down the D471. In the rich land of Brie, this pinnacle of period architecture – created by some of France's greatest artists, including Le Vau, Le Brun and André Le Nôtre – was the inspiration for Versailles. Here you will discover the full château splendour, from the kitchens to the magnificently decorated reception rooms (that have featured in many films).

BRITTIP
If you can visit Vaux-le-Vicomte on a Sat from May–Oct or Fri in Jul and Aug, you can enjoy the amazing Festival of Light, when some 2,000 candles are lit throughout the château and gardens.

Your visit should include a full tour of the château (complete with audio-guide), the extensive French gardens, designed by Le Nôtre, who was also responsible for the Jardins des Tuileries in Paris, plus the Carriage Museum and the Le Nôtre exhibition in the cellars. Every second and last Sat Apr–Oct, you can see the eye-catching Fountain Show from 3–6pm. For more details, call 00 33 1 64 14 41 90 from the UK or visit **www.vaux-le-vicomte.com**.

BRITTIP
A perfect complement to any visit to Vaux-le-Vicomte is dinner at the L'Ecureuil gourmet restaurant, which is open 11.30am–6pm (until 11pm on Festival of Light evenings).

195

THE ATTRACTIONS OF PARIS

Vaux-le-Vicomte

Melun: This nearby city is also worth exploring. The ancient capital of the Capétiens kings offers some interesting walks, an artistic museum and the listed building of St Aspais Church – plus its speciality, the Brie de Melun, often regarded as the ancestor of all Brie cheeses.

Château de Blandy-les-Tours: Just outside the city, this fortified château is a superb example of 16th-century military architecture and a little-known gem of the Ile de France.

Barbizon: The Bohemian Painters Village is about 70km/44mls away to the south (down the N104, A5B, N105 to Melun, N372 and the N37). Here, against a backdrop that various landscape painters have made utterly timeless, you can discover the **Auberge Ganne**, a museum-home of the 19th century and a tribute to an era of artists who influenced the world's landscape and colourist painters. Call 00 33 1 60 66 41 87.

Fontainebleau: Take a slight detour to the south-east and you come to another lovely town with its 16th-century château, home to the kings of France from the Middle Ages. Another major architectural and artistic gem in the panoply of French monuments, its extensive gardens and Napoleonic Museum of Military Art and History offer a fascinating glimpse into another world (**http://musee-chateau-fontainebleau.fr**).

Moret-sur-Loing: Travel still further (about another 10km/6mls south-east) and you come to a medieval city between the Seine and Loing rivers.

Versailles

Château de Fontainebleau

Wander the town and see why it was the inspiration for Impressionist painters like Monet, Renoir and, especially, Sisley.

BRITTIP
For more on all these locations, look up the special tourist website at **www.lesparisplus.com**.

Provins

The jewel in the region's crown, though, is the World Heritage Site and medieval city of **Provins**, some 60km/37mls down the D231 to the south-east. Pass the 12th-century ramparts and you are truly transported back to the Middle Ages, with narrow streets, half-timbered houses, monuments – and dungeons!

BRITTIP
Disney offers a day-trip to **Provins** with Tourism 77 Travel, including entry to many of the town's main attractions from Apr–Nov at £41 adult, £12 children. It departs at 10am most days and returns at 7pm.

Here you can try various medieval crafts, such as calligraphy and stained glass making, design coats of arms and watch the free-flying birds of prey. Provins provides the perfect setting for various period events (**http://provins. net**) organised every summer and, if you happen to be in the area during the last week of Aug, definitely stop by

Provins

to experience some of the week-long **Carnival**, which is one of the highlights of the Seine-et-Marne region. There are also 3 large-scale medieval shows, including a spectacular jousting competition.

Souppes-sur-Loing: Further south still you arrive here, with its stunning **Château Landon**, perched on a rocky outcrop overlooking the verdant valleys of the Fusain. The medieval city boasts a host of memorable monuments, including the Nôtre Dame church, the St Severin abbey, St Thugal tower, St Andrew priory and the beautiful Parc de la Tabarderie.

Or just visit nearby

Château de Ferrières: Nearer to Marne-la-Vallée (just off the A4 at Ferrières-en-Brie), you have this sumptuous pastiche of Renaissance architecture, embellished with one of the most extraordinary English parks in France.

Champs-sur-Marne: A town just to the west (on N34) boasts another stately home emblematic of the bourgeoisie in the Château de Champs-sur-Marne, the residence of Madame de Pompadour in 1757, with formal stately gardens, flower beds and ornamental lakes.

Coulommiers: Then travel east for 20km/12mls on the N34 to another medieval town whose commander's fortress-style residence was built by the Knights Templar in the 12th century. Visit the **St-Anne Chapel**, the round dovecote and the stunning **Capucins Park**. You can also enjoy some picturesque river trips from Coulommiers on the Grand Morin.

Meaux: A short drive to the north-east is an Episcopal city full of Middle Ages character. The impressive **St-Etienne Cathedral** is well worth a visit, along with the **Episcopal Palace** (which now houses the Bossuet Museum) and the **Jardin Bossuet**. On certain weekends in Jun–Sept you can also enjoy the stunning **Meaux Grand Spectacle Historique**, an epic event featuring 500 actors, dancers and equestrians, re-enacting the saga of the city.

Abbaye de Jouarre: In between Meaux and Coulommiers you will find the region's most outstanding sacred site, with 12th-century crypts displaying some astonishing early Merovingian sarcophagi. Food lovers will be interested in the Musée Briard, which traces the history of Brie's cheese-making traditions.

Auvers-sur-Oise

Art lovers may well be lured away to the north-west to spend a half-day or so in the charming village of **Auvers-sur-Oise**, the burial place of painter Vincent Van Gogh. Although the great artist lived here for only 3 months before his untimely death, his stay produced some of his most startling work, and its inspiring influence is still present today (not surprisingly, as Cezanne, Pissarro, Daubigny and others also painted here). The village also hosts an annual International Musical Festival (late May–Jun), which attracts some high-quality performers.

Start by visiting the Office de Tourisme on Rue de la Sansonne to see the 15-minute audio-visual presentation on the village and Van Gogh, then wander out and drink in the wonderful scenery, quaint farms and cafés that inspired so many of the great French painters. To reach Auvers-sur-Oise, take the A15 out of Paris to Exit 7 (Mery-sur-Oise), then pick up N184 alongside the River Oise into the village (**http://auvers-sur-oise.com**).

Now it's up to you!

And that, folks, is that. You now have the essential wherewithal to not only plan and prepare for your holiday in *Disneyland Paris*, but also to get the most out of it when you are there. As you can see from the last 2 chapters, there is a lot more to a holiday here than just theme park frolics (although, if you choose to do just that, you will still have a pretty good time!).

BRITTIP
If you know a little French (there are some translations but they are limited and not always totally fluent) and want a personal view of the city, have a glance at **www.myparisnet.com** for an insider's view.

It is a world of almost infinite charm and substance, a combination of Imagineering pixie dust and ages-old culture and allure. The Walt Disney Company wasn't that crazy when it brought its major slice of Americana to Europe and, while it was not an instant fit, the Franco-European influences now sit comfortably and enjoyably alongside the transatlantic ones.

Most of all, however, we hope you have taken on board how much artistry is involved in providing such obvious entertainment, whether it be on the rides, shows, restaurants or hotels. The resort is the product of more than 55 years of imagination, perspiration and inspiration, with some pretty amazing architecture and engineering thrown in along the way (not to mention the vast backdrop of Paris and its environs).

After numerous visits to Disney theme parks (we lost count many years ago!), we still find them absorbing, fascinating and downright fun. There is so much involved, we would hate for anyone to pay their hard-earned money and then miss some of the essential 'Magic'.

BRITTIP
Don't forget to email your favourite photos of *Disneyland Paris*, named with your name and email address, to marketing@foulsham.com if you want the chance for them to appear in the next edition of the book.

So, we challenge you to keep this book with you at all times, read and inwardly digest the contents before you go. And then get out there and have FUN!

Bonnes vacances…

10 Your Holiday Planner

Here is a way to help you decide what you can do given three or four days in *Disneyland Paris*. This planner is simply designed to give you an idea (from our own practical experience) of what a typical family might be able to achieve in the time allotted. Obviously, you are free to make up your own schedule (on the blank form at the end), but be aware of the different requirements of the theme parks and associated attractions. Have fun with your planning!

Example: 4-night/5-day coach trip with Leger Holidays

Day/time	Schedule	Notes
Day One		
Noon	Pick up from home bus station at midday	
1.30pm	Arrive Dover	
2.15pm	P&O ferry to Calais	Stock up with drinks and snacks on the ferry for the 4-hour coach journey to *Disneyland Paris*
4.30pm	Arrive Calais; brief stop at hypermarket	Don't forget the 1-hour time difference!
Evening	Long, rather boring drive through northern France	
9.30pm	Arrive at *Disney's Hotel Santa Fe*	Check in and go to room
Day Two		
8am	Up for hotel breakfast	Book character lunch at Cowboy Cookout Barbecue at hotel front desk
9am	Off to the *Disneyland Park* for the day	Get FastPass for Peter Pan
Morning	*Disneyland Park*	
1pm	Stop for lunch at Cowboy Cookout Barbecue	Have fun with Chip 'n' Dale, Goofy and Pluto!
Afternoon	*Disneyland Park*	
4pm	Catch the afternoon parade	
5.15pm	Time to Meet Mickey Mouse!	
6.30pm	Leave the park and head for *Disney Village*	

Day/time	Schedule	Notes
7pm	Dinner at Planet Hollywood	Only 10-minute wait for table
8.30pm	Slow wander back to hotel via *Disney Village*	
Day Three		
9am	Slow start this morning!	Book character breakfast for tomorrow at Café Mickey in *Disney Village*
10am	Head for *Walt Disney Studios*	
11am	Queue up for Tower of Terror	
Noon	Meet Stitch outside the Stitch Live! attraction, then head to CinéMagique	Just missed midday CinéMagique? Go on to Art of Animation instead
1.30pm	Stop for lunch at Restaurant En Coulisse	
2pm	Stop at concierge desk in Disney Studio 1	Book dinner at Silver Spur Steakhouse
2.10pm	Queue for 20 minutes to get in to 2.30pm Moteurs ... Action! Stunt Show	
3.30pm	Catch Disney's Stars 'n' Cars parade	
4pm	Stop for a drink at Studio Catering Co. outside after show	
5pm	Take in the Armageddon attraction	
5.30–6.30pm	Enjoy another hour at park	No queues for Magic Carpets ride and Rock 'n' Roller Coaster
7pm	Head next door and have dinner at Silver Spur Steakhouse	
8pm	Head back to Fantasyland for kids' favourite rides	
10pm	Bag a prime spot to watch evening Fantillusion parade on Main Street USA	Dad goes off to get drinks! Still long queues at most of the counter-service cafes
	Straight back to the hotel on the bus after the parade	
Day Four		
8am	Manage to get everyone up and out in time for breakfast at Café Mickey in *Disney Village*	
9.15am	Stop at City Hall in *Disneyland Park* to book dinner at Blue Lagoon	

YOUR HOLIDAY PLANNER

Day/time	Schedule	Notes
9.30am	Enjoy Fantasyland!	In the first 90mins, we do Peter Pan, Snow White, Pinocchio (twice!) and the Carousel beating most of the crowds
11am	Leave park for RER Station	
11.15am	Catch train for Val d'Europe	5-minute journey
11.30am	Visit Sea Life Centre	Spend 2 hours looking round all the exhibits, and children finish up in the soft-play area!
1.30pm	Have great lunch at pizza restaurant in Les Terrasses	
2.30pm	On to La Vallée outlet shopping village	Kids get to play in playground while parents enjoy a coffee!
4pm	Quick tour of Auchan hypermarket before catching RER train back to Disney	
5pm	Catch Animagique show at *Walt Disney Studios*	
5.30pm	Quick refreshment stop at Studio Catering Co.	
5.45pm	One last Flying Carpets ride	
6pm	Time to leave for *Disneyland Park*	
7pm	Dinner at Blue Lagoon	
8.30pm	Just time for another trip to Fantasyland!	
9.30pm	Back to *Disney's Hotel Santa Fe* on shuttle bus	Pack cases for coach tomorrow
Day Five		
8am	Up early and straight off to breakfast	
10am	Coach departs for Calais hypermarket; then on to ferry	
3pm	Ferry leaves Calais	2pm UK time
4.30pm	Arrive back at home bus station	Mission accomplished!

Your holiday – have fun now!

Day/time	Schedule	Notes

Index

INDEX